Mortal Friends, Best Enemies

A volume in the series

CORNELL STUDIES IN SECURITY AFFAIRS
edited by Robert J. Art, Robert Jervis, *and* Stephen M. Walt

A full list of titles in the series appears at the end of the book.

Mortal Friends, Best Enemies

German-Russian Cooperation
after the Cold War

CELESTE A. WALLANDER

Cornell University Press

ITHACA AND LONDON

First published 1999 by Cornell University Press

Printed in the United States of America

Library of Congress Cataloging-in-Publication Data

Wallander, Celeste A.
   Mortal friends, best enemies : German-Russian cooperation after the Cold War / Celeste A. Wallander.
      p. cm. — (Cornell studies in security affairs)
    Includes bibliographical references.
    ISBN 0-8014-3581-1 (cloth : alk. paper).—ISBN 0-8014-8608-4 (pbk. : alk. paper)
    1. Germany—Foreign relations—Russia (Federation) 2. Russia (Federation)—Foreign relations—Germany. 3. Russia (Federation)—Politics and government—1991–   4. Germany—Foreign relations—1991– 5. National security—Germany. 6. National security—Russia (Federation) I. Title. II. Series.
DD120.R8W25   1999
327.43047—dc21   98-47907

Cornell University Press strives to use environmentally responsible suppliers and materials to the fullest extent possible in the publishing of its books. Such materials include vegetable-based, low-VOC inks and acid-free papers that are recycled, totally chlorine-free, or partly composed of nonwood fibers.

Cloth printing   1 2 3 4 5 6 7 8 9 10

Paperback printing   1 2 3 4 5 6 7 8 9 10

to Jeff

Contents

Acknowledgments

.This project was conducted with fellowship and grant support from the German Marshall Fund and the National Council for Soviet and East European Research. I thank especially Robert Randolph of the NCSEER and Diana Fazari of the German Marshall Fund. Additional research support came from the Milton and Clark Funds at Harvard University, as well as the Weatherhead Center for International Affairs and Davis Center for Russian Studies. Follow-up research in Germany was made possible by Professor Helga Haftendorn and the Arbeitsstelle Transatlantische Außen- und Sicherheitspolitik. Leave time to support writing was provided by Harvard University and the WCFIA. Many individuals at Harvard were helpful and responsive through my field research and writing. I thank Tim Colton, Jorge Dominquez, Bob Putnam, Joe Nye, Anne Emerson, Ann Wigglesworth, Maureen Connors, Lis Bernstein, Deborah Clain, and Pat McVay for their patient support.

For hosting me during 1992 in Bonn, I am very grateful to the Deutsche Gesellschaft für Auswärtige Politik and the director of its research institute, Professor Karl Kaiser. In Moscow, both the Institute for the USA and Canada and the Diplomatic Academy provided me with office space and logistical support. I am grateful to Yuriy Davidov of ISKRAN and Aleksandr Gordievskiy of the Diplomatic Academy for their kind assistance in arranging interviews and accessing research materials.

[ix]

At several points I received help from the Moscow office of the Strengthening Democratic Institutions program, directed by Graham Allison, for which I am grateful. The project's Moscow director in 1992, Astrid Tuminez, was my center of knowledge about operating in Moscow, a research partner, travel companion, and great friend.

I was fortunate to have the opportunity to present portions of my research and arguments as they were evolving. I am grateful to the following research centers and their communities for hosting my talks: the WCFIA, Olin Institute, the DGAP, the Davis Center for Russian Studies, the Watson Institute at Brown University, the Department of Political Science at Rutgers University, PIPES at the University of Chicago, and the Osteuropa Institut of the Free University of Berlin.

I have also been lucky to have received written comments from friends and colleagues throughout the process of writing. Robert Keohane has read virtually everything I have written on this project, from grant proposal to final version. Although others might have wondered why I needed to write so much and change it so often, Bob put up with this as a normal and constructive process. He also helped me to realize one of the most important things I needed to know in order to finish this book: that it is okay to take a break and go for a run. I'm grateful for his insights, criticism, and friendship.

Lisa Martin has also read several versions of most of the manuscript, and no one writes better or more extensive comments. Lisa's insights and help on other people's work is one of the true public goods in the field of international relations. I am fortunate that she does not let rational choice get in the way of being a great colleague.

Robert Art read parts of the manuscript in the middle of the process and provided valuable advice that prevented me from taking some wrong turns. He also read the completed manuscript and helped me to argue better and more briefly, for which not only I, but all who read this book, must be very thankful.

Other friends and colleagues who have read portions of the manuscript and have offered advice, queries, and critiques are Randy Stone, Randy Schweller, Matt Evangelista, Iain Johnston, Chris Gelpi, Marc Busch, Jack Levy, Mike Desch, Page Fortna, Monica Toft, Henning Riecke, Louise Richardson, Mark Kramer, Michael Libal, and Peter Barschdorff. Their interest in the idea of a book on security institutions kept me writing when I sometimes wondered what I was doing. I am also indebted to Roger Haydon for reading portions of the manuscript as I developed them and for giving me several chances to get it right. Kay Scheuer was an excellent and tolerant editor; certainly better than I deserved. Pat Harahan was generous in providing the map in Chapter 5.

Acknowledgments

For research assistance at Harvard, I thank Jane Prokop, Mark Nagel, Brad Cuthbert, Geoff Suiter, and Lois Kaznicki. For assistance in Moscow in 1993 and for conducting additional interviews in late 1994 when I could not travel, I am very grateful to Oksana Antonenko-Gamota.

Anyone who has written a book knows that the personal side of the process is as important as the professional side. Not many authors, however, are fortunate enough to have a spouse who provides both personal support and the experience and insight of a tenured professor and author himself. I am forever grateful to my husband, Jeff Anderson, for reading so much of my work, translating when my German proved not up to the task, and doing more than his fair share in taking care of our children. I also thank Nathaniel, our post–cold war baby (born 20 November 1990) for putting up with a year of research in Europe and my frequent absences; Joey, for being a blissful baby and adaptable toddler so I could write the book; and Genevieve, for being patient so I could finish the final stages.

Most of all, I offer my deepest gratitude to the German, Russian, and Ukrainian officials whom I interviewed, and who remain anonymous. Although burdened by their own professional obligations and over-committed schedules, these people were generous with their time, knowledge, and insight. I hope that as a small return I have made clear their dedication in contributing to a peaceful post–cold war Europe.

C. A. W.

Cambridge, Massachusetts

Mortal Friends, Best Enemies

[1]

Balance and Institutions

On the highway into Moscow from the international airport a monument in the form of a massive tank trap marks the point at which Soviet forces stopped the German advance in 1941, only about thirty kilometers from the Kremlin and a mere twenty minutes' drive from the city. The first time I visited the Soviet Union my host pointed out the monument and told me its meaning; he told me it was where Soviet forces had stopped the "fascists" (*fashisti*), however, and did not use the word for Germans (*nemtsi*). Germans have their own reminders of the Russian military presence. As part of the 1990 agreements on unification, the German government pledged to preserve Soviet war memorials, including an impressive monument in Berlin dedicated to the Soviet forces lost in the 1945 assault on the city. Built from the marble of the destroyed Reich Chancellory, the monument stands just west of the Reichstag and not far from the Brandenburg Gate, in the midst of the new seat of the German government being built in central Berlin. It will be a permanent reminder of Russian military power.

The relationship between Germany and Russia has played a central role in European security for hundreds of years, and both nations remain deeply cognizant of their history of mutual destruction. Clashes between "Germans and Slavs" figured in European history as early as the Middle Ages, when Prince Aleksandr Nevskiy drove the Teutonic knights from Russian lands. German-Russian rivalry has been central to European conflict because of geopolitics: Russia's westward expansion created the potential for conflict with Prussia (and later Germany) over territory in central and eastern Europe, especially Poland and the

[1]

Balkans. More fundamentally, Russia's entry into the European state system in the eighteenth century gave it the military and diplomatic power to make or break Prussia as leader among the German states, and then later Germany in its various quests for European hegemony.

German-Russian conflicts have been central causes in European wars, but cooperation between the two nations has not always produced peace. German-Russian collusion has often worked against regional security. In the twentieth century alone, German and Soviet leaders cut separate deals in the Treaty of Brest-Litovsk, the Treaty of Rapallo, and the Molotov-Ribbentrop Pact, enabling both countries to threaten or destabilize their neighbors.

In more recent times, German-Soviet security relations were central to European security during the cold war. After World War II, a united Germany belonging solely to one side of the east-west divide was unacceptable to both the United States and the Soviet Union because of the implications for the balance of power in Europe. Given conflicting U.S.-Soviet assessments and requirements, a divided and semi-sovereign Germany became necessary for European security. Because Germany's division was fundamental to the cold war balance of power, German unification was bound to affect European security. The story of unification involves the calculations of many states, including West Germany's allies, but the country whose security was most affected and had to be accommodated by the terms of unification was the Soviet Union.[1]

After the cold war, Germany and Russia remain crucial to the prospects for European security. To the extent that western security policy relies ultimately on a military balance that entails American engagement, German integration, and the maintenance of lower levels of Russian conventional force capability, Germany must remain a NATO member but not threaten Russia. To the extent that western security policy aims for Russian reform and international integration, Germany's role—its economic resources, political links, and clear interest in stability to its east—is central to the policy. And to the extent that long-term European security depends on a cooperative security community, Russia and Germany both hold veto power over its success.

In addition to these broad post–cold war security issues, Germany and Russia faced numerous concrete problems that could have caused conflict in the past few years. Some directly involved military forces: Soviet troops remained on sovereign German territory at the time of unifi-

1. For a thorough overview, see Philip Zelikow and Condoleezza Rice, *Germany Unified and Europe Transformed: A Study in Statecraft* (Cambridge: Harvard University Press, 1995).

cation, and the breakup of the Soviet Union called into question the ratification of the Conventional Forces in Europe Treaty with its limitations on combat forces and military personnel. Other issues involved different problems for security: the demise of the Soviet Union created the risk of escalation from local conflicts within and among the countries of the former Soviet Union. The Soviet demise also had implications for German economic well-being, since large portions of German trade and substantial Soviet debt obligations to Germany hung in the balance. From the Russian point of view, the decision to embark upon a radical course of political and economic reform presupposed a western commitment to material aid, led by the United States but bolstered by German interests in and positive assessments of Russia.

Therefore, both distant and recent history draw our attention to this relationship as we try to understand the present potential for conflict and cooperation in Europe. But although past events serve as a useful guide, German-Russian history does not allow simple predictions about contemporary relations for two reasons. First, that past encompassed conflict, cooperation, and collusion, and any of those different outcomes could characterize German-Russian security relations today. The only constant factor arising from history is that relations between these two will never be a matter of indifference, either to Germany and Russia or to their neighbors.

The second reason is that German-Russian relations are affected by more than the perennial influences of power and national interests. Without doubt, Germany and Russia remain central to European security because national interest and national power—elements that have shaped German-Russian relations for hundreds of years—remain important. Although scholars may debate how to measure "power" definitively, Germany and Russia are undoubtedly among the most powerful states in Europe. Furthermore, no other countries were more directly and fundamentally affected by the end of the cold war, which completely reshaped their places in the European balance of power and recast their national security interests. The German Democratic Republic became part of the Federal Republic of Germany in October 1990, an event that altered Germany's position in Europe and enhanced its power. The Soviet Union was effectively eliminated in August 1991 and then formally dissolved in December 1991, creating fifteen successor states, Russia among them. This altered Russia's position in Europe and significantly diminished its power. Indeed, the end of the cold war is usually defined in terms of the unification of Germany in 1990, the breakup of the Soviet Union in 1991, or the combination of the two.

[3]

German-Russian relations are defined not only by their power and interests, however , but also by the large number of international institutions inherited from the cold war. Neither the balance of power nor national interest set German-Russian relations on an inevitable path, of either conflict or cooperation. A historical perspective suggests that context is crucial to the form security relations take, and that after the cold war that context includes international institutions.

In this book I develop a theory of institutions in security affairs that leads to different predictions about German-Russian strategies and relations from those made by theories in the realist paradigm, for which power and interest play the defining roles. The theory proposes that under certain reasonable conditions, German and Russian officials construct security strategies based not only on national self-interests and an assessment of balances of power, but on the constraints and opportunities international institutions create for effective policies.

THE ARGUMENT IN BRIEF

Theories in the realist tradition explain security relations in terms of power and anarchy. Anarchy means the absence of a sovereign authority in the international system. The implication of anarchy is that states have to provide for their own security, and they can use any means they choose to do so. As a result, states will focus on the use of military force and the balance of international power. States will not be able to cooperate in security relations because cooperating states chance being exploited and risking national security. Furthermore, states will not wish to cooperate because the focus on balances of power means states must be worried about relative gains—that other states will gain more from cooperation than they themselves do.

As a result, realist theories expect that concern for the balance of power will be central in any security relationship, particularly one as high stakes as that between Germany and Russia. This perennial concern has been sharpened since the end of the cold war, because the passing of the bipolar international system makes security and power calculations more complicated and more sensitive to small disturbances or mistakes. Although locked in a fundamentally hostile relationship during the cold war, at least the Soviet Union and the Federal Republic of Germany each knew where the other stood and could base its policies on the stable bipolar balance. With the historically brief and unusual period of the cold war behind them, Germany and Russia can be expected to return to more common historical patterns of shifting power balances carefully weighed and watched. In a departure from its cold war situation, when it was bound to the west as a junior partner, Germany is now free and potentially tempted to exercise security policies in the tradition of Bismarck, who constructed multiple alliances and could shift among them in search of the balance that would ensure Germany's security. However, noting that balancing produced not only Bismarck's brilliant diplomacy but numerous wars in the nineteenth century and the Great War in 1914, realist theorists predict that security through balance of power will be less stable and a threat to the neighbors of Germany and Russia.

If states were concerned only about power and interests, and if anarchy were the only condition affecting cooperation in security relations, realist theories might be correct in predicting a return to balance-of-power politics and instability in Europe. But this characterization of the international system and states' calculations in choosing security strategies is incomplete. In addition to states operating under anarchy, the international system is characterized by institutions of various types. Although institutions cannot force states to cooperate or act contrary to their interests, they enable states to cooperate when it is difficult yet in their interests to do so. States often have common, as well as competing, security interests, so concern for relative gains does not automatically rule out cooperation in security affairs. Furthermore, the use of military force is often costly or ineffective, so states may find it in their interests to choose other policy instruments.

Given these conditions, international institutions can enable states to choose cooperative strategies in security relations by reducing uncertainty about the power and intentions of other states and about the consequences of their strategy choices. Specific forms of institutions with different capacities and resources can help states to solve different kinds of obstacles to security, such as the need for monitoring and sanctioning others' behavior, coming to mutually acceptable agreements, increasing transparency about security interests and intentions, and creating incentives for cooperation when it is costly in the short term. Institutions will be valuable to states if they have features that enable states to overcome these obstacles to cooperation, known as problems of collaboration, coordination, assurance, and linkage. German and Russian decision makers will be able to choose rational, self-interested, cooperative strategies for national security when institutions that enable them to overcome these obstacles exist.

Therefore, an institutional theory of security relations expects different outcomes in German-Russian security relations after the cold war from those realist theories look for. Because Europe is an institution-rich environment, institutional theory predicts German-Russian security cooperation where there are common interests, where force is costly or ineffective, and where institutions provide the resources necessary for overcoming specific obstacles. Power and interests remain central to German and Russian security calculations. The patterns of their relations will differ, however, from those of the past when decision makers calculate not only the balance of power, but the opportunities for cooperation created by modern international institutions. We will see greater stability and more multilateral cooperation in German-Russian relations after the cold war than realist theories predict.

EVALUATING INSTITUTIONAL AND REALIST THEORIES OF SECURITY AFFAIRS

During the cold war it was difficult to assess the relative explanatory value of realist and institutional theories. The bipolar distribution of power coexisted with the set of international institutions created upon its structure. One could not discern whether decision makers were responding solely to the structural constraints and opportunities created by the distribution of power, or whether institutions had an independent effect. Both power and institutions favored stability, security cooperation within the western alliance, and bipolar competition moderated by avoidance of global nuclear war.[2] Therefore, it has been difficult to assess whether institutional challenges to realist accounts of international security relations offer added theoretical value.

Now, however, in light of the mix of structural change and institutional continuity at the end of the cold war, we can evaluate the effect of institutions on security strategies and outcomes. The structure of power has changed, undermining the sources of stability and security important in realist theory. If stability and cooperation characterize security relations, it may be a result of the independent effects of international institutions.

In principle, to evaluate the importance of institutions in security relations one would want to study as many countries in as many areas of the world as possible. In practice, this is impossible. If institutions affect se-

---

2. For an important analysis along these lines, see John Lewis Gaddis, "The Long Peace: Elements of Stability in the Postwar International System," *International Security* 10 (Spring 1986): 99–142.

curity relations, they do so by affecting the choice of state strategies. Therefore, we need to know how decision makers viewed their country's objectives, their options, and the constraints they faced, and why they chose the strategies and policies that resulted from this evaluation. Evidence of publicly announced policies provides information only about the outcome of this process and makes it at least difficult and probably impossible to discern the relative impact of power and institutions on strategies. The evidence we need can be obtained only by interviews with officials, which limits the number of countries that can be studied.

Thus my findings on Germany and Russia can be only suggestive, and not the final word on the relative explanatory value of realist and institutional approaches for security relations after the cold war. Context and particular German and Russian interests and perspectives will play a greater role in my explanation than is permissible for a general theory. As with any case study, I cannot generalize without acknowledging that important elements of German-Russian security relations may be unusual.

Nonetheless, because of the contradictory expectations of realist and institutional approaches about German-Russian security strategies in the new international system, mine is a crucial case for both theories. If power balancing, avoidance of multilateral cooperation, and the irrelevance of existing institutions are not major factors in German and Russian security strategies, then realism fails in a crucial domain of the theory. Furthermore, according to realist theories, institutions should be least relevant in such periods of change. Old institutions that are valuable to both Germany and Russia in a period of fundamental systemic change would be a major disconfirmation of realist expectations about security affairs.

At the same time, a role for institutions in security strategies is a "least likely" case.[3] The conditions for multilateral strategies are least likely to be met in security relations, because of the close relationship between power and security. Therefore, this study should be a difficult test for institutional theory.

Yet, although we need to devise difficult tests for an institutional theory of security relations, we also have to test it in a domain where its basic conditions are met. Since institutional theory claims that existing

---

3. See Harry Eckstein, "Case Studies and Theory in Political Science," in *Handbook of Political Science*, vol. 7: *Strategies of Inquiry*, ed. Fred I. Greenstein and Nelson W. Polsby (Reading, Mass.: Addison-Wesley, 1975).

institutions will survive the end of the cold war, the most important of these conditions is an institution-rich environment, such as Europe. If institutions are irrelevant to security strategies in Europe, they are unlikely to have any substantial effects elsewhere. Furthermore, Europe is the place where realist approaches and institutional expectations most clearly diverge. It would surprise neither institutionalists nor realists if institutions had little effect on security strategies in Asia or the Middle East, but if existing institutions do not significantly and systematically affect Germany and Russia, institutionalism will have failed where the theory's preconditions have been met. Although German-Russian relations cannot be a decisive test, it is an important one.

My substantive focus is not only the outcomes in German and Russian relations, but each state's security strategies. The focus on strategies permits a high degree of precision and immediate assessment. Although the absence of war in Europe is not a fair disconfirmation of realist predictions, evidence that decision makers are failing to respond to the end of the cold war by choosing unilateral and power-based security strategies would be. Although disagreement, competition, and the inadequacies of institutions to manage certain disputes in Europe do not constitute a fair disconfirmation of institutional predictions, evidence that decision makers ignore institutional mechanisms for monitoring, coordination, information, and linkage would do so.

Furthermore, strategies are the crucial phenomena to be explained in competing approaches to security relations. Both realist and institutional approaches are theories of rational social choice, although not all are formal theories.[4] They are theories of social outcomes as the result of the choices of individuals, groups, or states. The theories explain variation in strategies as a means to understanding outcomes, and offer different

---

4. The distinction is an important one: nonformal theories can be theories of rational choice. Both Hans Morgenthau and Kenneth Waltz assumed rationality on the part of decision makers. Morgenthau did this explicitly—it was one of his six realist assumptions: Hans J. Morgenthau, *Politics among Nations* (New York: Knopf, 1948). Waltz's use of the rationality assumption is more ambiguous. On the one hand, he claims that decision makers will rationally respond to their structural environment, but at other times he claims that structure affects state behavior by "punishing" those states that violate its strictures, through an international equivalent of natural selection. Even in this latter version, however, he expects that the odd violator will either learn to choose in accordance with international constraints or be eliminated: Kenneth N. Waltz, *Theory of International Politics* (Reading, Mass.: Addison-Wesley, 1979), pp. 81–88. Keohane's assumption of rational choice is explicit: Robert O. Keohane, *After Hegemony: Cooperation and Discord in the World Political Economy* (Princeton: Princeton University Press, 1984), chap. 5.

expectations about the effect of constraints on strategies. In short, to ignore states' security strategies would be to ignore the core of these theories and to dismiss a rich and crucial set of evidence.[5]

Therefore, the dependent variables in this book are security strategies and outcomes. Security strategies vary between unilateral, power-based strategies and cooperative strategies—those based on compromise and mutual adjustment. Outcomes in German-Russian security vary between the competitive balancing behavior expected by realist theories of security relations and the maintenance of and compliance with international agreements and commitments.

Instead of state strategies and outcomes, one might focus on institutions. But this approach would favor an institutional explanation because one would be looking for evidence where we would expect it to be strongest. State strategies already enmeshed in an institutional forum tell us nothing about the relative importance of institutions in a state's security strategies: we might be looking at a very narrow and insignificant set of state choices relative to the range of its security relations with other states. A focus on state strategies and on outcomes avoids predisposing the study to findings of strong institutional effects.

My focus on strategies also means that evidence should be based on real-time calculations, rather than post hoc recollections. Officials engaged in the process of weighing alternatives and choosing national security strategies will be able to explain that process in more detail and with greater reliability than if they are asked to remember those processes years later. Political figures and civil servants change jobs and cannot be expected to reproduce the perspectives of a different set of circumstances at a later time. Furthermore, we are all tempted to rationalize decisions and have them appear to have been inescapable after the fact in an attempt to justify failed policies and claim credit for successful ones. Contemporaneous interviewing cannot eliminate these problems, but it increases the chances of evidence that is true to real circumstances. A complete list of interviews, along with an essay addressing methodological issues on their use as evidence, is found in the Appendix. I also

5. It is important to note that I am not explaining Russian and German preferences or interests. I am taking them as given, although variable. Explaining the sources of variation in preferences and the effects on international relations could be the subject of a study of security relations after the cold war as well. For a discussion of the relationship between actors, preferences, strategies, and outcomes, see Jeffry A. Frieden, "Actors, Preferences, and International Relations," in *Strategic Choice and International Relations*, ed. David Lake and Robert Powell (Princeton: Princeton University Press, forthcoming).

rely to a lesser degree on some written sources: newspaper accounts, public government documents, and internal government documents given to me by some of the people I interviewed.

This book addresses three questions about the balance of power and institutions in German-Russian security relations: When (under what conditions) do institutions affect states' security relations? How do institutions affect states' security strategies? And when are institutions effective in facilitating security cooperation? Chapter 2 presents an institutional theory of security relations that gives answers to each of these questions and contrasts those institutional expectations with those drawn from realist theories. Chapter 3 explains how German and Russian officials saw their national security interests and problems in the context of international security issues and opportunities, and then takes up the first set of theoretical issues I have raised. It assesses whether variation in common and competing interests, the usefulness and effectiveness of military force, and the constraint of uncertainty affected the role of institutions in German and Russian security strategies as expected. Chapters 4, 5, 6, and 7 look at the main issues in German-Russian relations after the cold war. Each chapter explains the obstacles to cooperation and assesses whether, how, and why institutions played a role in cases of successful cooperation. Chapter 8 summarizes my findings and assesses the contribution of an institutional theory of security relations to security studies and neoliberal theories of international political economy.

[2]

An Institutional Theory of Security Relations

It is not difficult to describe German-Russian relations. More difficult—and far more interesting—is to explain why those relations take the form they do. A grasp of that form is useful not only for predicting the future but for understanding contemporary relations in light of the past. Since the past history of the relationship has varied so widely, we need an analytical basis for focusing on important questions and predicting likely outcomes.

In this chapter, I begin by outlining realist approaches to understanding security strategies and outcomes and deriving realist expectations on German-Russian security relations after the cold war. Although realism is better understood as a broad tradition than as a single coherent theory, its focus on power and national interests as causal variables produces distinctive predictions about German-Russian security relations.

The main part of the chapter develops an institutional theory of security relations. The theory is based upon an understanding of how uncertainty complicates a state's choice of strategies and how a state's self-interest in coping with uncertainty creates a role for institutions in security relations. The theory is conditional on the existence of common interests and on limited utility of the use of force. The core of the theory proposes that variation in the type of security problem states face affects both their choice of strategies and the institutional forms needed to support cooperation. This in turn implies that cooperation is most likely when the available institutional forms are appropriate to tasks, and when the layering of multiple institutions provides states with a repertoire of instruments in support of security cooperation.

REALIST THEORIES AND GERMAN-RUSSIAN RELATIONS

The realist tradition prevails in theories of security relations. Among these, structural realism provides the clearest prediction that the end of cold war bipolarity means an increase in uncertainty and instability.[1]

Structural realism expects security relations to be the result of the international distribution of power. In a bipolar distribution of power, only the two great powers can threaten each other. Each knows where the threat lies, and each can accurately assess what it needs to do to meet that threat. Balancing is easy and stable; consequently, great powers will not plunge into war. By contrast, multipolar distributions are rife with uncertainty. Any combination of great powers can join forces to defeat another; consequently, all must be highly sensitive to even marginal changes in the balance of power and to the alliance efforts of potential competitors. Balancing will be less stable than in bipolar systems, and therefore states are more likely to make mistakes in calculating the prospects for prevailing in disputes. Military conflicts among the great powers are more likely and system instability increases in multipolarity.[2] Today, since bipolarity disappeared with the demise of Soviet power, and the European security scene is populated by more nearly equal states because of German unification, change in the international system has transformed the prevailing security environment in Europe in a negative way.

Other realist theories combine analysis of the distribution of power in the international system with more specific analyses of power, interests, and uncertainty that lead to the same expectation. Although Stephen Walt's theory concerns revolutionary states and is not directly applicable to Germany and Russia, the theory's focus on uncertainty as cause of conflict has broad implications. Revolutions increase uncertainty in the international security environment because they alter the balance of power suddenly and bring to power new leaderships whose intentions are not known or are not stable. Consequently, revolutions are likely to increase hostility, conflict, and even war, because they produce greater uncertainty about the balance of power and states' intentions.[3]

Other variants of realism allow for variation in states' goals and intentions, ranging from satisfied status quo powers to dangerous and ag-

---

1. On the relationship between classical realism and structural realism, see Robert O. Keohane, "Realism, Neorealism, and the Study of World Politics," in *Neorealism and Its Critics*, ed. Robert O. Keohane (New York: Columbia University Press, 1986).
2. Kenneth N. Waltz, *Theory of International Politics* (Reading, Mass.: Addison-Wesley, 1979), pp. 168–170.
3. Stephen Walt, *Revolution and War* (Ithaca: Cornell University Press, 1996).

gressive revisionist states. According to theories that emphasize intentions, international conflict varies with the character of states which happen to inhabit the system: when revisionist states are absent, major conflict is unlikely.[4] In the late 1990s, theorists have begun to incorporate analysis of institutions into predictions about the international system and have set out an agenda for developing theories and testable predictions about institutions in security relations.[5] Like structural theorists, however, they expect that institutions will not have a substantial effect distinct from that of national power, that balancing behavior will predominate, and that institutions created under the bipolar distribution of power will not be effective under multipolarity unless they reflect underlying power.

Therefore in realist theory, German unification raises questions about whether Germany will resume its historical ambitions, while the demise of the Soviet empire increases uncertainty about Russian intentions and stability. Although the end of U.S.-Soviet rivalry might appear to create a more benign security environment, according to realist theory the prospect of conflict and instability is now greater. The loss of bipolarity and the appearance of states with more equal national power increase uncertainty about power balances. States will seek to create temporary alliances, but shifting intentions and power balances will make these alliances unstable and prone to conflict.[6] Change in Germany and Russia increases uncertainty about their intentions and ambitions. German-Russian conflict would threaten Europe, while German-Russian collusion or alliance could serve expansionism or the establishment of German and Russian spheres of influence.[7]

Some theorists in the realist tradition expect conflict to be less pervasive, an approach Charles Glaser calls contingent or "optimistic" realism.[8] Agreeing that much realist theory makes the mistake of equating

---

4. Randall L. Schweller, "Bandwagoning for Profit: Bringing the Revisionist State Back In," *International Security* 19 (Summer 1994): 72–107.

5. Randall L. Schweller and David Priess, "A Tale of Two Realisms: Expanding the Institutions Debate," *Mershon International Studies Review* 41 (May 1997): 1–32.

6. Waltz, *Theory of International Politics*, pp. 164–170.

7. John J. Mearsheimer, "Back to the Future: Instability in Europe after the Cold War," *International Security* 15 (Summer 1990): 5–57; Christopher Layne, "The Unipolar Illusion: Why New Great Powers Will Rise," *International Security* 17 (Spring 1993): 5–49; Kenneth N. Waltz, "The Emerging Structure of International Politics," *International Security* 18 (Fall 1993): 44–79. On the dangers of democratization, see Edward D. Mansfield and Jack Snyder, "Democratization and the Danger of War," *International Security* 20 (Summer 1995): 5–38.

8. Charles L. Glaser, "Realists as Optimists: Cooperation as Self-Help," *International Security* 19 (Winter 1994/95): 50–90.

security with power,[9] Glaser argues that, under certain conditions, common security interests and concern about self-defeating competition create incentives for states to cooperate in their security relations. If states can base military policies on defensive forces and if they can credibly signal benign intentions, security cooperation is possible.[10] Therefore, if Germany and Russia can meet these conditions, they can cooperate, but if they cannot, optimistic realists expect conflict. Like pessimistic realists, optimistic realists expect that states will be more likely to pursue self-defeating and conflict-oriented security strategies under conditions of great uncertainty.

Optimistic realism fails as a theory, however, in three important respects. First, while it may be the case that states can cooperate when they credibly signal their benign intentions, optimistic realism has not told us much about what affects their capacity to do so. Second, the argument assumes a level of information and a lack of ambiguity in divining intentions from actions and tacit signals which defy reality. It assumes, for example, that Russian attempts to secure a defensive balance of conventional forces relative to the countries of the former Soviet Union would easily be seen by Germany as nonthreatening.

Third, the argument does not take into account obstacles to cooperation other than fear of exploitation and uncertainty about intentions. Security problems are plagued by many factors not solved by credible signaling. Competitive bargaining, complex issues, and multiple participants are just a few of the important obstacles to cooperation the approach ignores.[11] As the results of my interviews show, even when German and Russian officials were relatively confident about the other country's intentions, they faced enormous obstacles to security cooperation arising from these other problems. Developments in realist theory have challenged traditional realism, but they have not replaced them with strong propositions which generate falsifiable hypotheses. Optimistic realists may not be surprised to observe security cooperation, but they have not (yet) developed a theory that can explain and predict it.

In addition to the greater uncertainty inherent in multipolarity, realist scholars identify two other important factors leading to conflict rather than cooperation: relative gains concerns and the ability to resort to mil-

---

9. Celeste A. Wallander, "International Institutions and Modern Security Strategies," *Problems of Communism* 41 (January-April 1992): 44–63.

10. Glaser, "Realists as Optimists," pp. 60–70.

11. Fen Osler Hampson (with Michael Hart), *Multilateral Negotiations: Lessons from Arms Control, Trade, and the Environment* (Baltimore: Johns Hopkins University Press, 1995); Lisa L. Martin, "Interests, Power, and Multilateralism," *International Organization* 46 (Autumn 1992): 765–792.

itary force. Relative gains concerns prevent cooperation because the central importance of power in anarchy means that states view gains for others as losses for themselves.[12] Relative gains concerns reduce all security relations to zero-sum interactions, and in such situations there is no possibility of cooperation. The use of force is an obstacle to security cooperation because elimination is a possible cost of cooperation. Because states seek survival, the use of force is always a possibility in security affairs; therefore, states will be highly unlikely to risk cooperation or reliance upon institutions to manage their security affairs because they fear that cooperation puts their survival at risk.[13] Combined with the effects of uncertainty, concern for relative gains and the ability to use force make cooperation virtually impossible and conflict ever-present.

Realist theories lead to clear predictions about state responses to the new post–cold war international system. They predict that concern for balancing power will be the central element of state strategy. They predict a greater preference for self-reliant strategies to cope with uncertainty, and cooperative security efforts based on a strict calculation of power, in identifying both potential threats and potential allies. Given the loss of bipolarity, they predict that existing international institutions will be irrelevant to security relations, or that they must reflect the realities of the new distribution of power. In either case, institutions will have no substantial independent effect on strategies and outcomes.

Optimistic realism expects that where cooperation does occur it will be based simply on a favorable offense-defense balance or on the ability of states to signal benign interests directly to one another, with or without the intermediary role of institutions. Optimistic realists should expect that states will be indifferent to the choice of institutions or to variation in institutional rules and procedures in choosing their security strategies.

AN INSTITUTIONAL THEORY OF SECURITY RELATIONS

Institutional theory is based on two propositions about the international system. First, the system is characterized by varying levels of institutionalization as well as different distributions of power. Second, under certain conditions institutions may affect the strategies of self-interested

12. Joseph M. Grieco, "Anarchy and the Limits of Cooperation: A Realist Critique of the Newest Liberal Institutionalism," *International Organization* 42 (Summer 1988): 485–507.

13. Charles Lipson, "International Cooperation in Economic and Security Affairs," in *Neorealism and Neoliberalism: The Contemporary Debate*, ed. David A. Baldwin (New York: Columbia University Press, 1993), pp. 72–73.

[15]

states by serving as monitoring, bargaining, information, or linkage mechanisms. Therefore, an institutionalist security theory predicts that states will use institutions in addition to self-reliance and power balancing in choosing their security strategies, and that states will choose multilateral cooperation when institutions can serve as instruments for achieving security. Institutionalist theory expects that institutions created during the cold war will survive and will reduce uncertainty in German and Russian security relations. Institutions' ability to reduce uncertainty means that states will preserve and use them to manage security relations even when the distribution of power which first created them has changed.

Institutionalists agree that the end of the cold war has increased uncertainty about states' power and intentions. They also agree that disputes and even conflicts will arise in the new security environment. Where they disagree with realists is over how those disputes and conflicts will be managed. They believe that the obstacles to multilateral cooperation are more likely to be overcome when there are institutions available to states, that rules and procedures do matter, and that patterns of success in effective multilateral security cooperation cannot be explained solely by power and interests but must take international institutions into account.

Institutions are explicit, persistent, and connected sets of rules that prescribe behavioral roles and constrain activity.[14] Institutions must be distinguished from cooperation, since the claim of institutional theory is that the former make the latter possible. Institutions may take the form of organizations, regimes, or conventions: NATO, the nuclear nonproliferation regime, and the regime established by the Conventional Forces in Europe Treaty are all institutions. International institutions by and large have no enforcement powers. They affect states' behavior by altering the strategic environment, rather than through enforcement.[15] Institutions serve as monitoring mechanisms, provide negotiating structures and focal points in cases of distributive bargaining, enhance the infor-

---

14. Robert O. Keohane, *International Institutions and State Power* (Boulder, Colo.: Westview Press, 1989), p. 3. See also Douglass C. North, *Institutions, Institutional Change, and Economic Performance* (Cambridge: Cambridge University Press, 1990), p. 3: "Institutions are the rules of the game in a society or, more formally, are the humanly devised constraints that shape human interaction."

15. Even institutions that operate on the domestic level, and therefore have enforcement power, affect social behavior largely as strategic constraints. See Ronald Rogowski, "Institutions as Constraints on Strategic Choice," in *Strategic Choice and International Relations*, ed. David Lake and Robert Powell (Princeton: Princeton University Press, forthcoming).

mation available to states assessing their choices of strategies, and allow states credibly to signal threats, promises, intentions, and capabilities.[16]

An institutional theory of security relations must address three issues. First, it must establish the conditions under which institutions will affect security relations. Second, it must explain how institutions affect the types of problems states face in their security relations. Third, such a theory must say something about the relationship between strategies, institutions, and outcomes. Before I develop this theory, I need to clarify what I mean by a security strategy.

SECURITY STRATEGIES

Strategies are policies chosen in the pursuit of interests or preferences, given available means and constraints.[17] Security strategies are the policies states choose in order to pursue their security interests and preferences. In choosing effective and efficient security strategies, states not only pursue what they want, but calculate what they can get in light of constraints.

German power, interests, preferences, and strategies constrain Russian choices, and the same Russian factors constrain German choices. Power constrains choice because economic and military resources can influence outcomes. The preferences, interests, and strategies of other states constrain a state's security strategy because decision makers have to calculate how others' choices will affect outcomes. This condition—in which outcomes are the result of the choices of two or more states—is called strategic interdependence.

---

16. North, *Institutions, Institutional Change, and Economic Performance*, p. 27; R. H. Coase, "The Problem of Social Cost," reprinted in Coase, *The Firm, the Market, and the Law* (Chicago: University of Chicago Press, 1988), chap. 2; Paul Milgrom and John Roberts, "Bargaining Costs, Influence Costs, and the Organization of Economic Activity," in *Perspectives on Positive Political Economy*, ed. James E. Alt and Kenneth A. Shepsle (Cambridge: Cambridge University Press, 1990), esp. pp. 60–66.

17. For discussions of strategy and "grand strategy," see Robert J. Art, "A Defensible Defense," *International Security* 15 (Spring 1991): 5–53, at pp. 6–10; Barry R. Posen, *The Sources of Military Doctrine: France, Britain, and Germany between the World Wars* (Ithaca: Cornell University Press, 1984), chap. 1; Edward Luttwak, *The Grand Strategy of the Soviet Union* (New York: St. Martin's Press, 1983); Richard Rosecrance and Arthur A. Stein, "Beyond Realism: The Study of Grand Strategy," in *The Domestic Bases of Grand Strategy*, ed. Rosecrance and Stein (Ithaca: Cornell University Press, 1993). This definition is broader than the technical meaning of the term in game theory, in which a strategy is a player's plan of action for the entire game, taking into account all possible contingencies. In this second sense, a state could really have only one security strategy, and it could never change, because any potential effects of institutions would have already been incorporated into the strategy. I am indebted to Robert Powell for this clarification.

In realist approaches, strategic interdependence in anarchy and uncertainty about other states' likely actions taken together lead states to assume the worst. States will always assume that other states have strongly competitive preferences—if not zero-sum, then those of a Deadlock or Prisoner's Dilemma game. Under these conditions, even a defensively motivated state will always choose strategies that ensure it will avoid being exploited.

But rather than assuming the worst, states have an interest in learning what others' intentions and choices might be. To understand why, think about what happens when state preferences can vary. In Figure 1, the first game matrix shows one state with Stag Hunt preferences and her partner with Deadlock preferences. Our Stag Hunt player knows that her Deadlock partner has a dominant strategy to defect. Therefore, our player is faced with a choice of her worst outcome if she cooperates, and her second worst outcome if she defects. In this case, she should choose to defect.

The second payoff matrix shows both players with Stag Hunt preferences. In this case, mutual cooperation will not only get both players their most preferred outcome, it is an equilibrium outcome: neither player has any reason to leave it, so it will be stable. If our player knows that her partner has Stag Hunt preferences, she can confidently cooperate. *Her preferences have remained constant, but her choice of strategies changes depending on what she believes the preferences, and therefore likely choices, of the other player to be.*

What if our player is not certain what kind of player she faces, and knows only that there is some probability that her partner has Deadlock preferences and some probability of Stag Hunt preferences? Realist the-

Figure 1. Uncertainty and security games

		Game One		
		Stag Hunt player		
		C	D	
Deadlock	C	2,4	1,3	(4 = best,1 = worst)
player	D	4,1	3,2	

		Game Two		
		Stag Hunt player		
		C	D	
Stag Hunt	C	4,4	1,3	(4 = best, 1 = worst)
player	D	3,1	2,2	

orists expect that our player will assume the worst and defect to avoid her worst outcome. But that is not an efficient security strategy: the player always sacrifices her most preferred outcome, even though there is some chance that she could do better. If there were mechanisms to reveal information on what kind of player she faces, we would expect our player to incorporate that information in her strategy rather than simply assume the worst. Such a strategy would be more efficient, relative to our player's own security interests. States want to avoid being exploited in security relations, but they need not ignore information.

Choosing security strategies, therefore, entails overcoming three difficulties. First, since they can never be certain that they will not be exploited, states need to pay close attention to the costliness and effectiveness of force. Second, although states can determine their own strategies, outcomes will be affected by the choices of other states. Therefore, states need information on the interests, preferences, and strategies of others. And third, although worst-case strategies can achieve a minimum form of security, those strategies may be inefficient or ineffective. Since I assume that states are rational, they will prefer more efficient strategies over less efficient ones.

So, what can institutions do in security relations that addresses these difficulties? Under certain conditions, institutions allow states to construct and choose more effective and efficient security strategies than would be possible through unilateral or power-based policies.

WHEN INSTITUTIONS AFFECT SECURITY STRATEGIES

Realist theorists posit that concern about relative gains, the use of military force, and the effects of uncertainty lead states to choose unilateral and power-based means to achieve security. This rules out any independent effect that institutions may have on security relations. But when relative gains concerns are eased and when force becomes costly or ineffective, institutions can aid in solving strategic interaction problems.

Common and Competing Interests

Hans Morgenthau believed that national interests were defined in terms of power.[18] Kenneth Waltz disagreed, and wrote that the "goal the system encourages (states) to seek is security. Increased power may or may

18. Hans J. Morgenthau, *Politics among Nations* (New York: Knopf, 1948), p. 4.

[19]

not serve that end."[19] In fact, both Morgenthau and Waltz explicitly state that the interests and goals of states vary,[20] but both failed to incorporate that variation into their theories and to explain how it would affect strategies and behavior.[21]

Security interests range across a continuum. When relative gains concerns are severe, relations between states will be zero-sum (one state's loss will be another's gain). Competing claims to territory, the equation of power with security, and the presence of an expansionist state generate zero-sum interests.[22] Clearly, institutions can play no role in state strategies when all interests conflict in this way. Since international institutions cannot force states to abide by rules, they cannot coerce outcomes. When states have strictly competing security interests, they will rely upon power and unilateral measures. Such situations, however, are rare. Even the United States and the Soviet Union at the height of their conflict judged themselves to have a common interest in avoiding nuclear war.

In other cases states have some common as well as conflicting interests, but the competitive nature of their interests is such that they prefer even mutual defection over mutual cooperation. In a game such as Deadlock (see Figure 2), we would not expect to see cooperation. Since states can achieve a mutually preferred and stable outcome by following their dominant strategies, we would not expect institutional mechanisms to affect security strategies.[23]

As security interests move toward those characteristic of Prisoner's Dilemma, common interests increase even as competitive interests re-

19. Waltz, *Theory of International Politics*, p. 126.

20. Morgenthau, *Politics among Nations*, pp. 8–9; Waltz, *Theory of International Politics*, pp. 91–92.

21. Walt's alliance formation theory does incorporate this variation, because perception of threat (and thus variation in compatibility of security interests) plays the central causal role in security strategies. Stephen M. Walt, *The Origins of Alliances* (Ithaca: Cornell University Press, 1987).

22. Randall L. Schweller, "Neorealism's Status-Quo Bias," *Security Studies* 4 (Fall 1994): 225–258.

23. It is interesting that recent discussion of the relative gains problem in security affairs has not focused more on the Deadlock game. Critics of institutionalist theories may actually have in mind Deadlock preferences in their arguments about the importance of relative gains. For a summary of the debate, see David A. Baldwin, "Neoliberalism, Neorealism, and World Politics," in *Neorealism and Neoliberalism*, ed. Baldwin. In fact, it is puzzling that discussions of Deadlock are quite rare in security studies, even though this game probably underlies many security problems such as arms races. See George W. Downs, David M. Rocke, and Randolph M. Siverson, "Arms Races and Cooperation," in *Cooperation under Anarchy*, ed. Kenneth A. Oye (Princeton: Princeton University Press, 1986), pp. 122–132. Oye chastises researchers on this point: see Kenneth A. Oye, "Explaining Cooperation under Anarchy: Hypotheses and Strategies," in *Cooperation under Anarchy*, p. 7.

Figure 2. Security games

		Player B		
		C	*D*	
Prisoner's Dilemma				
Player A	C	3,3	1,4	(4 = best, 1 = worst)
	D	4,1	2,2	

		Player B		
		C	*D*	
Deadlock				
Player A	C	2,2	1,4	(4 = best, 1 = worst)
	D	4,1	3,3	

		Player B		
		C	*D*	
Stag Hunt				
Player A	C	4,4	1,3	(4 = best, 1 = worst)
	D	3,1	2,2	

		Player B		
		C	*D*	
Chicken				
Player A	C	3,3	2,4	(4 = best, 1 = worst)
	D	4,2	1,1	

main. Relative gains per se cannot be the obstacle to cooperation in simple Prisoner's Dilemma, because states prefer mutual cooperation to mutual defection, even though they have a dominant strategy of defection. However, variation in the *degree* to which states fear exploitation, prefer cooperation, and would benefit by exploiting others affects their willingness to cooperate in a repeated game of Prisoner's Dilemma. Variation in the size of the payoffs affects the severity of the dilemma and thus the prospects for avoiding or ameliorating it through mutual cooperation.[24]

Security relations involving bargaining or distributional issues also have a mix of common and competing interests. States are faced with

---

24. Robert Jervis, "Cooperation under the Security Dilemma," *World Politics* 30 (January 1978): 167–214, at p. 171: Joanne Gowa, *Allies, Adversaries, and International Trade* (Princeton: Princeton University Press, 1994), pp. 52–53.

competing incentives: in order to gain preferred outcomes they need to coordinate strategies, but they have competing preferences for different outcomes. Suppose Helmut will get $100 and Boris will get $50 if both name heads, Boris will get $100 and Helmut $50 if both name tails, and neither gets anything if they make opposite choices. This is a coordination game, characterized by conflicting interests as well as common interests—the situation in the familiar security game of Chicken (see Figure 2).

The obstacles to cooperation in these cases lie in the incentives for states to compete for different outcomes. Obstacles are even more severe when agreement today will establish the pattern of cooperation far into the future. The distribution of the gains to be realized in any agreement is important, and this can lead to hard bargaining about the terms of the agreement. The dilemma states face is that in pursuing distributional advantage they may fail to come to any agreement, which is an even worse outcome than accepting a less-than-favorable agreement.[25]

Distributional problems are important in security relations. Stephen Krasner has argued that distributive issues are pervasive and that power plays an important role in settling these issues.[26] Although there are obstacles to cooperation, the important point here is that nonetheless states can have a common interest in reaching certain outcomes, even while competing interests persist as well. Power may play a role in determining which deal will be struck, but even the powerful have a reason to avoid failure to cooperate. Under these circumstances, institutions may be a more efficient instrument for the pursuit of self-interest.

Thus, as common interests in a security relationship increase, we expect that institutions *can* play a role in security strategies when security interests combine a mix of common and competing elements. But this is a rather weak claim: we need to know when institutions *will* play a role in security strategies.

Usefulness of Military Force

Institutions will not be important in security strategies if force is low-cost and effective. When states believe, however, that others are constrained by the ineffectiveness or costliness of force and when they find

---

25. On the pathologies of the incentives in bargaining, see Howard Raiffa, *The Art and Science of Negotiation* (Cambridge: Harvard University Press, 1982), and Steven J. Brams, *Negotiation Games: Applying Game Theory to Bargaining and Arbitration* (New York: Routledge, 1990).

26. Stephen D. Krasner, "Global Communications and National Power: Life on the Pareto Frontier," *World Politics* 43 (April 1991): 336–356.

themselves constrained by these factors, multilateral strategies become effective. Under these conditions, institutions play a role in security relations. Although a state with military power can always resort to force, that it will always do so is not foreordained. Russia could certainly impose nearly any outcome it would like on Estonia, Latvia, and Lithuania, but military occupation of the Baltics would be costly. As the cost of force options increases, states will look to alternative strategies to pursue their security interests.[27] A preponderance of power does not guarantee that the use of force is a viable security instrument.

Furthermore, while force can always be used, it cannot always guarantee that a state's objectives will be achieved. The use of military force may be highly effective for defense or acquisition of territory. It also may be effective for defeating and occupying a threatening state and replacing its regime with one more benign. But the traditional threat and use of force is far less effective for other possible security problems. It is unlikely to be useful when arms control or disarmament is a security objective. The smuggling of nuclear weapons material and technology cannot be effectively addressed by traditional use of force when the problem is one of lack of control by an incompetent government. Threats may be effective in a strategy of nuclear deterrence, but they cannot prevent an accident.[28]

Institutions cannot prevent the use of military force by outlawing it, or play a role when rewards are high or a state is determined to use military power whatever the cost. It would be absurd to think a security institution such as the Organization for Security and Cooperation in Europe (OSCE) could have prevented World War II.[29] But the dominant studies of the origins of World War I, with their focus on the role of miscalculations about the state of offensive military technology, the effectiveness of offensive military doctrines, and the effects of alliances,

27. Thomas C. Schelling, *Arms and Influence* (New Haven: Yale University Press, 1966), chap. 2; Robert Powell, *Nuclear Deterrence Theory: The Search for Credibility* (Cambridge: Cambridge University Press, 1990), chap. 2; Robert Jervis, *The Meaning of the Nuclear Revolution: Statecraft and the Prospect of Armageddon* (Ithaca: Cornell University Press, 1989), pp. 38–41.

28. For a related discussion that focuses on power's limited fungibility, see David A. Baldwin, "Power Analysis and World Politics: New Trends versus Old Tendencies," *World Politics* 31 (January 1979): 161–194.

29. The Conference for Security and Cooperation in Europe (CSCE), created by the Helsinki Final Act in 1975, changed its name to the OSCE in December 1994 to reflect the increasingly formal nature of the institution. I refer to it as the OSCE to be consistent. The officials whom I interviewed before the change used the older term, of course, and where I quote them directly I preserve their usage.

imply that some degree of marginal change in the effectiveness or costliness of military force would have altered states' calculations and possibly prevented the descent toward war.[30]

So for many security problems, force is ineffective or is costly relative to cooperative strategies, and in such cases states should be willing to rely more on the latter. Although stronger, this claim is still weak for making predictions about German-Russian security relations after the cold war: we still need a clear prediction of when existing institutions will play a role in sustaining multilateral security strategies.

Uncertainty

As I have argued, despite the focus on power, uncertainty also shapes a state's security strategies according to realist theory. In structural realism, variation in uncertainty determines which international systems are stable. Waltz argues that multipolarity is unstable because uncertainty is high: it is easy to make miscalculations about the balance of power.[31] Variation in uncertainty also plays a central role in theories of the security dilemma. When the actions states take to enhance their security can reduce the security of other states, they are in a security dilemma.[32] If states could distinguish between offensive and defensive capabilities, deploy only defensive capabilities, and thereby demonstrate their exclusively defensive intentions, the security dilemma would disappear.

If uncertainty can vary, and if states are able to alter their strategies when it does, states should find it in their own interests to seek ways to reduce uncertainty. This is the point at which realist and institutional theories of security relations clearly diverge. Realists argue that, given anarchy, states can do no better than assume the worst. Institutionalists argue that uncertainty creates incentives for states to get information and that institutions can serve that purpose.[33] Since information permits the choice of better strategies, German and Russian decision makers will seek it. When they can reduce uncertainty by distinguishing dangerous states from benign ones, they can choose better strategies.

---

30. Stephen Van Evera, "Why Cooperation Failed in 1914," in *Cooperation under Anarchy*, ed. Oye; Jervis, "Cooperation under the Security Dilemma," pp. 172–174, and 178–179.

31. Waltz, *Theory of International Politics*, p. 118; Thomas J. Christiansen and Jack Snyder, "Chain Gangs and Passed Bucks: Predicting Alliance Patterns in Multipolarity," *International Organization* 44 (Spring 1990): 137–168.

32. John H. Herz, "Idealist Internationalism and the Security Dilemma," *World Politics* 2 (January 1950): 157–180; Jervis, "Cooperation under the Security Dilemma."

33. Keohane, *After Hegemony*, pp. 100–102.

Information asymmetries and the problems they create for choice are pervasive in social life. In the "market for lemons" the seller of a used car knows more about it than the potential buyer. The buyer knows this and will tend to value the car less given the chance that it is a lemon (it has defects that reduce its actual value). Sellers of "creampuffs" have an interest in proving that the cars they offer for sale are not lemons, but this is difficult because lemons and creampuffs are not distinguished by appearances. Institutions such as "lemon laws" provide information that allows buyers to distinguish lemons from creampuffs and creampuffs to distinguish themselves from lemons. Good deals are more likely to be made and bad deals are more likely to be avoided, so strategies are more efficient.[34]

What would a "lemon" in security relations look like? A security lemon would be a state with strongly competitive or even aggressive interests that seeks to enter multilateral arrangements only to exploit other states. The realist prescription is to assume every state is a security lemon. As in the market for used cars, the costs for a deal will be higher and beneficial deals will be missed. Because of the lemon problem, states will be suspicious of the declared intentions of other states and of information other states reveal unilaterally.

Security lemons, of course, have an interest in maintaining uncertainty and misinformation about their capabilities and interests, but in doing so they reveal themselves. Iraq and North Korea, for example, revealed their determination to develop nuclear weapons capabilities by thwarting international inspections of nuclear facilities. If states that are not security lemons can credibly reveal themselves, they can achieve gains from cooperation. Iran, for example, allayed the concern of many states by agreeing to safeguards and inspections of nuclear facilities. Therefore, institutions can be important if they serve as the informational and signaling mechanisms that permit states to get more information about the interests, preferences, intentions, and security strategies of other states. They ameliorate uncertainty by providing symmetric and credible information.[35]

In the absence of institutions, realist approaches which claim that states will respond to uncertainty by assuming the worst are probably

34. Beth Simmons, "Why Innovate? Founding the Bank for International Settlements," *World Politics* 45 (April 1993): 361–405. On markets and lemons, see George Akerlof, "The Market for Lemons: Quality Uncertainty and the Market Mechanism," *Quarterly Journal of Economics* 54 (August 1970): 488–500.

35. Kenneth A. Shepsle, "Institutional Equilibrium and Equilibrium Institutions," in *Political Science: The Science of Politics*, ed. Herbert Weisberg (New York: Agathon, 1986), p. 75; Keohane, *International Institutions and State Power*, pp. 5–6.

correct. But given the importance of information for good security strategies and given the role of institutions in providing information, the response of states to uncertainty in an institution-rich environment will be to use those institutions to get information. States with benign or defensive security interests will wish to identify similar states and ways to cooperate. They will also want to identify security lemons and avoid being exploited.

Institutions reduce uncertainty in several ways. When states abide by informal institutions such as respect for sovereignty and diplomatic immunity, they signal that their intentions are not in conflict with fundamental assumptions under which other states operate. Modern formalized institutions such as the United Nations, the OSCE, or NATO provide for regular contact among states in which policies are discussed and debated in public and—probably more important—in private. As ongoing arenas for multilateral discussion, these organizations can allow states to exchange information *and* provide a framework for assessing the reliability of that information. An established framework of negotiation makes it easier for states to evaluate patterns of policies, and thus intentions.

Uncertainty is not limited to intentions and capabilities. Behavior can also be unclear. If a state chooses to exploit others' cooperative strategies, that behavior might escape detection. Security institutions can increase the likelihood that opportunistic behavior will be noticed. Most arms control regimes define quite clearly what types of behavior would constitute violation of institutional norms and rules.[36] The Intermediate Nuclear Forces (INF) treaty had no enforcement power or authority, but provided standards for behavior and information mechanisms that permitted the United States and the Soviet Union to assess intentions and compliance.

States may also avoid security cooperation because of uncertainty about the future. Although international agreements are binding on countries, not governments, changes in the latter can clearly affect a state's security policies. While institutions cannot guarantee future intentions, they can enhance a state's capacity to detect changes: if another state breaks institutional rules, it is a sign that its intentions have changed.

How might institutions affect uncertainty about the future in a way that supports multilateral strategies? One way is by reducing the

---

36. On the importance of rules in arms control negotiations and regimes, see Steve Weber, *Cooperation and Discord in U.S.-Soviet Arms Control* (Princeton: Princeton University Press, 1991).

chances that states will abandon established patterns of behavior which have benefited them. Since institutions are difficult and costly to construct and yet provide benefits to members, states have a stake in remaining members and sustaining them.[37] That institutions provide members with benefits allows the members to be more confident that multilateral security strategies today will obtain anticipated benefits later. Combined with increased confidence that exploitative behavior will be detected, greater confidence about future interactions enables states to choose cooperative multilateral security strategies.

Optimistic realists would question whether states need institutions to reduce uncertainty. States can monitor capabilities and actions and infer intentions from them; such self-reliant information gathering is what states have done throughout history. The problem with tracing behavior back to intentions, however, is that the meaning of individual actions is likely to be unclear or ambiguous. Institutions help states ascribe meaning to actions and patterns of behavior through established norms, rules, and procedures.[38]

Thus, under uncertainty, choosing security strategies is difficult. Anarchy and the use of force create incentives for states to assume the worst about other states' intentions and to depend on more self-reliant and power-based security strategies. These strategies will probably guarantee fundamental security values such as territorial integrity, but are likely to be inefficient because they will rule out the adoption of strategies that take into account variation in states' intentions.

But in an institution-rich environment, states will be able to ameliorate uncertainty by using institutions to get credible information. They will be able to identify security lemons, take measures to protect against them, and identify states with whom they have common interests This will enable them to choose security strategies more efficiently.

EXPLAINING VARIATION IN THE ROLE OF INSTITUTIONS

Although uncertainty is a constraint on efficient security strategies, dealing with it gets states only part of the way toward security cooperation. Information about other states' intentions does not necessarily solve security problems; it may only help states to identify the problems and threats they

---

37. Keohane, *After Hegemony*, chap. 6; Shepsle, "Institutional Equilibrium," p. 75.
38. Keohane, *International Institutions and State Power*, p. 6; Simmons, "Why Innovate?" pp. 369–370.

face. A stronger institutional theory of security relations must show how institutions allow states to deal with security problems and threats.

Different types of security problems arise from four different strategic situations: collaboration, coordination, assurance, and linkage. In collaboration situations, states need to detect exploitation and be able to retaliate. In coordination games, they seek to avoid fruitless competition by agreeing upon mutually acceptable if not mutually optimal outcomes. In assurance games, conflict prevention is the goal. In linkage situations, states need to alter the structure of incentives that makes them vulnerable to demands for unconditional cooperation. Institutions can function as instruments of security policies if they can serve as resources in solving the types of problems each of these situations poses.

Collaboration and Deterrence

When states prefer an uneasy peace over conflict, or seek outcomes that can be achieved only through joint action such as mutual arms reductions, they can achieve gains in security interests through sustained, if wary, cooperation. These strategic situations are known as collaboration games and take the common form of Prisoner's Dilemma.

The simplest form of collaboration is mutual deterrence, in which states maintain mutual cooperation by threats of retaliation.[39] Allies also face collaboration problems when they are tempted to free ride on their partners' defense efforts. Security institutions play a role in collaboration problems in both situations: they monitor behavior and allow for sanctioning. That is, they create or support the features of an iterated Prisoner's Dilemma in which conditional cooperation is a rational and efficient strategy.[40] The problems collaboration games pose for security are commonly illustrated by obstacles to strategic arms control.[41]

Collective defense and collective security are collaborative strategies for deterring attack and aggregating capabilities.[42] Alliances for collec-

39. Arthur A. Stein, "Coordination and Collaboration: Regimes in an Anarchic World," in *International Regimes*, ed. Stephen D. Krasner (Ithaca: Cornell University Press, 1983), pp. 115–140.

40. Robert M. Axelrod, *The Evolution of Cooperation* (New York: Basic Books, 1984); Robert Axelrod and Robert O. Keohane, "Achieving Cooperation under Anarchy: Strategies and Institutions," in *Cooperation under Anarchy*, ed. Oye.

41. On monitoring and arms control regimes, see Bruce M. Russett, *The Prisoners of Insecurity: Nuclear Deterrence, the Arms Race, and Arms Control* (San Francisco: W. H. Freeman, 1983).

42. Arnold Wolfers, "Collective Defense versus Collective Security" (1959), reprinted in Wolfers, *Discord and Collaboration: Essays on International Politics* (Baltimore: Johns Hopkins University Press, 1962), p. 182.

tive defense increase the likelihood that the collaborative outcome (mutual deterrence) will be sustained because, by improving the allies' defense capabilities, they increase the likelihood of punishing an aggressor and reduce what an aggressor can gain. Collective defense institutions also must ameliorate problems of collective action among members. By creating a small group, supporting side payments (that is, supplementary deals and payoffs outside the rules of the game itself), and exposing who is contributing to collective defense, an alliance can overcome collective goods problems among allies. The more highly institutionalized a collective defense arrangement, such as NATO, the less likely its members are to abandon one another, and the more securely collective action problems among allies will be solved.[43] The role of institutions such as NATO in overcoming collaboration problems among adversaries and among allies can be quite substantial.

Collective security arrangements must deal with both the adversary and ally collaboration problem at the same time because potential aggressors are also members. *Collective* security means that a threat to any member of the system is a threat to all others.[44] States commit themselves to joint action against any member that might seek to exploit the others rather than arming against specific adversaries. Consequently, collective security meets the definition of a public good more closely than does collective defense. Therefore, collective security is more prone to failure than collective defense because all members may find it difficult to agree on a response, and free riding is more likely. There is a trade-off, however: although comprehensiveness reduces sanctioning effectiveness, it increases information about potential violators because they are members. It is easier to anticipate defection in collective security arrangements than outside them because members are not armed to the teeth against one another and are expected to prefer a defensive status quo. Therefore, it should be easier to identify likely security lemons in a collective security institution because their behavior deviates from nonthreatening norms.

Despite these differences, the solution to collaboration problems remains the same: repeated interaction, monitoring, and sanctioning.[45] Although defection is the chosen strategy in a single game of Prisoner's

---

43. Glenn H. Snyder, "The Security Dilemma in Alliance Politics," *World Politics* 36 (July 1984): 461–495.

44. Wolfers, "Collective Defense versus Collective Security," p. 183. See also Charles A. Kupchan and Clifford A. Kupchan, "Concerts, Collective Security, and the Future of Europe," *International Security* 16 (Summer 1991): 114–161, at p. 118.

45. Axelrod, *Evolution of Cooperation*; Oye, "Explaining Cooperation under Anarchy."

Dilemma, when the game will continue indefinitely, it is rational to choose cooperation as long as others do. Monitoring allows each state to be certain that it is not being exploited and that others are cooperating, and the potential for sanctioning creates a disincentive for trying to exploit others. Most institutional work on issues of international political economy has focused on collaboration problems, so the institutional resources needed for their solution are well known.[46]

Realist approaches lead us to expect that in the face of collaboration problems in security relations, states will rely on what they can achieve unilaterally. They will guard against being exploited and will try to exploit other states—they will choose a strategy of defection. They will focus on achieving what they can through power rather than risking cooperation.

An institutional theory of security relations expects that when faced with collaboration problems in their security relations, states will try to sustain conditional multilateral strategies of cooperation in an ongoing relationship. The dynamics of collaboration problems will require that institutions provide for monitoring and sanctioning. When decision makers seek to rely upon multilateral cooperation in collaboration situations, we expect that they will be able to do so if institutions with strong monitoring and sanctioning capabilities are available.

Coordination, Bargaining, and Distribution

Security problems may arise from competitive political and military interests even in situations where jointly acceptable outcomes exist. In contrast to collaboration, the cooperative outcomes in coordination situations are stable. Nevertheless, cooperation is not easy: states have incentives to bargain in order to get the most advantageous distribution of benefits from a settlement. The degree of competitive interests in coordination situations can vary quite substantially. For example, in mutual nuclear deterrence, as modeled by the game of Chicken (see Figure 2), both players seek to avoid mutual defection, but each would prefer to prevail while the other backs down. Participants would find multiple outcomes acceptable, but their interests are competitive because each seeks to achieve its best outcome. In order for them to arrive at a stable outcome, some outside factor must intervene. In classic discussions of Chicken, authors usually speak of "resolve" or "bargaining power." In nuclear crises during the cold war, the equilibrium that was favored

---

46. Keohane, *After Hegemony*, chaps. 4–7.

most often was that associated with the status quo. Alternatively, outcomes in coordination or bargaining might be determined by power.[47]

Crises often create coordination and bargaining problems because the parties share some common interest (usually, in coming to an agreement short of total or large-scale military conflict), yet have competing interests over the terms of the agreement. In situations of competitive interests there is no point at which the parties can all achieve their most preferred outcomes. They have strong incentives, therefore, to make maximum demands and to avoid stable compromises. Insofar as threats to security in Europe can arise from the spillover effects of conflicts in neighboring lands (including refugee problems), they are bargaining problems with important distributional effects.

Arms control negotiations may also be coordination rather than collaboration problems when they include multiple dimensions on which states have different preferences. For example, in the Conventional Forces in Europe Treaty negotiations, both sides (NATO and the Warsaw Pact) sought to reduce high levels of armaments, which produced offensive postures and threatened crisis stability. But because of the different weapons profiles and advantages of the two military alliances, the Warsaw Pact sought limits on naval and air forces while NATO focused on limiting tanks and artillery. Although overall limits on the two sides were to be symmetric, symmetric numerical limits would have had asymmetrical military effects.

Whereas resolution of collaboration problems requires monitoring and sanctioning, solutions to coordination and distributional situations require bargaining structures and some method to identify a focal point.[48] Monitoring and sanctioning are not necessary because once achieved, agreements are stable. The obstacle in coordination problems is that the distributional implications of an outcome can hinder states in coming to an agreement, not only preventing resolution but possibly escalating the dispute.

Realist approaches lead us to expect that in the face of coordination problems in security relations, states will rely on power to achieve favorable distributional outcomes.[49] Since Russia and Germany are powerful

---

47. Schelling, *Arms and Influence*, pp. 116–125; Krasner, "Global Communications."

48. Stein, "Coordination and Collaboration," pp. 125–127; Martin, "Interests, Power, and Multilateralism," p. 776. On focal points in security competition, see Thomas C. Schelling, *The Strategy of Conflict* (Cambridge: Harvard University Press, 1960), chap. 3.

49. Krasner, "Global Communications," pp. 336–337. Krasner notes that bargaining and distributional concerns are usually triggered by changes in power. Since my cases were chosen because of their centrality to changes in the international distribution of power, coordination problems ought to be important in German-Russian security relations.

states and since they are powerful in different respects (militarily and economically, respectively), we would expect those resources to play a predominant role in their security strategies for coordination problems, Russia pressing its advantage in military issues and Germany using its economic resources.

An institutional theory of security relations expects that when faced with coordination problems in their security relations, states will try to come to agreement through multilateral strategies that use institutions as frameworks for negotiation and institutional norms, principles, and precedents as focal points. The dynamics of coordination problems will mean that decision makers value institutions as instruments to solve bargaining problems. When decision makers seek to rely upon multilateral strategies to resolve distributional and coordination security problems, we would expect them to be able to do so if institutions with established negotiation frameworks and focal points are available.

Information and Assurance

Security problems may arise from defensive actions taken by states in the face of uncertainty about the intentions of others. In games such as Stag Hunt (see Figure 2), the parties have no interest in launching a war or threatening other states, since they most prefer mutual cooperation. Once achieved, mutual cooperation will be sustained because it is an equilibrium outcome, so exploitation is not a problem and there is no temptation to cheat. Mutual defection is also an equilibrium outcome, however, so if states have established a pattern of noncooperation, they are trapped there without some mechanism outside the framework of the game. In assurance problems, states prefer to cooperate but historical, political, or military conditions make them wary of being exploited.

Another way to conceive of assurance problems is to recall that in realist theories, anarchy and the incentives for self-help security strategies it creates mean that states must assume that there is some probability that others have aggressive intentions, even if they do not.[50] For example, the German-Polish border question in 1990 was an assurance problem. The history of relations and border changes created suspicion that Germany might seek to acquire lost territories, and the German government sought (after some uncomfortable and unpleasant domestic political complaints) to make clear its preference for the existing border and to commit itself to its maintenance.[51]

50. Jervis, "Cooperation under the Security Dilemma," p. 168.
51. Jeffrey J. Anderson and John B. Goodman, "Mars or Minerva? A United Germany in Post–Cold War Europe," in *After the Cold War: International Institutions and State Strategies in*

Assurance mechanisms reassure states that other states' underlying preferences favor mutual cooperation. The task is not to provide the conditions for retaliation, but to provide information and transparency, which allow states to cooperate. In contrast to problems of coordination in security relations, the task here is not to mediate among potentially cooperative yet also competitive bargaining outcomes, but to help states reveal their cooperative intentions and thereby foster cooperative relations.

Established arms control agreements may entail assurance problems. The need in this case is not monitoring and sanctioning to guard against cheating, but transparency and information to assure members that intentions are nonexploitative. Deviations from the norms and procedures of an institution meant to provide transparency and assurance can lead states to reevaluate intentions and suspect noncompliant states.

While the difference between collaboration and coordination problems on the one hand and assurance problems on the other may be clear in analytical terms, in practice identifying whether a potential dispute results from competitive objectives or from uncertainty, mistrust, and fear is very difficult. Therefore, institutions designed to provide information and transparency will be weak. Being willing to accept that other states have assurance preferences makes a state very vulnerable to exploitation. Should other states change their preferences, or should their deception in claiming to have assurance preferences be revealed, members of an institution designed for transparency need to be able to change strategies quickly. Most important, they will want to have back-up sanctioning options. As I will argue, effective institutions for transparency are unlikely to stand alone. They will be linked to institutions that guard against exploitation and provide for retaliation and protection.

Realist approaches generally do not allow for assurance problems in security relations, or they hold that the constraints of anarchy are so great that states must treat even slight uncertainty about assurance preferences as an assumption of Prisoner's Dilemma.[52] Even if a state did prefer mutual cooperation over all other outcomes, it would choose security strategies to guard against the chance of being exploited.

An institutional theory of security relations leads us to expect that when a state has assurance preferences, it will try to ascertain whether others do as well, and if it can get reliable information that this is the

Europe, 1989–91, ed. Robert O. Keohane, Joseph S. Nye, and Stanley Hoffmann (Cambridge: Harvard University Press, 1993), pp. 30–31.

52. Jervis, "Cooperation under the Security Dilemma."

case, it will choose multilateral strategies and security cooperation. The nature of the assurance problem will mean that decision makers value institutions for transparency and information. When decision makers seek to rely upon multilateral strategies to sustain assurance outcomes, we expect that they will be able to do so if institutions with substantial information and transparency capacities are available.

Linkage

Security problems and threats may arise from situations in which one of the players has an exploitable or exploitative dominant strategy. A state's strategy is exploitable when it favors cooperation unconditionally, as in a Suasion game (see Figure 3). Because player A has a dominant strategy that favors cooperation, player B can choose to defect in order to get her most preferred outcome, leaving player A with her second-worst outcome. B could do better only by threatening to behave irrationally, or through tactical issue linkage.[53] A state's strategy is exploitative when it favors defection unconditionally and its partner is forced to cooperate merely to avoid its worst outcome, as in a Coercion game (see Figure 3). As in the Suasion game, player A can avoid being exploited and being stuck with her worst outcome only if she can change the payoffs through linkage.[54]

Figure 3. Linkage dilemmas

		Suasion		
		Player B		
		C	D	
Player A	C	4,3	2,4	(4 = best, 1 = worst)
	D	3,2	1,1	

		Coercion		
		Player B		
		C	D	
Player A	C	3,3	2,4	(4 = best, 1 = worst)
	D	4,1	1,2	

53. On suasion and linkage strategies, see Martin, "Interests, Power, and Multilateralism," pp. 777–779.
54. Downs, Rocke, and Siverson, "Arms Races and Cooperation," p. 127.

Suasion or Coercion situations are familiar in security studies, as familiar as is the strategy of linkage to try to deal with them. Powerful states usually have advantages in linking behavior across issue areas bilaterally because they have the resources to provide side payments or impose costs.

Institutions can also effect linkage, however. Although they are a response to inefficiencies in social interactions (overcoming market failure, providing information, and so on), institutions also may be valuable to states because they *create* market imperfections.[55] This is the case with linkage strategies in security relations. Institutions distort the "market" and incentives. They can provide resources for side payments very directly. The International Monetary Fund (IMF) and the World Bank offer financial and developmental assistance to countries that comply with institutional rules. The North Atlantic Cooperation Council (NACC) and Partnership for Peace offer training and education resources for military establishments to members in good standing. Through their institutional rules, they can enhance the credibility of members who threaten to withhold resources if targets do not comply. Institutions can link benefits in different issue areas and exchanges. While states may not want to comply in a specific instance, they may value an institution's set of benefits and reciprocal obligations strongly enough to deter exploitative behavior.[56]

Realist approaches expect linkage to be an important strategy in security relations, but linkage must be bilateral and depend on preponderant power. In particular, we would expect powerful countries such as Russia and Germany to seek to impose linkage in areas in which they were powerful, but not to allow themselves to be constrained by institutional rules or incentives.

Institutional theory expects that when a state is exploited because of asymmetrical interests, it will choose multilateral strategies to construct linkage and achieve a cooperative outcome. Linkage requires institutions with substantial economic, political, and military resources to offer as benefits, and with strong rules and principles that can help establish credible commitments. When decision makers seek to rely upon multilateral strategies to sustain linkage strategies, we expect that they will be able to do so if institutions with substantial resources and performance rules are available.

If institutions matter in security relations, then decision makers should not be indifferent to them in choosing security strategies to deal with

55. North, *Institutions, Institutional Change, and Economic Performance*, p. 7.
56. Martin, "Interests, Power, and Multilateralism," p. 779.

each of the four strategic situations I have outlined. Because the four situations pose different obstacles that require different resources, decision makers should find that different institutional designs solve the various problems. The variation in the types of obstacles and institutional features should be reflected systematically in the responses of the German and Russian officials I interviewed.

EXPLAINING OUTCOMES

Ultimately, we are interested in international behavior. We study international relations because we seek to understand the causes of peace, stability, and conflict. Even if institutions reduce uncertainty and affect strategies as I have proposed, we cannot consider them important in security relations without some evidence that they affect patterns of behavior. In this section I propose two conditions under which institutions sustain multilateral security strategies: security institutions have to be efficient and effective, and they must mitigate fears of exploitation.

The Right Institution for the Task

States wishing to cope with a security problem must choose a particular strategy depending on the different underlying security tasks they face. Institutions will be effective in sustaining multilateral security strategies when decision makers match security problems, strategies, and institutions. Since different institutional features and capacities are needed to support different strategies, states must rely upon the right institutions for efficient and effective strategies.

If states are to avoid conflict in collaboration games such as collective security and collective defense, they require mechanisms that prevent undetected cheating and allow states to retaliate in order to avoid being exploited. Successful management of competitive bargaining in political or military disputes requires strong principles, norms, instruments for mediation, and focal points. States seeking to deal with assurance tasks need institutions that reliably reveal foreign and domestic policy processes.[57] Linkage requires resources for side payments and credible commitment mechanisms to alter incentives.

It would be difficult to imagine one multilateral security institution that could address all four of these tasks. International institutions vary with respect to their memberships, objectives, guiding principles, and

57. Martin, "Interests, Power, and Multilateralism," pp. 781–782.

organizational capacities, and, therefore, with respect to the security tasks they can effectively address. Multilateral strategies will be ineffective and even counterproductive when decision makers either misidentify security problems or rely upon institutions that do not have the appropriate features for solving the underlying problem.

Moreover, these four tasks are not always compatible, making it difficult for one institution to handle all of them. Bargaining strategies may be exploited by a state bent on exploitation or cheating because negotiations can provide time and cover to gain territory or political advantage. Such a situation calls for a clear deterrent threat if military action is to be prevented, but negotiations send quite a different signal and can lower the costs and risks an aggressor faces. Like bargaining, transparency strategies designed for assurance may be used by a state with exploitative intentions. If you send information that you do not threaten a neighbor and that your military capabilities are limited, this knowledge can be used by an aggressor to increase its chances of success.

Mixing coordination and assurance can escalate political or military disputes. In all bargaining situations, the parties have every interest in strategically misrepresenting their minimal demands in order to get the best deal possible. Should one of the parties have access to information about the other state's minimal demands, it can use that information to great advantage by offering no more than those minimal terms, secure in the knowledge that its competitor would rather agree to that minimal deal than no deal at all. Therefore, the transparency and information mechanisms useful for solving assurance problems can be an obstacle in distributional and bargaining problems, unless they are strictly applied to all the parties and have symmetrical effects so that no one has a bargaining advantage as a result.

National security decision makers will be wary of multilateral security strategies and institutions, although they will use them when they can. Evidence of failure or self-defeating multilateral strategies will lead decision makers to fall back on unilateral and power-based security strategies. Therefore, institutions cannot affect security behavior substantially unless they are effective and efficient. They will be neither effective nor efficient when they do not have the form and function to enable states to solve their security problems.

Layering of Institutions

Although security problems vary and require different multilateral strategies and institutions to sustain solutions, they are linked in a state's overall security relations. While certain aspects of a bilateral relationship require a linkage strategy, others may entail distributional problems, and still others transparency issues. For example, Russian policies toward Germany simultaneously entailed linkage of troop withdrawal to economic assistance, bargaining over the terms of debt repayment, and implementation of transparency provisions of the CFE treaty. Since, as I have argued, no single institution could solve all these problems, several were necessary for sustaining multilateral strategies. Institutional variation is important to meet different tasks.

Just as important for effective strategies, however, are the formal and informal connections among institutions, because states need to have fall-back positions in case ambitious multilateral strategies fail. Recall that my argument depends on two crucial conditions: the degree of common and competing interests in state interactions and a state's confidence that the use of force will not determine outcomes. From a state's point of view, reliance on multilateral strategies requires comprehensive coverage to protect against the possibility of playing the wrong game and being exploited. A rich net of institutions, with their connections and overlap of memberships, is an insurance policy. In particular, states need protection against using coordination, assurance, and linkage strategies when faced with a partner with Prisoner's Dilemma or Deadlock preferences because cooperative strategies leave a state vulnerable to exploitation.

A network of institutions with formal or informal connections does two things to support multilateral strategies. First, it maximizes information about the range of intentions and strategic situations states face. An arms control regime that requires strong monitoring rules and procedures, such as that under INF or Strategic Arms Reduction Treaty (START) I, would provide warning of changes in intentions and exploitative behavior that might be important in ongoing negotiations for a new arms control treaty. Since the configuration of intentions is crucial for the form and sustainability of multilateral strategies, when states have many streams of information about the behavior and intentions of others, they can be more confident about detecting exploitation or unilateral strategies.

Second, a network of institutions reinforces the availability of defensive strategies in the face of shifting intentions or exploitative behavior. States can afford to participate in security institutions designed for transparency and mediation if they can count on the monitoring and sanctioning capabilities of an institution designed for collaboration as well. Institutions are difficult and costly to create, and states do not want to leave to the moment of necessity the construction of institutions to enable them to deter and retaliate against exploitative behavior. They want

[38]

those options in place. Germany can afford a strong multilateral strategy supported by organizations such as the Council of Europe, the OSCE, the Baltic Council, and NACC precisely because it can count on the resources and common defense efforts of NATO. As a result, Germany has been quite successful in taking the lead in solving problems of coordination, assurance, and linkage in central and eastern Europe. In contrast, Russia lacks a similar network of strong security institutions. If multilateral strategies were to fail, Russia would be left with little but traditional military and diplomatic responses to exploitative strategies. As a nuclear great power, Russia retains the option of such responses, but dependence on them erodes Russia's ability to rely on multilateral strategies for the variety of other security problems it faces.

Contrasting Realist and Institutional Hypotheses

In summary, realist and institutional theories produce contrasting expectations about the role of international institutions in German-Russian security relations after the cold war.

Realist hypotheses:

- Because of structural change and greater uncertainty, concern for balancing power will be central to states' strategies and states will tend to rely on unilateral, power-based strategies in security relations.
- States will be indifferent to variation in institutional form and function.
- Institutions will not have substantial independent effect on strategies and outcomes.

Institutional hypotheses:

- Given common interests and costly or ineffective use of force, greater uncertainty increases the value of institutions to states after the cold war for choosing efficient and effective security strategies.
- Because security problems and the conditions needed to solve them vary, variation in institutional form and function matters. States will choose cooperative strategies when institutions are available with the appropriate form and function for these problems:
  1. colloboration problems require institutions for monitoring and sanctioning;
  2. coordination problems require institutions that establish negotiating forums and focal points;

[39]

3. assurance problems require institutions for information and transparency;
4. linkage problems require institutions with resources and strong conditional rules and procedures.

- Institutions will be effective in producing security cooperation when they have the appropriate forms for solving the relevant security problem and when there are formal or informal connections among them.

[3]

Intentions, Power, and Uncertainty

This chapter first explains German and Russian definitions of their national interests after the cold war. I then assess the evidence on whether the two necessary conditions for an institutional role in security relations are met: the prevalence of common as well as competing interests, and the costliness and limited effectiveness of force. Finally, I evaluate my institutional hypothesis that as uncertainty in states' security environment increases, they will not abandon preexisting institutions but value and attempt to rely upon them to an even greater extent. This directly contradicts realist expectations on the role of institutions.

German and Russian Security Interests

German-Russian relations began on a positive note in 1991. Although Gorbachev's Soviet Union had negotiated German unification, German gratitude transferred to the Russians. Good feelings were strengthened because Russia appeared to be on a fast track toward economic reform, democratization, and disavowal of the historic Russian empire. For their part, Russians saw Germany as taking the lead in supporting the general program of Russian political and economic reform. Furthermore, Germany was Russia's single largest donor of humanitarian assistance through 1992.[1]

---

1. Sergei Karaganov, *Whither Western Aid to Russia* (Gütersloh: Bertelsmann, 1994), p. 85.

German security interests in 1992 were defined in terms of stability rather than threats. Political and government elites saw no state that posed a traditional threat to German security in the form of territorial demands or disputes, pressure to conform to a different foreign policy line, or deliberate harm to German economic well-being.[2] Germany no longer had a hostile and heavily armed Soviet Union on its borders. This does not mean that the security outlook was entirely benign; Germany faced several problems that involved control of its territory and the functioning of the nation-state.

Germany focused on two objectives: preventing instability in central and eastern Europe, and establishing reformed democratic and market-oriented countries there. Ethnic conflict, economic chaos, and mass immigration are salient and important security issues to the German elite.[3] Germany's security interests demonstrate the distinction between threats and vulnerabilities. Threats have to do with the intentions of other states, vulnerabilities with points of weakness at which a state may be harmed by others. Although Germany faces few threats, the reform of the communist states has made it more vulnerable to the east's instability.[4] Russia, as the country with the greatest military power and greatest economic potential for development as a great power, was a particular focus of German concerns and efforts. Therefore, traditional German national security interests in protecting national territory from external attack have been supplemented by security interests in the economic and political development of states in central and eastern Europe.[5]

2. This is the general and overwhelming conclusion of experts on German security and foreign policy. See Wolfgang F. Schlör, "German Security Policy," *Adelphi Paper* no. 277 (London: International Institute for Strategic Studies, 1993); Josef Joffe, "After Bipolarity: Germany and European Security," *Adelphi Paper* no. 285 (London: International Institute for Strategic Studies, 1994), pp. 37–38; Hilmar Linnenkamp, "The Security Policy of the New Germany," in *The New Germany and the New Europe*, ed. Paul B. Stares (Washington, D.C.: Brookings, 1992), pp. 93–125.

3. American academics may be highly skeptical that democracies are more pacific than other states, but that is not directly relevant to the question of how the national security elites of Germany and Russia evaluate their interests after the cold war. On the academic skeptics, see Christopher Layne, "Kant or Cant: The Myth of the Democratic Peace," *International Security* 19 (Fall 1994): 5–49, and David E. Spiro, "The Insignificance of the Liberal Peace," *International Security* 19 (Fall 1994): 50–86. For a succinct statement of Germany's definition of its national interests, see Christoph Bluth, "Germany: Defining the National Interest," *The World Today*, March 1995, pp. 51–55. On stability as Germany's security objective, see Schlör, "German Security Policy," p. 46.

4. Beverly Crawford, *Economic Vulnerability in International Relations: East-West Trade, Investment, and Finance* (New York: Columbia University Press, 1993), pp. 5–6.

5. Hans-Peter Schwarz, "Germany's National and European Interests," *Daedalus* 123 (Spring 1994): 81–105, at p. 99.

Although Germany does not possess nuclear weapons itself, Germany security interests involve nuclear issues in two respects. First, it has a strong interest in preventing nuclear proliferation. As a nonnuclear weapon state, Germany had no direct role in START negotiations, but it did play a role as a party to the treaties which would assure that Russia alone would be the nuclear successor state to the Soviet Union.

Second, nuclear threats and dangers do not lie only in the direct effects of blast and explosion, but also in the effects of radiation. This had been a concern throughout the cold war, given that Germany would have been the nuclear battlefield in an east-west conflict, but it took on new dimensions with the Chernobyl accident in 1986. German security interests have come to include preventing nuclear reactor accidents in central and eastern Europe.[6]

Economic issues play a role in the national security policies and interests of all states, and no less in the case of Germany because of the importance of exports to the German economy.[7] Although German trade with the countries of central and eastern Europe was limited, its growth potential was substantial.[8] Furthermore, German trade with countries of the former Soviet Union was concentrated in the hands of eastern German firms vulnerable to marketization, so the trade issue played an important role in bilateral relations.[9]

Russian national security interests in 1992 were problematic. All the sources of its foreign policy were changing: its security and geographical environment, its economic structure, its domestic politics and political

---

6. See Hans W. Maull, "Großmacht Deutschland? Anmerkungen und Thesen," in *Die Zukunft der deutschen Außenpolitik*, ed. Karl Kaiser and Hans W. Maull (Bonn: Forschungsinstitut der Deutschen Gesellschaft für Auswärtige Politik e. V., 1992), pp. 64–65.

7. Dieter Senghaas, "Verflechtung und Integration," in *Die Zukunft der deutschen Außenpolitik*, ed. Kaiser and Maull, pp. 35–52.

8. Schlör, "German Security Policy," p. 21.

9. So strong is the link between Germany's national interests in trade and its foreign policies that many scholars do not distinguish interests and strategies as I do. See, for example, Peter Katzenstein, "Taming of Power: German Unification, 1989–90," in *Past as Prelude: History in the Making of a New World Order*, ed. Meredith Woo-Cummings and Michael Loriaux (Boulder, Colo.: Westview Press, 1993), pp. 59–81; Jeffrey J. Anderson and John B. Goodman, "Mars or Minerva? A United Germany in Post–Cold War Europe," in *After the Cold War: International Institutions and State Strategies in Europe, 1989–91*, ed. Robert O. Keohane, Joseph S. Nye, and Stanley Hoffmann (Cambridge: Harvard University Press, 1993); Schlör, "German Security Policy," pp. 6–7; Gunther Hellmann, "'Einbindungspolitik': United Germany and the Promise of Foreign Policy Continuity," paper presented at the International Studies Convention, 21–25 February 1995, Chicago; Harald Müller, "German Foreign Policy after Unification," in *The New Germany*, ed. Stares, pp. 126–173; and Beverly Crawford and Jost Halfmann, "Domestic Politics and International Change: Germany's Role in Europe's Security Future," in *The Future of European Security*, ed. Beverly Crawford (Berkeley: University of California, International and Area Studies, 1992), pp. 216–259.

institutions, and the relation of society to the Russian state. Consequently, Russian foreign policy statements have often appeared unstable and internally contradictory. A clear case of instability was the transition from a relatively idealistic and internationalist foreign policy articulated largely by Foreign Minister Kozyrev in early 1992 to a more nationalist and "realist" policy articulated by a broader government leadership by 1994.[10] Official Russian policy in this period wavered between Kozyrev's goal of joining the "civilized" international system and an April 1993 document asserting the Russian prerogative to protect the rights of Russian minorities in the countries of the former Soviet Union.[11]

However, Russian *policy* must be distinguished from Russian national *interests*, and these latter were considerably more stable than conventional wisdom implies. Official Russian foreign policy became more assertive in claiming traditional security interests (those involving territory, geopolitics, and military power) along with economic goals. But all these elements were present in the responses and discussions I had with Russian officials, politicians, and scholars in 1992. The shift was more of degree than kind.[12]

From the beginning the definition of Russian national and security interests included many elements. Economic reform was the preeminent

10. For analyses of Russian foreign policy in this period which explain and document this transition, see Alexei Arbatov, "Russian National Interests," in *Damage Limitation or Crisis? Russia and the Outside World*, ed. Robert D. Blackwill and Sergei A. Karaganov (Washington, D.C.: Brassey's, 1994), pp. 55–76; Alexei K. Pushkov, "Russia and America: The Honeymoon's Over," *Foreign Policy*, no. 93 (Winter 1993–94): 76–90; Bruce D. Porter and Carol R. Saivetz, "The Once and Future Empire: Russia and the 'Near Abroad'," *Washington Quarterly* 17 (Summer 1994): 75–90; Kyoji Komachi, "Concept-Building in Russian Diplomacy: The Struggle for Identity from 'Economization' to 'Eurasianization'," Working Paper No. 94–3, Center for International Affairs, Harvard University, 1994; Suzanne Crow, "Why Has Russian Foreign Policy Changed?" *RFE/RL Research Report*, vol. 3, no. 18 (6 May 1994): 1–6; and S. Neil MacFarlane, "Russian Conceptions of Europe," *Post-Soviet Affairs* 10 (July–September 1994): 234–269.

11. For a published translation of Kozyrev's February 1992 speech, "Vystupleniye na prakticheskoi konferentsii 'Preobrazhennaya Rossiya v novom mire,'" see the reprinted version in *International Affairs* (Moscow) (April–May 1992). On the April 1993 document, see Sergei Karaganov, *Where Is Russia Going? Foreign and Defence Policies in a New Era* (Frankfurt am Main: Peace Research Institute Frankfurt, 1994), pp. 19–22.

12. For a similar argument see Franklyn Grifiths, "From Situations of Weakness: Foreign Policy of the New Russia," *International Journal* 49 (Autumn 1994): 699–724, esp. pp. 706–707. One of the strongest analysts and advocates of Russia's clearer assertion of its national interests is Sergei Karaganov, deputy director of the Institute of Europe and a member of Yeltsin's influential Presidential Council. Yet in 1992 he wrote: "Russia and other republics still want a favorable international climate, but their definition of the term 'favorable' has changed. . . . traditional international priorities will to a large extent become secondary as the domestic agenda becomes internationalized": Sergei A. Karaganov, "Implications of German Unification for the Former Soviet Union," in *The New Germany*, ed. Stares, pp. 331–364, at p. 352.

concern, but regional stability and relations with the new states of the former Soviet Union were high priorities as well. Atlanticism was a function of the government's public and practical emphasis on getting western support and financial assistance for domestic reform. Russia's interest in economic reform and prosperity created a set of supporting interests in trade, integration, currency convertibility, and international financial credibility.[13] In order to reform the economy, the Russian government sought western financial and technical resources and access to the international economic and trading system, and it tried to reassure the countries providing these resources that it did not pose a military threat to them.

Russia's national security interests, however, are defined by economic reform *and* by the realities of its strategic environment: disintegration and the complexity of the multipolar system. In private discussions, I found that official concern about stability, Russian minorities, and the problem of the former Soviet states were active issues from the beginning.[14] Although the former Soviet states do not pose a traditional military threat to Russia, Russian security depends on its military, political, and economic relations with its new neighbors and their foreign and domestic policies. This includes their policies toward Russian minorities, which can create migration problems for Russia and regional conflicts. Focus on the west and traditional security interests should not obscure the importance to Russia of the former Soviet states.[15] Russia is threatened by weak and unstable countries on its borders.

Similarly, Russian security depends on developments in central Europe. Although Russia opposes the extension of NATO into central Europe, its interests are not served if western Europe turns away from that region's instability, migration, and conflicts.[16] Russia's regional interests are to limit conventional forces, prevent the emergence of an anti-Russian coalition, and cope with the new strategic buffer zone between itself and

13. For the interrelation of these interests given a basic interest in market economies and prosperity, see John Williamson, "The Economic Opening of Eastern Europe," in *Currency Convertibility in Eastern Europe,* ed. Williamson (Washington, D.C.: Institute for International Economics, 1991), pp. 361–431.

14. Komachi argues along the same line. See "Concept-Building in Russian Diplomacy," esp. pp. 6–7.

15. Steven E. Miller, "Russian National Interests," in *Damage Limitation or Crisis? Russia and the Outside World,* ed. Robert D. Blackwill and Sergei A. Karaganov (Washington, D.C.: Brassey's, 1994), pp. 77–106, at pp. 82–85; Nikolai Travkin, "Russia, Ukraine, and Eastern Europe," in *Rethinking Russia's National Interests,* ed. Stephen Sestanovich (Washington, D.C.: Center for Strategic and International Studies, 1994), pp. 33–41, at p. 35.

16. Karaganov, "Implications of German Unification," p. 353; Karaganov, *Where Is Russia Going?,* pp. 3–7.

the most important countries of Europe.[17] Russian security interests are also bound up with the issues, roles, responsibilities, and problems Russia inherited from the Soviet Union, such as debt, arms control commitments, and nuclear nonproliferation.[18]

Furthermore, these security interests do not necessarily contradict interests in economic reform. External stability along its new borders is all the more important to Russia precisely because pursuing economic reform and solving its economic problems are a priority.[19] Interest in economic reform and prosperity can coexist with military security interests. For example, Russia's interest in economic well-being and prosperity does not preclude an interest in international arms sales.[20]

Russian security interests also involve a nonmaterial, subjective dimension. Survival and prosperity are easy to identify as national interests, but less tangible interests are also bound up with the nature of Russia's domestic political, economic, and social system.[21] For this reason, the idea of "Eurasia" and Russia's role as a great power are important in thinking about Russian security.[22] One should not, however, exaggerate the significance of identity in Russian security interests during the period covered by this book. Many elements of foreign policy were uncertain and changing in this difficult time, domestic politics and interests among them. Identity was just one of many elements and just one over which elites and political figures disagreed.

Thus, Russia's national interests clearly encompass traditional concerns of military security.[23] But its national economic and political inter-

---

17. Arbatov, "Russian National Interests," p. 69.

18. Alexei Arbatov, "Russia's Foreign Policy Alternatives," *International Security* 18 (Fall 1993): 5–43, at pp. 6–8 and 26; Sergei Rogov, "Military Interests and the Interests of the Military," in *Rethinking Russia's National Interests*, ed. Sestanovich, pp. 68–82, at pp. 70–71. For a later formulation of Arbatov's analysis which remains consistent with this earlier statement, see Alexei Arbatov, "Russian Foreign Policy Priorities," in *Russian Security after the Cold War: Seven Views from Moscow*, ed. Teresa Pelton Johnson and Steven E. Miller (Washington, D.C.: Brassey's, 1994), pp. 1–42. For a useful catalog of Russia's foreign policy inheritance, see Dmitri Rurikov, "How It All Began: An Essay on New Russia's Foreign Policy," in *Russian Security after the Cold War*, pp. 125–164, at pp. 160–161; Sergei B. Stankevich, "Toward a New 'National Idea'," in *Rethinking Russia's National Interests*, pp. 24–32, at p. 28.

19. Stankevich, "Toward a New 'National Idea'," p. 27.

20. Pushkov, "Russia and America," pp. 86–87.

21. See Francis Fukuyama, "The Ambiguity of 'National Interest'," in *Rethinking Russia's National Interest*, ed. Sestanovich, pp. 10–23; Stankevich, "Toward a New 'National Idea'."

22. Celeste A. Wallander, "Russian Security Concepts at the Millennium," paper prepared for the conference "Conflict or Convergence: Global Perspectives on War, Peace, and International Order," 13–15 November 1997, Cambridge, Mass.

23. Paul A. Goble, "Russia as a Eurasian Power: Moscow and the Post-Soviet Successor States," in *Rethinking Russia's National Interests*, ed. Sestanovich, pp. 42–51, at pp. 45–48.

ests affect its function as a nation-state and thus touch upon its national security. To ignore these problem would be to misunderstand crucial issues in German-Russian security relations after the cold war.

COMMON INTERESTS AND CONCERNS FOR RELATIVE GAINS

The distinction between *threat* and *risk* is fundamental to an understanding of the effect of common interests on German and Russian security strategies after the cold war. When I asked about the threats they faced, Russian and German officials would correct me, using "risks" as the way to think about security problems. German officials pointed to the NATO Rome declaration of 8 November 1991, at which the alliance members declared the end of "the old threat of a massive attack" and oriented the alliance toward "any potential risks to our security which may arise from instability or tension."[24] In April 1992, German Chancellor Helmut Kohl told a German newspaper, "Security is no more against one another but rather with one another."[25]

This was a widely held view within the German government with a well-established rationale. A German official (9) said that the government now does "risk assessment" rather than threat assessment because the former is a function of instability, which can arise from forces such as ethnic and economic migration.[26] He explained the shift to risk assessment as a response to the fact that "the whole area is unpredictable." Stability is a focus of German security interests because of the potential for large movements of people fleeing ethnic conflict or economic deprivation, he said. A German foreign office official (43) said that German security interests depended on stability in Europe, which in turn depends on the absence of conflict along "the France-Germany-Poland-Ukraine-Russia line." Another official (20) said that instability in Russia raises the prospect of genuine security problems for Germany because Germany's proximity to Russia makes it vulnerable to new nuclear dangers arising from instability. "The difference between nuclear weapons and Chernobyl is almost nonexistent," he observed. A German official (8) argued that because of the potential for social breakdown after communism,

---

24. "Rome Declaration on Peace and Cooperation," Issued by the Heads of State and Government participating in the meeting of the North Atlantic Council in Rome, 7–8 November 1991 (electronic version).

25. "Erweiterte EG und GUS sollen kooperieren," *Süddeutsche Zeitung*, 4 April 1992, p. 2.

26. The numbers in parentheses correspond to the numbered lists of German and Russian interview subjects in the Appendix.

and because "there is no longer a Wall to protect ourselves, we cannot be only western-oriented: we have neighbors in the east and a very difficult history with them."

German politicians consistently spoke about a lack of intentional Russian threat. One Social Democratic (SPD) Bundestag member (16) said, "the main threat is instability" from various sources, the most important of which are nationalist conflicts, "and the incapacity of the existing structures in those countries to handle tensions and change in social interests—there is a chance of them exploding." A Christian Democratic (CDU) Bundestag member (60) said that certainly security in terms of safety from intentional attack had improved over the past few years, but that "the task now is one of stabilization." A CDU parliamentary staff analyst (14) told me that the CDU parliamentary group has agreed *not* to use the term "threat," but rather to speak of "risk." That means, he explained, we exclude the intentional aspect of a military threat. Of course, he added, there remain "people with their fingers on the trigger," but those in Bosnia, Armenia, Azerbaijan, Moldova, Georgia, and Russia are all threats to one another. "These are risks to our security, but not threats." An SPD staff analyst (52) said that the concept of threat was no longer operative for security policy because "we are now no longer a country at the dividing line." An SPD Bundestag member (25) listed domestic instability and the proliferation of arms and military technology out of the former Soviet Union as the most significant problems in German relations with Russia. He observed that all of these were matters of common interest. When asked explicitly about a military threat, he answered, "I cannot see it for the west, although for the CIS states among one another, yes."

This view was official German policy, as well as widely held. One official (53) explained, "There is no more threat; or rather, the potentials are still there, lying around, which produces a type of risk, but the intentional threat is no longer there." Another (63) answered my question about NATO as a continuing instrument of defense against a potential Russian threat: "We do not consider Russia as an enemy. We are doing everything to help." Subsequent interviews in 1996 confirmed this German view of Russia, which had even strengthened given the condition of the Russian military, German officials said.[27]

The distinction between threats and risks and common interests in stability were also clear in official Russian policy and its underlying ratio-

27. German interviews 65 and 66.

nale. When asked about threats to Russian security, a Russian politician (31) said we need to deal with the real dangers in Europe, such as nationalism and immigration, "not state threats, but risks." Russian policy distinguishes between "threats" and "challenges," a foreign ministry official (46) said. A challenge exists when a country or a group of countries is capable of doing damage to Russia but does not want to do so. A "threat" exists when a country or a group of countries has both the means to do harm and the intention to do so. This was the view not only of the foreign ministry, but also of the military. Russian military analysis identifies no imminent military threats to Russia, despite the fact that many countries (including Germany) and groups of countries (including NATO) have the capabilities to harm Russia. In contrast, however, Russia faces many challenges, and these form the basis of Russian military planning. A defense ministry official (45) said, "The problem with geopolitics is not how we view it, but how reality presents it," and in that regard, Russia does not face threats from western Europe. The threats to Russia arise from regional conflicts and instability, he said, not from global conflicts and power as was the Soviet concern. This assessment was also that presented in the ministry of defense document on military doctrine, approved by Yeltsin on 2 November 1993.[28]

Even Russian conservatives did not believe that Germany was a threat. One (11) told me that today's German leaders understand the disastrous result of past policies, especially the push for *Lebensraum* in eastern Europe. This does not mean, he said, that they are not interested in central and eastern Europe: the difference is that now there is "a real possibility for German influence in the east without war." Did this not worry him? No, he said, because now Germany sees these countries as independent and sovereign. An adviser to the vice president (36) offered three reasons why Germany is not a threat: Germany values stability above all, it seeks economic presence and preponderance rather than political influence or military expansion, and Germany's economic efforts in the region are in Russia's interests as well, especially German economic interests in Russia. Germany, he observed, "needs things to be all quiet on the eastern front."

When asked whether German interests in Europe were not a threat to Russia, officials and politicians alike responded in the negative. A foreign ministry official (12) said, "I do not see it: we have the same visions

28. "Osnovnye polozheniia voyennoi doctriny Rossiiskoi Federatsii (izlozheniye)," internal Russian government document, 34 pp.

of security in Europe and favor the same mechanisms." A political adviser (19) said that Germany recognizes that "the key problem of European security is stability in Russia and the former Soviet Union." A defense ministry official (30), asked about potential conflicts with Germany, said, "It is not the security only of east or west." A nationalist politician (21) said, "We have in common with Germany an interest in stability in eastern Europe," so Germany is either neutral or a potential source of help. Recognition of Slovenia and Croatia was a case of traditional German policy and behavior, he said, but Germans had seen they made a mistake in this case by moving on it alone and were now trying to rectify the error through cooperative policies. A foreign ministry official (26) said Germany would be a threat if it asserted territorial claims in eastern and central Europe, but he saw no likelihood of this.

So German and Russian officials thought of their relations in terms of risks rather than threats for two reasons: they saw each other's intentions in relatively benign terms, and they were most concerned with instability. Combined with geopolitical realities, the political and economic dislocation caused by the breakup of the Soviet Union meant that potential common security interests were most important to the officials I interviewed. The shift from "threat assessment" to assessment of "risks" and "challenges" meant that common interests played a larger role in security relations.

Given their past history of conflict, it is important to understand the reasons for these low threat assessments. Russians claimed to see fundamental compatibility in their relations with Germany, with historical episodes of hostility caused by aberrations. Typical was the claim of an official (40) who spoke of close economic and cultural relations between Germany and Russia over some two hundred years. When asked about World War II, he replied, "More important in contemporary German-Russian relations are the common interests." An analyst (29) called Germany "our old partner" and "our neighbor": when reminded of the two world wars, he replied that they were anomalies. Other Russian officials and politicians saw the cold war period as an aberration in which the division of Germany itself created threats: without the division, the sources of conflict in security interests disappeared.[29] A foreign ministry official (24) noted that Germany was the first of the G–7 countries to recognize Russia as the legal successor state to the Soviet Union and that Kohl and Gorbachev on the anniversary of the German attack in June 1941 had issued a statement observing that the countries had overcome

29. Russian interviews 9, 12, and 16.

their past history. Thus, he concluded, by 1991 "the things that held back German-Russian relations were all gone." Russian officials also claimed that the long history of strong relations between the countries means that Germans understand Russia better than do Americans. A Russian politician said that "Germans for Russians are foreign, but close" and this meant partnership rather than threats.[30] A conservative politician said that because Russia is a "Eurasian" power, over time its relations with a country like Germany were far more important than those with the United States. Russia has, he said, "objective interests" in relations with Germany, whereas Russian relations with the United States were a function of the Yeltsin-Kozyrev preferences.[31]

In addition, Russian officials recognized German concern with instability and concluded it generates common interests. In particular, they focused on German interests in European stability and Germany's priorities in supporting Russian reform. An official (40) said that German-Russian relations held neither an ideological nor a political basis for conflicts, and that the two countries had a common interest in stability in Europe. A politician (31) pointed out that Germany has long-term interests in Russian development, and that German interests in supporting Russian reform created a kind of "common brotherhood." Looking into the next century, he observed, German interests clearly were served by a switch to investment rather than just aid, which meant a long-term relation with Russia and an emphasis on stability. Observing that the key problem in European security is stability in Russia and the former Soviet Union, one Russian government adviser (19) told me that therefore countries such as Germany find it in their interests to support reform.

Russian officials tended to see German long-term interests in central Europe as a source of stability. One (11) was unconcerned when asked about German interests in central Europe: "They see the future, they orient themselves in this direction, and they remain on this continent." Another official (24) said German interests in stability require economic development in the east and protection of minority rights. Confidence in Germany's interests in stability was generally present across the political

30. Russian interview 31. A German official (48) spoke in strikingly similar terms, saying of Russians "They are not neighbors, but are close."
31. Russian interview 36. His view was not based on a rosy picture of German interests and policies. He criticized Germany for causing the war in Yugoslavia by recognizing Croatia and Slovenia, and observed that if it turned out that American and Russian forces ended up fighting on opposing sides, Germany would be the cause of this World War III. However, he pointed out, the Germans understand this and they do not want a bigger war, so they are trying to prevent escalation. German interests, he argued, lie in its natural long-term economic relations in central and eastern Europe.

spectrum, although its precise form varied. Liberal and reformist officials and politicians saw common security interests in preventing conflicts, enhancing stability, and supporting reform in the former communist world. Moderate and conservative officials and politicians were less preoccupied with "common" interests and more likely to frame the issue as one of asserting and pursuing Russian interests, but even so, they saw those as generally compatible with Germany's.[32]

These assessments might imply a return to "the spirit of Rapallo" in German-Russian relations: common interests would lead to collusion in Russian-German relations and threaten European security. But I found little evidence of such a possibility. Conservative Russian political figures and, to a limited extent, government officials did see something of a "special relationship" and saw it largely in historical terms.[33] But the issues that might have formed the basis of German-Russian collusion— the Volga Germans and Kaliningrad—proved unimportant, as I explain in Chapter 6. In general, in fact, Germany was not a major concern for Russia in 1992. A foreign ministry official (13) said that Russian foreign policy priorities were "one, the U.S.; two, Europe; and three, not Germany." Instead, the Russian foreign policy community was preoccupied with the instability and risks generated by the breakup of the economic, military, and political system in which it had been embedded. Kozyrev was strongly criticized for neglecting the instability and problems of Russia's new neighbors in the "near abroad" in his speech to the February 1992 conference on foreign policy which emphasized relations with the west.[34] A parliamentary adviser (5) told me that the largest failure of Russian foreign policy was its neglect of the most important set of foreign relations and sources of security problems, the countries of the former Soviet Union.

Another reason for the low threat assessment was geography. Germany and Russia occupy Europe's most historically disputed and conflict-

---

32. Unlike liberals, conservatives did tend to see greater common interests for Germany and Russia than for Russia and the United States. A foreign ministry official (10) was positive about German-Russian relations because they have "more points of coincidence" than Russian-U.S. relations.

33. This was especially clear in Russian interviews 21 and 7. The former declared "In Europe, Germany comes first: Germany is the most important for Russia in Europe."

On each side, many officials and politicians voiced widely shared views on some subjects, and it would be tedious to list every interview in which these were expressed. When I discuss such broadly held views, therefore, I cite only specific interviews in which they came across particularly strongly or from which I quote directly.

34. A major shift in Russian foreign policy emphasis to the countries of the former Soviet Union was the first change in Russian policy following Kozyrev's replacement by Yevgeniy Primakov in December 1995.

ridden territory, but in 1992 officials were preoccupied with the common interests that stemmed from geopolitical realities. As one German foreign office official (29) said, "You know, 50 percent of politics in Europe is geography and you cannot simply move away! Moscow will be there, no matter what happens." Another (56) said that Russia is a large neighbor, and "we are right under the hill." Many German politicians and officials said that Germany has a stronger interest than some other western countries in solving the security problems which arise from instability, lack of reform, and nationalist conflicts because of its proximity.[35] One official (56) said, "For us, *Ostpolitik* is not a spectator sport." Russian officials and politicians also repeatedly raised the issue of proximity as a factor in generating common security interests. "The Germans are always in the middle," was a typical observation, as was "they are right next door."[36]

Yet, although the two are part of the same neighborhood, officials pointed out the importance of a comfortable distance. Both Germans and Russians noted their lack of common borders as a reason for the absence of mutual threat.[37] Officials in both states perceived the existence of a true buffer zone (as opposed to Stalin's "buffer" of states controlled by the Soviet Union) as having removed a primary source of conflicts of interest. A Russian official (40) observed, "Russia has no borders with Germany! But for others I can see there may be concern." This opinion supports the optimistic realist view that variation in the degree to which states pose concrete offensive threats to one another is important for variation in security cooperation.

Economic issues played a role in German and Russian perceptions of common interests, but these were less important and had far less direct effect than one might expect. In the period from the fall of the Berlin Wall until 1992, many in both countries expected that the potential for trade and investment in Russia would lead Germany to conceive of security interests in terms of common economic interests. But by 1992 it was clear how limited the economic potential was in Russia, and German policy adapted accordingly. One German official (62) observed that the obstacles in Russia were great, "so the east is overrated as economic market; it is all security. Of course, this is not what is said in public and not what is in the mind of public opinion."

Russians, in contrast, continued to hold optimistic views throughout 1992 and into 1993: only in 1994 did greater skepticism appear. Liberals

35. German interviews 3 and 16.
36. Russian interviews 7 and 21.
37. Russian interview 12; German interview 43.

and conservatives, officials, politicians, and academics alike were inclined to be enthusiastic about the potential for German-Russian trade and for German investment.[38] They were also not inclined to see conflicts of interest in economic relations. What they worried about most of all was German neglect and lack of interest.

Economic relations did generate common interests in German-Russian relations, but in a complex way. Traditional issues and economic issues become quickly intertwined when one talks about Russia with German officials because of the link between stability, reform, and economic relations. Asked about security relations overall, one official (44) quickly turned to economic relations. Germany gets over one-third of its energy imports from Russia, he said, but at the same time the Russians know that the largest share of their hard currency earnings comes through energy exports to Germany. We could easily get oil and gas elsewhere, he said, "but it is also in our interests for stability to buy energy supplies from Russia." Thus trade relations with Russia, he said, are based on the goal of stability, the imperatives of geography, and "Germany's difficult history in relation to Russia and the east." The link between economic relations and security issues in generating common interests was reflected in the frequency with which the term "exposure" came up. In an economic sense, it meant exposure to default on Soviet debt and to a fall in trade.[39] In security terms, it meant refugees, migration, nuclear safety, and generally spillover from conflicts in the east.[40]

A common concern with stability, however, did not rule out competing interests, and this was most clear in divergent German and Russian diagnoses of how stability could be achieved in the former Soviet states. On the one hand, Russian officials would acknowledge that the former Soviet republics were clearly sovereign states; but on the other hand, the same officials when pressed argued that these independent countries would have to behave in a certain way if they expected to have good relations with Russia.[41] One Russian official (6) when asked about Russia's most important security problems answered reflectively that "We are faced with the question of whether borders or self-determination is more important."

German officials likewise saw the former Soviet Union as a source of conflicting as well as common interests. One (31) said that Germany and Russia would not agree on the aims in all Russia's disputes with the

38. Russian interviews 1, 3, 7, 9, 22, 33, and 36.
39. German interviews 33, 37, 41, 52, and 61.
40. German interviews 15, 43, and 52.
41. Russian interviews 5, 16, 40, and 59.

other countries of the former Soviet Union, and said that he expected this to be a real problem in western relations with Russia in the future. But it is also the case, he added, that Russia can play a constructive role in some of those conflicts. Another official (59) said that Russian interests in settling these conflicts was consistent with German interests, but not if Russia's policy took on an imperialist cast.

Officials were also increasingly wary about conflicts of interest in Yugoslavia. Russian officials noted the limitations and problems of German involvement there because of Germany's history in Yugoslavia during World War II and criticized the German initiative in recognizing Croatia and Slovenia as a major cause of escalation in the fighting.[42] But these officials expressed no alarm about Germany's interests. One Russian (40) expected problems over Yugoslavia in German-Russian relations and was critical of Germany's position, but concluded, "All—Germany, Russia, and the U.S.—sit in the same boat." In a similar vein, another official placed crises and regional conflicts at the top of his list of security issues and offered as the prime causes for concern Nagorno-Karabakh, Moldova, and Yugoslavia, all cases in which Russian priorities and preferences were clearly diverging from Germany's.[43]

So Russians did not wear rose-colored glasses when it came to recognizing conflicts of interest, even early in 1992. A nationalist politician (21) observed that in Europe "our partners are the same as our opponents," and added that although it is good now for Russia that the Germans are in eastern Europe, "Russians do worry—it is an intuitive feeling." Another politician (31) pointed to German-Russian differences on the Baltic states, and added further, "Germans should not participate in Russian-Ukrainian relations." Even a rather liberal scholar (20) warned in the context of the near abroad, "Russia should not add to German ambitions." A foreign ministry official (6) said, "There will be and are conflicts of interest—but not a German threat." A senior foreign ministry official (38) said that Russia's need is to learn how to combine democracy with protection of its national interests: "Our difficulty is to decide what our national interests are and how we may defend them" (the Soviet Union, he noted dryly, did not have this problem).

Therefore, the typical view of officials responsible for Russian policy and analysts influential in Russian politics was less sanguine about the "new world order" than public government statements. In confidential

---

42. Russian interviews 12, 15, 21, 40, and 41.

43. Russian interview 12. However, because he saw these conflicts in terms of the common interests Russia had with other countries in preventing instability, he favored crisis management and multilateral political cooperation.

interviews, politicians, officials, and analysts alike believed Germany to be pursuing its own interests and seeking influence in Europe. However, because they also perceived that German and Russian security interests had common as well as competing elements, they tended not to favor reliance on unilateral strategies. One Russian official (16) emphasized that although he thought Germany's policy on Yugoslavia wrong and counterproductive the solution to the problem was to work together for stability and resolution of the crisis: "We cannot get involved and take sides as in World War I."

Yet, the fact that German and Russian officials saw substantial common interests did not in itself explain why relative gains concerns failed to dominate their calculations. Officials could see common interests and seek to pursue them and benefit from them, but still remain concerned and constrained by fears that their cooperation could be turned against them in the future.

The reason for discarding relative gains considerations came down to domestic politics. For the most part, Russian officials were sanguine about successful security cooperation with Germany because they were relatively confident about Germany's domestic political and economic system, and what that meant for the future. As one official (16) said, "Why should Germany be seen as a threat? It is clear that Germany has undergone serious internal changes from Nazi times." Another official (6), asked why he was not concerned that Germany would benefit from cooperation in Europe and then use its advantages against Russia, answered "Because the government of Germany is not totalitarian." An analyst said that the Russian government does not worry about security cooperation with Germany because it is a democracy, and "You know, no democracy has fought another democracy in the twentieth century."[44] A politician (21) said, "This government in Bonn is not German, but European—although the next generation may be different given the change in German power," while at the same time observing "Russia is not friendly with anyone and has no friends; it is too big."

While German officials did not believe that Russia *would* use gains from cooperation against Germany in the future, they were aware that it *could*. The indexes they repeatedly invoked to assess this likelihood were their assessments of Russian domestic politics. In particular, the transition to a market economy, according to German officials, created domestic interests that supported trade and cooperation with the west, while

---

44. Russian interview 14. He was not pleased when I replied that I did not think that Russia was a democracy yet, and that democracies fight nondemocracies quite often.

the transition away from the Soviet political system created constraints on aggressive policies in Europe. Though far from irreversible, these conditions formed the basis for judgment that Russia sought cooperation for its benefits themselves, not for advantages that could be turned against others.[45]

Even so, German officials and politicians did not assume that Russia had to be a certain kind of liberal democracy in order for Germany to feel secure. A politician (25) said, "If there were to be a authoritarian government, I would regret it, but it would not automatically lead to Russian international expansionism." Such a government might try to collect what it saw as Russian lands, he said, but that is different from a threat to the west. I am confident, he said, that the Russians "will discover that we are the best agent and partner in Europe and the EC, regardless of who is running their government," and this is the basis for long-term, stable relations. A foreign office official (29) said that if reforms failed or were set back, "we would not close the door; we did not close the door to Brezhnev." But the goal is to generate internal support for democracy and participation in a cooperative security system, officials said repeatedly. Domestic politics and priorities are a source of common interests, and monitoring these factors is key to assessing Russian intentions. As long as Russia is on the road to reform, the chances that gains from such cooperation would be turned against Germany were perceived as low. A CDU official (34) said, "We are interested in talking to Russia and dealing with it not as it is today, but with the knowledge that it will be a great power again." Therefore, he said, we are interested in supporting reform. Was he not worried that aiding Russian development and return to great power status was counterproductive? Not at all, he said; "There are no good points in trying to keep Russia a developing country."

German and Russian officials were not ignorant of the potential for relative gains. They could readily speculate on more dangerous futures: Russians worried about the post–Genscher/Kohl generation who might not have the same memory and understanding of World War II, and Germans were concerned about a Russian society driven by instability, poverty, insecurity, and memories of superpower status to pursue a hostile foreign policy. But neither set of officials saw these futures as likely; they did not deem preoccupation with such futures to be productive, realistic, or necessary; and they did not think using strategies to pursue

45. German interviews 21, 28, 45, and 56.

common interests would be dangerous or irresponsible. That is, multilateral cooperation could be efficient, practical, self-interested, and responsible.

Instead, German and Russian decision makers thought in terms of the information that they could acquire about the other's intentions and common interests. They were aware of the potential for a more dangerous future and monitored indicators that could warn if the benefits of security cooperation were being used against them. In many areas of policy, however, concern for "relative gains" made little sense at all. What could it mean, for example, for states to be prevented from cooperating to solve problems of political instability in border regions when stability is in both countries' interests? Concern for relative gains would appear to be an artifact of the wealth generated by trade, but in considering future contingencies, states take into accounts baselines from where they begin. While perhaps a rich Russia could produce the sorts of military forces Germany should and would fear, that Russia is decades away, and to German officials it makes little sense to sacrifice sensible self-interested policies for distant contingencies, especially if those contingencies can be guarded against. Although a richer Germany could become a military superpower, the fact that an already wealthy Germany had not sought to do so, had indeed constrained its own military options, and had built a domestic political system that precludes foreign adventures was far more important for Russian thinking about common interests, relative gains, and efficient security strategies.

USE OF FORCE

Even believing that risks were more salient than threats and that their security relations encompassed substantial common interests, German and Russian officials would have been inclined to avoid cooperative multilateral security strategies if they thought using military force would be low cost or effective. This would be true even if each country preferred to pursue security relations via multilateral strategies, because each would have to worry that its multilateral strategies could be exploited. German and Russian assessments of the likelihood of the other's resorting to force were low, although not nonexistent.

None of the Russians had much doubt about German *power*, but that did not translate automatically into concern about Germany's use of military force. One politician (31) said, "The role of Germany in Europe will of course be dominant, (but) the question is, will this be constructive dominance or destructive dominance?—I think the former." Although many officials and analysts noted that Germany was reducing its military forces and would have to deal with the assimilation of the former GDR for some time to come, they usually pointed out that Germany was still a powerful country. One official (37) said that Russian government and foreign policy circles were thinking in terms of a ten-year framework, in which the estimation of the likelihood of a German use of force was low: "But Germany is a country with immense military potential, and a national sense, a nationalism that brought Germany twice into world wars and thus to Russia—it is a question that must be examined all the time. But for now we see no dangerous moves."

That Germany is a democracy was crucial to many Russian officials and analysts in assessing the use of force. Many also pointed out that modern Germany has a different kind of leadership from those which launched military attacks against Russia and the Soviet Union in the past.[46] Others observed that Germany would not use force because it is now a "normal" country in the sense that it is unified and fully sovereign. One official (26) said, "Germany is like France and Italy. Five years ago it was a country to be checked or controlled, to be worried about. Now it is just like any other country in Europe." A politician (33) pointed to Germany's deep internal opposition to the use of force and its constitutional debate on "out-of-area" missions as indicators of the low likelihood of its unilateral use of military force.

Germany's interests in an international order in which the use of military force would be costly also played a major part in the Russian assessments. One (40) conceded that German foreign policy had a violent past, but argued that the new Germany's stronger interest in economic relations and cooperation is more significant in its contemporary foreign policy. Another official (24) explained that he did not assess the use of force as likely because it would be costly to Germany. Germany has to focus on economic development because of unification, he argued, which will take at least ten to fifteen years. Since this will cost the German government a lot of money, they will not have funds for the military. Furthermore, he said, "Germans have learned in history that with military means they cannot win," and therefore Germany does not have a "power policy."

Another reason Russian officials gave for their government's low estimates of the likelihood of Germany's using force was the geopolitical situation in Europe, particularly distance as a function of the buffer zone

---

46. Russian interviews 16, 32, 40, and 61.

between Germany and Russia. Officials often referred to the "double-belt of countries"[47] separating Russia from Germany: that is, first the countries of central and eastern Europe such as the Czech Republic and Poland, and second the countries of the former Soviet Union including the Baltics and Belarus.

Russian views on the potential for German use of force thus were bound up in traditional ways with assessments of geopolitics. This conjunction of traditionally oriented analysis with conclusions that German use of force was unlikely was puzzling. One analyst explained that the German question meant for Germany unification, but for the Soviet Union it meant the build-down of the military threat from German territory. This problem was solved through the agreement in 1990 with Gorbachev, which declared that Germany would not aid any aggression against Russia.[48] The 1990 German pledge was an essential form of guarantee because of the territories that the Soviet Union had taken from Germany. Compounded by the issue of Polish acquisition of German lands, territorial guarantees have been quite a serious matter in Soviet and now Russian security calculations. A foreign ministry official (24) confirmed that these arguments were correct. Russian assessments of relations with Germany begin on the foundation of the October 1990 treaties, he said. They regulated questions of German unification, established the basis for economic relations, and settled the question of the timing and manner of the withdrawal of former Soviet military forces from Germany. "Then we could continue with the practical work, with abstract questions settled." He added that the territorial bases of Russian concerns about German use of force meant that it was crucial that members of the Soviet General Staff had participated both in the bilateral discussions with Germany and in multilateral forums where recognition of the territorial status quo was affirmed.

While Russian views of the low likelihood of Germany's using military force was a precondition for Russian willingness to try multilateral strategies in security relations, the conclusion is complicated in an important way because institutions themselves played a significant role in Russian confidence. Many officials included German membership in NATO as a reason for their low assessment of the likelihood of German use of force. One official (11) said, "Germany is bound to NATO; it is under control that it otherwise would not be." A defense ministry official (30) said that because Germany is bound to NATO and seeks secu-

---

47. Russian interview 11.
48. Russian interview 35. He noted that Russia does not have a similar commitment in its relations with France.

rity through cooperation, "we do not consider the armed forces of Germany as a threat." By 1998, of course, Russian views of NATO have become quite negative, cast in terms of threat, and bound up with higher assessments of the likelihood of force options.[49] This was a result of the policy of enlargement, however, not a reaction to NATO per se. In 1992 and 1993, Russian officials and politicians consistently believed that neither NATO nor a united Germany in NATO increased the likelihood of the use of force against Russia.

German commitment to multilateral institutions and to its international obligations to limit military capacity were cited by numerous officials and experts as a reason why Russians do not see German power as equivalent to a high likelihood of the use of force. One official (24) said, "We just do not see a military threat from Germany," because of the treaty on unification which limited Germany to 370,000 troops. I pressed one expert (35) on whether such legal obligations were really seen in Russian security community circles as serious. He was surprised that I was doubtful and assured me that they were taken quite seriously within the government.

German officials similarly assessed the likelihood of Russia's using military force as low but not nonexistent. A major reason why German officials were concerned with "risk assessment" rather than "threat assessment" was their estimation of the low likelihood of Russian use of force against the west. One official (9) said, "No one believes that Russia will attack, and furthermore it is not like before, when they could in a few days attack and surprise us and be here." An SPD official (52) said that the residual threat was "a long way to the east."

Concerns about the still substantial Russian military capability were evident, of course. Although by 1998 the Russian military has crumbled, it had not done so in 1992. One official (9) said that the military potential of Russia is enormous and cannot be ignored, so we must be realistic about the capabilities that are left. "I do not believe that any attack will come, but in case of a coup or a resurgence of military thinking, as is the case already a little today, then again there is a bigger risk." A politician (26) said that of course the threat of military force would become real again if the Russian military were to use the political chaos to take control of the government and return to the threatening policies of the past; "The Soviet army is not yet gone or undone—it still has a unified command under CIS forces." But when asked to name the greatest danger to Germany from Russia, even he responded by citing "political, social,

---

49. This was clear in my subsequent interviews in 1994.

and economic chaos—that the way pressure is building up in those countries will be uncontained and spread out from the east to western Europe," and not Russian reliance on its military forces.

Because of the low estimation of the likelihood of intentional attack, German officials were far more preoccupied by the threat of military conflict arising from instability in the former Soviet Union. They saw the Russian army as the only former Soviet institution left intact and functioning, and social unrest within its ranks was a real concern. A politician (16) acknowledged that the state of Russian military forces meant there is a military threat, but it lies in "the explosion of weapons, not their use, and their spread."

Assessments of the use of force as a security instrument are important not only for evaluating the likely actions of other states, but also for considering one's own options. Russian officials assessed Russia's own use-of-force options as certainly viable, but also as quite costly or ineffective relative to other strategies (this even before the debacle in Chechnya). Of course, Russia must restructure its military forces and maintain the capacity for defense, said a Russian defense ministry official (30). But, he went on, the official view of the defense ministry is that the usability of military forces is limited. When I expressed some skepticism he conceded that this was "a difficult evolution," but maintained that it was true. A foreign ministry official (40) observed that it was clear that the positive trends in European security in the past few years had slowed, but added, "but all could be worse if we seek a military solution." Although it is always a difficult process, he said, there is a fundamental commitment in the Russian government to "sit down at the same table" and work at negotiations.

Russian protestations about the limited value of the use of force are, of course, more than a little disingenuous given Russian military actions in Tajikistan, Georgia, Moldova, and Chechnya. But two points should be kept in mind: the distinction between the "near" and "far" abroad in Russian resorts to force, and variation in the costliness of force. An analyst of security affairs (15) who interviewed military officers about Russian defense strategies said that the 14th Army could take control of Moldova in several days, "but it cannot do it in one day, and that is why nothing is done." The use of force was clearly an active option and has at times been the Russian strategy of choice in dealing with the near abroad. But this does not mean that the military option can work in other regions or for all security problems.

German officials and politicians talked consistently of the ineffectiveness of military force for the security problems most pressing in Europe, and saw the use of force as a costly instrument. One official (45) argued that there is an underlying feeling that there cannot be war in Europe. Clear in interviews with German officials was the conclusion that once you define security interests in terms of market reform and democratization, unilateral and power-based strategies are ineffective. Internal support for democracy and economic reform can come only from security cooperation, one official told me, and "a system of multilateralizing security—to create an internal situation where democracy works smoothly, where the connection between [internal] military power and political rule is broken."[50] Another official (58) said that while the threat of nuclear attack from the Soviet Union no longer exists, "the breakup of the Soviet Union creates new nuclear threats—safety, proliferation, use of nuclear weapons in the east." In these conditions, he concluded, military forces are not useful for security.

Another official (45) put things very clearly:

> Here, we mean security in the broader sense, not the traditional military balancing. That is, then, stability, which in turn is democratic institutions and economic development. We recognize that foreign policy is a function of the internal situation. We are just not talking here of security in terms of a military balance—which is in the past.

Ultimately, the point is not that German officials are not worried about the Russian threat to their security. The point is that given the focus on "risks" in place of "threats," and given the assessment that substantial and important areas of common interests exist, a security strategy based on engagement with Russia serves German interests best. Therefore, the use of force remains a crucial issue in post–cold war European security, and in German-Russian security relations, but assessments of the costliness and effectiveness of use-of-force options vary considerably. That variation affects the choice of security strategies, because when the use of force is seen as costly or ineffective, officials and politicians are more likely to think about multilateral cooperation approaches to national security. Germany and Russia are concerned with the balance of power, but they can rely upon institutions as well as national military power to achieve and maintain that balance.

---

50. German interview 29. My insert, from a follow-up question asking him to clarify what he meant by "military power."

RESPONSE TO UNCERTAINTY

As the evidence I have presented in this chapter makes clear, uncertainty increased in both the German and the Russian security environments in 1992, as we would expect from both systemic and state-focused theories of international relations. Uncertainty about Russian intentions and capabilities was most striking, because of the combined effects of the breakup of the Soviet Union and the transition from the Soviet political and economic systems. Russia was in large measure a new country with a new mix of domestic political and economic interests. Although the basic line of the leadership favored democratization and marketization, the stability of that coalition was not certain. One German official (9) admitted, "One can try to assess and guess at what they might do or what might happen, but no one knows." Russian leaders had less change to cope with in Germany, but changes were considerable nonetheless. Unification brought new internal problems and priorities, while the alterations in the international system created potential for German assertiveness. As we saw in the previous section, though Russians were not deeply concerned about a German threat, they were aware that the changes in Germany's interests and in its power could have implications for German strategies. One Russian official (37) said, "We know Germany's past and the threat it has posed to Europe; it has to be watched all the time."

In addition, the end of the cold war created new issues and linked old ones in ways that made the tasks of foreign policy incredibly complex. As we will see in greater detail in subsequent chapters, assumptions about the effects of conventional and nuclear arms control, the causes and control of weapons proliferation, the effects of internal civil conflict on international security, and the relationship between reform and stability were thrown into question. As a result, German and Russian decision makers faced increased uncertainty about the relationship between their policy choices and likely outcomes.

Realist theories, remember, expect that greater uncertainty leads states to rely upon unilateral strategies and balancing, and to avoid security cooperation. In contrast, I argue that greater uncertainty creates incentives for states to rely upon international institutions to get information necessary for choosing efficient and effective security strategies.

So, have German and Russian responses to uncertainty been to escape from institutions, to rely upon self-help, or to engage in classic balance of power politics? In the German case, not at all; in the Russian case, it depends. Faced with uncertainty about the intentions of its smallest and most vulnerable neighbors, and about the potential for escalation, military conflict, and refugee problems, Russia turned toward self-reliant, unilateral, and power-based security strategies. Faced with uncertainty about the role of the west in the political and military alliances of these countries, the Russian government has threatened balancing western force with CIS force and even invasion and occupation of the Baltic states. Russian intervention in the less extreme cases of Moldova, Georgia, Nagorno-Karabakh, and Tajikistan was part of a trend toward asserting a "Russian sphere of influence."

Nonetheless, faced with uncertainty about intentions and capabilities, with instability, and with unclear implications of new conditions and new policies in central and western Europe, Russian officials have clearly and consistently sought to use and adapt international and regional institutions. They have done so both to get information about the intentions, capabilities and policies of other states and to signal information about Russia's intentions, capabilities, and policies. This is not only *also* true of Russian relations with Germany, it is *especially* true. Russian officials are sanguine about German interests because of Germany's institutional memberships and the multiple and overlapping constraints on its military forces, political policies, and economic strategies. Russians said that Germany's multilateral military commitments are a force for stability and security in Europe and that institutions placed constraints on German options.[51] Similarly, Germany' membership, commitments, and policies in multilateral economic organizations (including the EU, IMF, Paris Club, and G–7) demonstrate the rules by which it plays and its interest in economic reform and prosperity in the east.

Russian officials relied upon existing institutions also because they embodied and guaranteed certain German commitments to the Soviet Union inherited by Russia, crucial in the uncertain transitional period. These included restraints on German military deployments during Russian military withdrawal from the former GDR, maintenance of trade credits and special financing arrangements for former GDR-Soviet trade inherited by the two countries, and renegotiation of Soviet-Russian debt under the Paris Club. While much about these arrangements was technically bilateral, Russian officials saw German strategies and policies as being conducted always in negotiation and consultation with the other members of its strongest institutions—so there would be no surprises,

51. Russian interviews 10, 11, 12, 23, 40, 42 and 59.

no sudden reversals. As one official (37) told me in 1992, "What we need now is stability and support while we are trying to change everything."

As for Germany, it is difficult, and indeed impossible, to find any area of security policy in which it sought to escape the constraints of institutions. Integration and assurance had been the basis for German cold war security policy, and they remained so under the changed circumstances of the post–cold war world. Germany had sought to achieve unification in 1990 through assurance based on multilateral commitments and constraints, and it sought to cope with the demise of the Soviet Union in the same manner. Institutions were crucial to the strategy. An official in the chancellor's office (31) explained that Germany has very clear security interests which require an active policy in eastern Europe for stabilization, but added that it is also very clear that Germany cannot take the lead in this region because of fears about German intentions. At best, Germany can contribute to multilateral efforts to support reform and stability in formerly communist countries, "and given our history, that is best." A foreign office official (40) said that Germans face an enormous number of new security issues, so German policy relies upon the "net" of institutions to catch crises and problems: "The more that happens, the more consultations that go on, the more work that gets done, the tighter the net becomes and the less chance that anything will fall through."

German reliance on integration and assurance was meant not only to signal information about Germany's benign interests and intentions, but to reinforce the process of transforming Russia into a neighbor with benign intentions. Far from seeking to escape institutions and go it alone, Germany became the most consistent advocate of extending membership and integrating Russia into a variety of institutions, including the G–7, European Union, and Council of Europe. One official (44) said, "In the final analysis, it is in the interests of the western world to pass through the transition period with as little upheaval as possible, and within that period to get them integrated into European and global western structures as much as possible."

Where does this leave our analysis of the choice of balance versus cooperation in German-Russian security relations? Officials did remain concerned about the balance of power. The Russian defense ministry based its estimate of the value of cooperation with the west in areas of common concern not only on the factors already discussed in this chapter, but also on an assessment that the balance of forces in the region continued to support doctrine and forces based on "reasonable sufficiency,"[52] a term which in Russian military doctrine means sufficient for

---

52. Russian interview 30.

defense. A conservative Russian politician (7) spent some time explaining that it was in American security interests to sustain those of Russia in order to counterbalance a rising Germany. A foreign ministry official (27) discussed policy in terms of balance:

> But there must remain a careful balance between joint European and U.S. forces, because each set has its own perceptions of interests and balances the other. U.S. forces should stay in Europe for five years, in case of hot spots, crises, accidents—for purposes of stability. Conservatives may use the fact that U.S. forces are still in Europe, but they are not taken seriously. However, the number of U.S. forces should be reduced because the threat has become smaller. Especially for the internal Russian audience, this is important.

German officials also answered in terms that made clear the continuing role of balancing in security strategies. One analyst (52), pointing to "residual risk" in the form of Soviet arms and (in 1992) 300,000 Russian soldiers in the former GDR, said that explains why NATO is still needed. A politician (60) said that this is not a new era of peace and freedom, but rather one of serious security problems so we must "keep our powder dry. . . . we have to see to the worst case, not only to the best case."

But to conclude from evidence of balancing calculations and concerns that German and Russian officials therefore choose noncooperative security strategies and disregarded international institutions fundamentally misunderstands both their security environment and the role of institutions in security relations. Institutions played a central role in the "balancing" calculations and strategies of both German and Russian officials. To the extent that Russia did formulate a policy to balance German military power, constraints on German forces and deployment options through international institutions were integral to the Russian strategy. Even officials in the defense ministry told me that since it was clear that Germany would remain in NATO, its power would be contained, and that the Russian military was satisfied with the "balance of forces" achieved through commitments to the Soviet Union and through international agreements in the process of agreeing to German unification.[53] Far from seeking to escape the commitments and processes developed during the cold war, Russian officials sought to retain them because of the stability they contributed for thinking about the western balance of forces and western intentions.

---

53. Russian interviews 30 and 45.

Similarly, the "balancing" aspect of German security strategies was neither unilateralist nor self-help. The politician (60) who told me that we have to prepare for the worst case and not merely the best continued: "These are not German problems, but international problems with German involvement. This should not lead us to a German national policy, but to German initiative within international policy." A foreign office official (43) said, "It is important that whatever is done in European security should not be done unilaterally or in secrecy." Institutions were one way to ensure that Germany would not be left alone in dealing with Russia, and being constrained was better than being alone. When I asked about the difficulties in getting common EU decisions on Russia, a politician (25) said, "I am not worried that other countries are involved in the east. In the longer run, we must be concerned that we will not be alone there. . . . The more friends they have, the better."

Furthermore, to return to the point with which this chapter began, institutions were valuable to the German and Russian governments because the uncertain security environment after the cold war appeared to be one in which "risks" played a bigger role than "threats." A favorable balance of power may have been a necessary condition for national security, but it was far from sufficient. A minimalist security policy of relying upon the balance of power, according to a wide variety of German and Russian government officials and politicians, would not solve the kinds of security problems that they faced after the cold war. Risks cannot be deterred, but rather need to be addressed. For this process, more active and cooperative security policies were on the table, and as this chapter has shown these were the potential choices and efforts which most concerned decision makers. A Russian defense official (30) said that he was concerned about the "real danger of war in Europe," but since the source of the danger lies in instability and escalation from local and ethnic conflicts, what is needed to meet it is cooperation, mutual assistance, and stability.

So while officials did think in terms of power balances and greater uncertainty made such calculations and strategies more difficult than in the simple world of cold war bipolarity, neither Germany nor Russia responded by falling back on unilateral, self-reliant strategies. German and Russian officials pursued a far more complex strategy that combined balancing through multilateral strategies sustained by institutions with consultation, negotiation, information gathering, and assurance. They did so because they perceived important common interests in their central security relations and because military force was seen as limited in its effectiveness and potentially extremely costly for national security interests in Europe. This is not to argue that the core realist argument that the balance of power is central to states' security strategies is wrong: a balance of power was crucial to both Germany and Russia. However, given the existing set of multiple international institutions, two departures from traditional realist expectations were clear in German and Russian responses to uncertainty: (1) institutions played a role in the balance of power, even though those institutions were created under different conditions of power, and (2) strictly self-reliant security strategies were seen as potentially less efficient and effective than multilateral strategies, which entailed aspects of security cooperation as well as competition.

[4]

Balances and Troop Withdrawals

This chapter and the next examine issues in German-Russian relations most characteristic of traditional security concerns: the numbers, deployment, and disposition of military forces. The withdrawal of formerly Soviet forces from German territory was primarily a bilateral concern and the weightiest military security issue in German-Russian relations in the cold war's immediate aftermath. It differed in important ways from broader issues of military balances and their potential use, and this justifies a separate and detailed treatment that is the subject of this chapter. The chapter also outlines the problems surrounding the withdrawal of formerly Soviet forces from the Baltic countries for comparison.

RUSSIAN TROOP WITHDRAWAL FROM GERMANY

Although Germany regained its sovereignty on 3 October 1990 in accordance with the "2 + 4 treaty," foreign military forces remained on German territory under three separate arrangements. NATO forces were (and continue to be) governed by the alliance's Status of Forces Agreement. U.S., British, and French forces in Berlin—not part of NATO but rather a residue of their occupation rights—were governed by a clause in the 2 + 4 treaty which provided that they would remain until all Soviet forces had left German territory.

Soviet—and later Russian—military forces in the former GDR (the Western Group of Soviet Forces before December 1991 and simply the Western Group of Forces thereafter) were another matter. Although they were technically no longer occupation forces after the Soviet Union granted the GDR sovereignty in 1954, the deployment and privileges exercised by the "friends" (as the east Germans called them) were those of an occupying force. For example, Soviet forces owned and operated a 11,500km "private road" network restricted to the Soviet military. This network served combat and training operations, with main routes running east-west for moving troops and equipment to the western front.[1] This quasi-occupation status could not continue; Soviet military forces would have to be withdrawn and their interim status governed by a German-Soviet treaty.

The problem was quite substantial. In 1989, there were 550,000 people associated with the WGF, including 337,800 military personnel, 44,700 civilians, and 163,700 family members. The forces comprised 5 armies (16 divisions) and one air army (5 divisions) deployed in 1,100 locations on territory which equaled that of the Saarland (a western German state), and were equipped with 4,100 tanks, 7,900 armored vehicles, 3,500 artillery, 600 combat aircraft, 700 other aircraft, and 800,000 tons of ammunition. In 1991 the Soviet army overall had 3.4 million military personnel and 54,000 tanks, so the organization was faced with having to move some 10 percent of its soldiers and roughly 7.5 percent of its equipment in four years. When the Soviet army broke apart in 1992 and the numbers of the Russian army dropped to 2.2 million personnel and 29,000 tanks, the operation became a proportionately larger undertaking, absorbing some 15 percent of total Russian military personnel and equipment. Withdrawal was an enormous military undertaking fundamentally affecting the European balance of power.

Over the summer and fall of 1990, Germany and the Soviet Union negotiated a bilateral treaty on the terms of the withdrawal, and a bilateral agreement covering transitional measures which would come into effect upon unification.[2] The main provisions of the treaty obligated the Soviet

---

1. German interview 32. I was shown a Soviet map of this road network, with the "private" roads marked in red. So extensive was the network that no piece of eastern German territory was much of a drive from it. After unification, Russian forces were no longer permitted to use the whole network, and it was shortened to 750km covering roads mainly from Russian barracks to their training grounds. "We stopped that military tourism," another official (18) told me. After unification German access to GDR defense documents demonstrated Warsaw Pact planning for military conflict on a truly astonishing scale. For example, the Bundeswehr reported Soviet plans to use, in any initial phase of conflict on German territory, some 840 tactical nuclear weapons. "Warchauer Pakt plante massive Atomangriffe," *Süddeutsche Zeitung*, 1 February 1992, p. 2.

2. For the treaty and agreement, see "Vertrag zwischen der Bundesrepublik Deutschland und der Union der Sozialistischen Sowjetrepubliken über die Bedingungen des befristeten Aufenhalts und die Modalitäten des planmäßigen Abzugs der sowjetischen Truppen aus dem Gebiet der Bundesrepublik Deutschland" and "Abkommen zwischen der

side to withdraw all its forces from Germany by 31 December 1994, delineated the conditions under which Soviet forces would remain on German territory in the interim period, and specified the terms that would govern how the withdrawal would be accomplished. The agreement covered amounts of and procedures for German financial assistance for the withdrawal.

The financial arrangements were for the most part quite straightforward. In recognition of the fact that the WGF after German unification would have to function in a hard currency economy, the German government agreed to contribute a 3 billion DM grant and a 3 billion DM interest-free loan (for five years) toward stationing costs. A special bank account for the WGF was established, and its officials could make contracts on their own for goods and services such as food and trash removal, and then pay from this account. The WGF itself held direct responsibility for this money. The credit was granted in two phases: DM 2 billion in October 1990 and DM 1 billion in October 1991. The Russians were to repay the credits by October 1996—"if they ever do," observed one German official (17). The 3 billion DM grant was paid in stages as well: DM 1.2 billion in 1991, and the remaining DM 1.8 billion in quarterly installments from 1992 to 1994. To assist with the costs of the withdrawal, the German government made a 1 billion DM contribution directly to the Russian government, calculated as the cost of transporting WGF personnel and equipment to the borders of the Soviet Union. That sum was also paid in installments, with amounts and times determined by a joint commission.

The German government also agreed to a 7.8 billion DM grant for a housing program in the Soviet Union for returning officers and their families, with a target of 36,000 apartments to be built with German funding. Ultimately 45,000 apartments were built in thirty-five locations. The German contribution was meant to assist the program, not fund it entirely, and the Russian side was supposed to build an equal number of apartments. The housing program was handled by the Kreditanstalt für Wiederaufbau (the successor institution to the agency for reconstruction established by the Marshall Plan to administer U.S. credits to Germany). A joint German-Russian committee solicited competitive bids on contracts and decided on the best proposals. When the work was done, contractors sent the bills to the Kreditanstalt, which paid the firms di-

Regierung der Bundesrepublik Deutschland und der Regierung der Union der Sozialistischen Sowjetrepubliken über einige überleitende Maßnahmen," both printed in *Presse- und Informationsamt der Bundesregierung Bulletin*, no. 123 (17 October 1990), pp. 1281–1300.

rectly—"so that this huge amount of money does not get into Russian hands," a German official (17) pointed out.

Finally, Germany also contributed 200 million DM to a training and education program for the soldiers, civilians, and dependents. The bulk of this money was to be spent in the former Soviet Union, but programs were also run in Germany for personnel and families before they left. These included courses in computers, market economics, and similar skills in anticipation of economic reform in Russia.[3]

The treaty and agreement together covered the complex and comprehensive system governing the withdrawal. The actual withdrawal, begun in January 1991, was overseen both by Russian and German civilian ministries (including foreign, finance, economics, and environment among others) and by the Bundeswehr Verbindungskommando zu den sowjetischen Streitkräften (led by Maj. Gen. Hartmut Foertsch) and the WGF itself (commanded by Gen. Boris Snetkov until December 1991 and thereafter by Col.-Gen. Matvey Burlakov).[4] The overall Joint Commission, which met three to four times each year, was supplemented by permanent working groups in specific areas, such as the legal affairs, construction, environment, training, and transport. The withdrawal was supervised entirely by the German government (primarily the Bundeswehr liaison) and the WGF. NATO was not directly involved, nor were Germany's western allies, other than through the 2 + 4 treaty which provided for the legal presence of western allied forces in Berlin while the WGF remained in Germany. An official (32) noted, however, that although NATO and the Western European Union play no direct role "of course, we keep them informed as alliance partners." Another official (18) explained that the Berlin stationing provision for British, French, and American forces "was a link to show the Soviets the continuing commitment of the NATO allies to Berlin: it is a sign to the Russians." By the same token, a Russian official (37) told me, the CIS had nothing to do with the operation, because Yeltsin had declared that the Russian Federation took control of all former Soviet forces outside of the former Soviet Union.

The withdrawal schedule had been agreed to in January 1991 by a joint German-Russian working group: 30 percent of the forces would be withdrawn in each of the years 1991, 1992, and 1993, with the remaining 10 percent leaving in 1994. Withdrawal proceeded roughly one division

---

3. "GUS-Offiziere in früherer DDR werden umgeshcult," *Süddeutsche Zeitung*, 8 April 1992, p. 2; "Wegtreten zur Marktwirtschaft," *Süddeutsche Zeitung*, 9 April 1992, p. 6.

4. Burlakov had commanded the withdrawal operation from Hungary. One official referred to him as a "withdrawal expert" (German interview 15).

at a time, with forces leaving first from the south, then from the north, then from the middle of the country, those in and near Berlin going last. No specific operational military criteria were used to determine the pattern of withdrawal, other than some Russian planning to conform to CFE provisions and Russian insistence that the withdrawal be accomplished in such a way that all forces would remain in intact combat formations.[5] In planning each quarterly and monthly operation, the WGF stated in joint commission meetings where it intended to withdraw, although the German command also on occasion conveyed requests from local German civilian authorities, which the WGF was usually able to accommodate. For example, at German request the WGF withdrew earlier than it had planned from *Land* capitals.[6] In another instance, the WGF agreed to speed up the removal of two missile brigades of SS-21s after a German request: they agreed, said a German officer (19), as a sign of good will.

Withdrawal was monitored in accordance with procedures agreed upon in the treaty. For all categories of WGF forces (soldiers, civilians, families, tanks, artillery, aircraft, and so on) a plan for the year, each quarter, and each month was agreed upon. The Bundeswehr and the WGF then reported and checked their figures on the actual withdrawal each month, and percentages of the plan completed were calculated. For example, at the end of September 1992, the WGF had accomplished 87.8 percent of the planned personnel withdrawal for 1992, and 119.7 percent of the planned 1992 tank withdrawal.[7]

The treaty also specified rules for the conduct of the WGF and the Bundeswehr. The WGF was obligated to behave as a treaty partner, rather than an occupation force, which meant that it had to operate under the same legal conditions as German and NATO allied forces. For example, during artillery exercises the WGF could no longer shoot from one range or practice ground to another when that entailed (as it almost always did) shooting over a town or village. The WGF was also obliged to restrict its training exercises to 7:30 A.M.–5:30 P.M. Monday through Friday, and WGF aircraft could fly no lower than German and NATO forces were permitted to. Most important, the WGF's authority was restricted to its installations: it could no longer go off-base to search for defectors or suspects, but had to rely on German police and authorities.[8]

---

5. German interviews 19 and 32; Russian interview 18.
6. German interview 32.
7. From an internal German government document, November 1992.
8. German interview 18. He told me that for the most part, the Russian military accepted these rules in good spirit. On one occasion, he said, they even tried to use the rules to their own advantage, by complaining that WGF tanks had to observe traffic laws on the Auto-

Constraints on the conduct of its forces was something the Russian military slowly and gradually came to accept. In 1991, it became known that, much to German surprise, still deployed on eastern German territory were nuclear weapons. In April 1991 a German major was shot during an enhanced surveillance mission of a suspected WGF nuclear depot. Whether he was outside the marked security zone, as the Germans claimed (and thus permitted to observe), or had entered the WGF installation, as the Russians held, the incident made clear that the withdrawal itself could entail tangible security risks. By June 1991, all nuclear weapons had been withdrawn, the WGF permitted short notice inspections of suspected sites, and joint working groups had clarified the legal constraints on WGF defense measures (namely, that they were not permitted to shoot *out of* their installations, only within them).[9] Similarly, by 1992 WGF officials had accepted that any Russian personnel accused of violating German law would have to be tried under German law in civilian courts. In one incident, a Russian soldier attacked by five Germans who had shot and killed one of his attackers was tried under German civilian law, and found innocent on the basis of self-defense. In another incident, Russian pilots engaging in reckless behavior crashed their aircraft and were held liable under German civil law for the damages. All these cases were managed by joint Bundeswehr-WGF commissions.[10]

The withdrawal was far from problem-free. The important problems were not in direct German-Russian relations, however, but were difficulties created by new factors that threatened to undermine the will or capacity of the Russian side to fulfill its commitments.

First, the loss of Soviet hegemony in eastern Europe made the operation more complicated and expensive than the Russians had anticipated. For instance, the Polish government withheld approval of agreements on transporting the WGF through Polish territory as leverage to try to get an early withdrawal of the Northern Group of Soviet Forces from Poland. This undermined Russia's ability to fulfill its commitments, and it sought German help in dealing with Poland. The German government

---

bahn—in particular, that they could not just stop on the highway for breaks—but American forces did not. When the Germans replied that this was untrue and that American tanks were subject to the same rules, "the Russians pulled out satellite photos showing American military convoys taking a rest on the German autobahn in western Germany." The Germans pointed out that the American forces had indeed followed the law by pulling over and stopping only at rest areas.

9. German interview 18.

10. German interview 18. "Jugendlicher Angreifer von GUS-Posten erschossen," *Süddeutsche Zeitung*, 13 April 1992, p. 5.

refused to become involved in the Russian-Polish dispute, citing the provisions of the agreement which made the organization of the withdrawal itself entirely a Russian responsibility. The equipment of the WGF was withdrawn instead by sea, and the personnel by air. When the Polish government changed its policy later in 1991, the Russian command stayed with the revised arrangements, since they were less expensive. The Russian military learned other quick lessons in the operation of market forces: Lithuania demanded transport fees for carrying former Soviet forces over its territory, and as eastern Germany joined the west's market economy, prices for goods and services increased. The costs of the withdrawal began to climb.

Second, the breakup of the Soviet Union created problems because issues concerning the withdrawal, housing, and breakup of the Soviet military could not be easily disentangled. The original plan had been to return personnel and equipment to the far western reaches of the Soviet Union, primarily to Belarus and Ukraine, and to build housing primarily in those regions. By mid-1992, ten sites were under construction, including two major installations in Ukraine. In the original plans, seven of the original sites were in Russia, seventeen in Ukraine, and eight in Belarus. The housing program became a prize which the former Soviet republics sought. Ukraine argued that the original housing allocation plans should be fulfilled. Russia's position was that since the forces would be returned to Russia, it should get all the housing, and it demanded that the allocation be changed so that Russia would get fifteen housing installations, Belarus seven, and Ukraine two.[11] Although ostensibly about apartments, the issue was more serious, a German diplomat (5) in Kiev said, "because it is about soldiers," and the problem was discussed at the highest levels by Ukrainian president Leonid Kravchuk, Kohl, and Yeltsin. Russian officials were adamant that Russia retain ownership of the WGF, its advanced equipment, and housing entitlements.

Russian officials hoped that the German stake in a smooth withdrawal would create an incentive for Germany to support Russia's views in these transport and housing disputes. But the German government refused to become involved in Russia's disagreements with its Baltic or CIS neighbors, and the Russians quickly reconciled themselves to the German position, which was to fall back on the existing agreement.[12] German officials insisted that where the troops were to be returned and

---

11. "Streit zwischen Moskau und Kiew über deutsche Gelder," *Süddeutsche Zeitung*, 6 May 1992, p. 8.
12. Russian interviews 6 and 24.

where the housing was to be built were not German concerns and that once Russia and Ukraine decided the housing issue, the construction would continue. When asked about these problems, one official (17) said, "Russia is the successor of the Soviet Union, including with respect to troops in Germany. We have not heard any complaints from the other republics on that, and the Russians say that all the troops return to Russia." If the Baltics now want hard currency, he added, that is not our responsibility. Eventually, Kohl, Yeltsin, and Kravchuk signed a joint letter stating that the housing matter was to be decided between Russia and Ukraine, and funds for construction were freed.

These delays in the housing program were exacerbated by Russia's failure to begin construction on its projects. As of 1992, virtually no Russian housing construction had begun. The reasons were largely financial, but also most Soviet construction industry factories had been located in the Baltic states, and now those countries were demanding hard currency payments for housing materials. Technically, then, Russia was not fulfilling its part of the agreement. Russian officials complained of obstacles beyond their control to agitate for German involvement and—more important—more German financial assistance.[13] Since Germany had a strong interest in the withdrawal's going smoothly, the Russians might have gained some bargaining leverage. But German officials chose not to interpret the delay as an obstacle to implementing the agreement, or as a deliberate Russian "defection" from the agreement. The government did not view Russia's failure to live up to its side of the agreement as a reason to suspend the German contribution to the housing program. One official (15) pointed out that Germany had no interest in creating more problems in fulfilling the agreement than existed. Another (17) indicated that the failure to live up to the commitment was not a result of any Russian decision to violate the agreement, but because the Russians simply did not have the money and because of the turmoil caused by the Soviet breakup. They are only hurting themselves, he said, not us.

The Russian lack of money brings us to the other major problem in effecting the withdrawal. The German-Soviet agreement had provided that the WGF could sell its "immovable" property such as barracks and other military buildings. The WGF did not own the land itself, but under its agreements with the GDR it did own the buildings. According to Russian sources, by 1990 the Soviet Union had built some 20,000 apartments, 700 barracks, and 28 airports, valued by Russian sources at DM 10 bil-

---

13. Russian interviews 24 and 40.

lion.[14] The agreement specified that the property would be sold "on market conditions," with the actual sales handled by a joint working group. The agreement also provided that costs for environmental and other damage caused by the WGF would be deducted from the profits; proceeds from the sales were to be held in an account until all damage claims could be calculated and deducted.

The WGF and the Russian government had counted on the proceeds from these sales to help finance costs of the withdrawal and their portion of the housing construction program.[15] However, two major obstacles arose. The first was Russian inexperience with markets. There was very little demand for the installations, especially not at the prices the Russians were asking. Many of the properties were dilapidated and substandard given German building codes. Some installations, such as modern facilities for repair of weapons, cars, and other equipment, found eager prospective buyers. Often when potential purchasers could be found, however, they were interested in the valuable land underneath and saw the Russian property in negative financial terms because the buildings would have to be destroyed. Although the German government had many interested buyers (as it owned the land), the deals could not go through because the Russians refused to accept the offered prices.[16] Further complicating the sales, the ownership status of the land in many cases was itself questionable because of claims against Nazi, Soviet, and GDR expropriations of property.

Second, the Russians severely underestimated the costs of the environmental damage that the WGF had inflicted on eastern Germany. Soviet military practices had included failure to dispose properly of spent ammunition and conventional trash, dumping kerosene and oil into water and soil, and failure to dispose safely of toxic waste.[17] Many towns

14. "Slukhi o shantazhe neskolko preuvelicheny," *Izvestiya*, 15 February 1992, p. 5; "Burlakov Interviewed on Withdrawal from FRG," *Pravda*, 12 March 1992, p. 5, in FBIS-SOV-92–053 (18 March 1992, pp. 5–6); Pavel Felgengauer, "Kvartira v obmyon na oruzhiye," *Nezavisimaya gazeta*, 23 June 1992, p. 2. Plans to sell Soviet installations and equipment for cash to fund housing and social services may also have figured in the large-scale and notorious corruption of the WGF command. It was widely known that officials of the procurement and financial divisions of the WGF were corrupt, for example demanding kickbacks from suppliers of consumer goods and food to whom they awarded contracts. These accusations were being investigated by Dmitriy Kholodov, a journalist who was killed in 1994 by a bomb placed in a briefcase that supposedly contained incriminating documents on the WGF scandal.

15. Russian interview 10.

16. German interview 17; "Die Liegenschaften der Sowjetarmee sind schwer verkäuflich," *Frankfurter Allgemeine Zeitung*, 13 October 1992, p. 17.

17. "Birkhuhn und Ölschlamm auf dem Truppenübungsplatz," *Frankfurter Allgemeine Zeitung*, 12 May 1992, p. 8. Under pressure not to make things worse in the former GDR so

near Soviet military installations had polluted ground water as a result. Local politicians in the eastern regions began to investigate the claims for damage against the WGF. In mid-1992 it was not clear that the value of the military assets was even enough to cover the environmental damage, let alone that it would generate a surplus to pay for the costs of the withdrawal.[18]

These financial obstacles threatened to delay the operation. Claims and counterclaims concerning property and environmental damage issues played a predominant role in 1992, to the point where several officials told me that the issue of the withdrawal had virtually ceased to be a military matter, and was a problem of economics.[19] Over the course of the year, Russian estimates of the value of the property dropped from DM 10 billion to a couple of billion. Seeking a solution that would resolve the impasse and put money into Russian coffers, Yeltsin at one point sent a letter to the German government proposing that it make a lump sum payment to Russia in exchange for Russia giving up all claims to the property. As one official (17) told me, the German government was open in principle to such a change, but by that point the estimates of the environmental damage were so high that "we calculate that the value of the Soviet property is not greater than the damage done. So the 'lump sum solution' is zero."

These unanticipated delays and problems put Germany in a difficult position. While it clearly did not have to change the rules or adapt to Russian complaints and demands, insisting on strict adherence to the terms of the agreement was not necessarily in Germany's security interests. The financial advantages of inflexibility were clear, but these had to be weighed against German interests in a successful withdrawal. The removal of former Soviet forces from German territory was a core security objective and requirement. Given the delays in the withdrawal and the growing political-economic turmoil in Russia, there was some risk that former Soviet forces could still be stationed on German territory if a more conservative, nationalist, or even communist government were to replace Yeltsin. By late 1992 some 130,000 Russian military personnel were still in Germany, hardly the Soviet threat, but, a Bundeswehr officer (18) said, "If you talk about any troops with weapons, they are of course dangerous." At 50 percent withdrawal, the Bundeswehr considered the

---

that the WGF could limit its financial liability for the environmental cleanup, the WGF began to adopt Bundeswehr practices for safe disposal of wastes such as motor oil.

18. For estimates, see "Milliarden Kosten durch Umweltsünden," *Süddeutsche Zeitung*, 7 May 1992, p. 6.

19. German interviews 17, 19, and 40.

WGF no longer an offensive-capable military force, especially given its lack of logistical and backup support. Nevertheless, both politicians and foreign office officials cited the residual WGF on German territory as one of Germany's biggest security problems.[20]

Furthermore, although the conventional military threat to Germany decreased with reduction of forces, in many respects the problems increased. The number of military personnel without housing back in Russia mounted, and the consequent risk of social instability from an already aggrieved Russian military which felt itself under siege greatly worried both Russian and German officials. Moreover, as the deadline for withdrawal drew nearer, the risks increased that desperate Russian soldiers would defect and that crime would increase as many sought to profit from their remaining time in Germany.[21] Reports of Russian personnel selling military equipment and cooperating with organized crime in the former GDR were extensive.

Although Germany wanted the forces out on time, the longer-term and larger security context had to be taken into account as well: German officials wanted the withdrawal to be accomplished in a cooperative spirit. While seeking to reach their objectives on the terms agreed to in 1990, they also sought to deal with the issues and problems that arose in such a way as to not harm German-Russian relations. In particular, they were concerned that the experience of the Russian military with Germany be a positive one.

Russia's position, in contrast, should have been very advantageous. The presence of the WGF in Germany had proved useful in wresting financial assistance from Germany and the troops' continuing presence ought to have created some leverage. Though Russians complained bitterly that Gorbachev had given away too much, in fact the agreement was unprecedented in having Germany pay for something that would have to be accomplished in any event. The sense of German obligation and responsibility to contribute to a resolution of the cold war divide and to Russian well-being was strong. German officials made it clear that two things made the program acceptable to the German government and public: gratitude for the ultimate Soviet role in making unification possible and, far more fundamental, a sense that Germany still owed a debt to the Soviet Union for World War II. One official commented that these payments were Germany's "reparations" to the Soviet Union, and Russian officials told me this as well.[22] Furthermore, al-

---

20. German interviews 25, 43, 56, and 60.
21. German interview 15.
22. German interview 62; Russian interviews 11, 24, and 40.

though the Russian government was criticized for failing to negotiate larger payments, the amounts were substantial (some DM 15 billion in total).

Nevertheless, the costs to Russia of implementing the agreements were great, and they were not only economic, but also political. As the date for the final withdrawal drew near in August 1994, Russian television aired repeated and public complaints by Russian officers, including highly critical comments by Defense Minister Pavel Grachev. During a special ceremony in Moscow, he pointed out that had Russia conducted the withdrawal according to the standard set for Western troop reductions it would have taken fifteen years. At a time when Yeltsin had grown increasingly dependent on the Russian military for political support, and nationalists and communists were making inroads in domestic politics by claiming that Yeltsin was sacrificing Russia's national interests by pandering to the west, the domestic political costs of the withdrawal became very high. Even by the time the troop withdrawal was accomplished, only 60 percent of the apartment construction had been completed, and over 60,000 military officers were left without homes. Nearly 85 percent of returning officers were expected to be dismissed from the armed forces without job guarantees. Russian officials feared that this situation could lead to major social unrest.[23]

At the same time a deep economic crisis was causing drastic cutbacks in the military budget. Funds that were allocated for military purposes in budgets from 1992 through 1995 had to be stretched to cover withdrawal and redeployment. Rapid withdrawal from Germany and simultaneously from the Baltics made it nearly impossible to provide for the returning troops, Russian officials claimed.[24] While the military budget was shrinking, the numbers of Russian troops deployed at home grew as a result of the withdrawals from Germany, the Baltics, and other countries "anxious to free themselves of our troops," as one military expert (17) dryly put it.

So for the Russian government, the political, economic, and social costs of the withdrawal were proving enormous. In contrast, the military security costs of delay or even intransigence would have been negligible. Russia did not suffer from a lack of military personnel and equipment at home, and was attempting to reduce its armed forces. A Russian defense ministry official (30) explained that the withdrawal was not a problem or

---

23. Russian interviews 19 and 65; Yevgeniy Shaposhnikov, "The Long Road Back from Berlin," *Moscow News*, 16 September 1994, pp. 1–2.
24. Russian interviews 53, 58, and 61.

threat to Russian security because it was a part of the larger reduction of conventional forces in Europe "from the Atlantic to the Urals." It is based on a balance of forces, he said: fewer military forces are needed in Europe with the end of the cold war. Asked whether the withdrawal was then not simply an inevitable response to objective conditions, he disagreed. The withdrawal was possible because of changed conditions in Europe, he said, but without an agreement between Germany and Russia it would not have happened. We needed, he said, to accomplish the withdrawal in the context of cooperation and partnership and with a view to the long-term German-Russian relationship.

A Russian politician (31) also spoke of the importance of the tangible German aid for the withdrawal. Of course, he added, Germany has its own interest in this—it is not merely a gift. But clearly Germany is interested in developing good relations and long-term ties. It is also important, he said, that the aid for the withdrawal is part of an agreement and a partnership; it is not just that Germans are giving money and Russia just needs help. This is a problem we share, and we are solving it through cooperation and mutual exchange.

Furthermore, the difficulties with the withdrawal had the effect of worsening Russia's regional relations. Because the withdrawal had proved so expensive, a disproportionate share of the departing forces were deployed to Kaliningrad, since this was Russia's westernmost point. Their presence there worried Poland and the Baltic states, since it looked to them like a Russian military buildup on their borders. Greater numbers of WGF forces than originally planned were also withdrawn to the Leningrad military district, which created problems for Russia's ability to comply with the limits on forces in the "flank zones" under the CFE treaty (see Chapter 5).

Yet at no point in the course of the withdrawal did the WGF or the Russian government delay or refuse to implement its commitment. Russian officials complained and demanded and proposed: while assuring that the withdrawal would continue, both officials and politicians insisted that adjustments to the agreements had to be made because of changed circumstances and increased costs.[25] One official (37) pointed out explicitly that the Russian government believed that Germany would not press for the withdrawal as originally agreed if it meant undermining Germany's policy of supporting Russian economic reform.

But the withdrawal went precisely according to plan and often ahead of schedule. This was true even when Russian forces were being re-

25. Russian interviews 7, 24, and 40.

moved in winter and Russian military families put in tents to live, or when movement of equipment to western Russia created problems for compliance with CFE destruction obligations. The withdrawal proceeded on schedule and was accomplished on 31 August 1994, four months early. Yeltsin attended a ceremony in Berlin marking the departure of the last Russian forces. On 8 September 1994, Germany, the United States, the United Kingdom, and France held a ceremony marking the withdrawal of foreign western forces from Berlin.

Along the way, Germany and Russia had agreed to four adaptations in the original agreement. First, in December 1992 on a visit to Moscow, Kohl agreed to supply an additional DM 550 million for housing construction, in exchange for an accelerated withdrawal completion (31 August instead of 31 December 1994). Second, beginning in 1992 Germany allowed the WGF to access 50 percent of the proceeds from immovables sales without waiting for all damage claims (the remaining 50 percent went into an account to be assessed against damage claims, as originally agreed). The aim was to get more money into Russian hands for building housing to facilitate the withdrawal, and to create incentives to get the Russians to agree to sales.[26] Third, the German environment ministry began an action program to teach the WGF how to clean up environmental damage, and the WGF eagerly adopted the program, at one point allocating it some 30,000 of its soldiers, in order to reduce its financial liability.[27] Fourth, in the end the German and Russian sides did agree to a "zero sum" arrangement that granted Germany ownership of remaining WGF property in exchange for making no further damage claims against Russia.

RUSSIAN TROOP WITHDRAWAL FROM THE BALTIC STATES

When the Soviet Union broke apart in December 1991, the Soviet withdrawal from central and eastern Europe was under way but far from complete. Soviet troops began to withdraw from Hungary in March 1990 and the withdrawal was completed in July 1991, as was that from Czechoslovakia. The withdrawal from Poland was somewhat more contentious and delayed by disputes about timetables and payments, but these were resolved relatively easily, and the forces had all departed from Polish territory by October 1992.

26. German interview 19.
27. German interview 19.

In the Baltics, the situation was different. All three states sought a speedy withdrawal and made no claims for formerly Soviet forces on their territory (as did, for example, Ukraine). Political leaders in the Baltics were entirely unequivocal in viewing any presence of former Soviet forces as a direct national security threat. When conflicts emerged in the former Soviet Union in which residual Soviet military forces appeared to play an active part in destabilizing the new countries or limiting their sovereignty (as in Moldova and Georgia), these concerns proved well founded.

Russia agreed early in 1992 in principle that the troops would be withdrawn from the three Baltic countries. Even without actual treaties or agreements in effect, Russian troops began to leave. Publicly (and in private discussions as well), the Russian government claimed that the problems in accomplishing speedy withdrawals arose from two sources: concerns for the "human rights" issues involving the Russian minorities in the Baltics, and the lack of housing in Russia for the returning forces. The first issue was the problem of defining both citizenship and the rights for noncitizen residents. Lithuania had passed a law in 1989 guaranteeing citizenship for all residents at the time of independence, but Estonia and Latvia sought to impose highly restrictive laws that would discriminate against Russian minorities. Their laws granted citizenship to those who had been citizens before Soviet occupation in 1940 and their descendants, but otherwise citizenship would be difficult to obtain. In Latvia the obstacles centered on ten-year residence, language requirements, and annual quotas. In Estonia, the problem was a two-year period in which noncitizens could apply for residency and work permits before they would be required to leave the country

Russians officials publicly began to link withdrawal of forces to these "human rights" issues. In addition, they demanded that the Baltics contribute to the costs of building housing, retract claims for territorial adjustment, give up claims for damage inflicted by the Soviet occupation, and in some cases, permit long-term basing rights. Privately, some Russian officials and politicians admitted that the issue had become bound up with growing nationalist sentiment and the government's perceived weakness in defending the rights and safety of Russians abroad.[28] This was the real reason for Russia's decision to create difficulties. Genuine security concerns were not the issue, since the withdrawal had actually begun and continued (although often at a very slow pace) throughout this period. Indeed, even at times when Russian politicians were declar-

28. Russian interviews 5, 37, 38, and 46.

ing that the withdrawal would be halted, it actually went on. By 1993 only about 40,000–50,000 Russian troops remained of an original total of 150,000. Russia did obtain control of the radar station at Skrunda in Latvia until 1998, but eventually conceded its demands on other basing rights.

Thus at issue was not the withdrawal in principle, but the terms of the withdrawal. Russia sought Baltic contributions toward housing expenses, changes in citizenship and residence requirements to ease the situation of Russian émigrés and military retirees, and leverage against Baltic territorial claims. One of the reasons the withdrawal from Lithuania went well was that its government paid for the construction of apartments in Kaliningrad. Even the positive outcome in Lithuania proceeded within the context of a highly public and forceful government media campaign to stand against Russian-directed "apartheid" and "ethnic cleansing" at a time when nationalist and communist opposition forces were launching their campaign against the Yeltsin-Kozyrev foreign policy.[29]

The Baltic states brought their complaints to the international community and directly to western countries. Russia, after all, was bound by its commitments under the OSCE not to deploy troops in foreign countries without the consent of those governments. Russia, in turn, proved willing to use the international stage to make counterclaims about violations of international norms protecting human rights and ethnic minorities. Russian officials claimed that noncitizens in the Baltic states were being discriminated against in employment and housing, that there were risks to personal security not being met by government responses, and that proposed citizenship and residence laws working their way through the Baltic legal systems violated international standards.[30]

The international community did become involved. In May 1992, NATO countries agreed in principle to assist Russia in the withdrawal. At the Helsinki summit in July 1992, the OSCE adopted a declaration calling for the speedy, orderly, and complete withdrawal of foreign troops from the Baltics. The topic was raised with Yeltsin by Kohl at the G–7 summit in the same month.[31] In addition, however, OSCE and

29. See Dzintra Bungs, "Progress on Withdrawal from the Baltic States," *RFE/RL Research Report*, vol. 2, no. 25 (18 June 1993): 50–59 for a discussion of the specific proposals and demands.

30. Russian interviews 5, 7, 12, 22, 32, and 38.

31. "NATO unterstützt Rußland bei Truppenabzug," *Süddeutsche Zeitung*, 9 May 1992, p. 10; "Kohl sieht in der Konferenz von München ein Signal der Ermutigung und der Hoffnung," *Frankfurter Allgemeine Zeitung*, 9 July 1992, p. 1.

Council of Europe missions began to consult with the Baltic governments on their citizenship laws and protection of ethnic minorities. Both Latvia's quotas and Estonia's residency restrictions came under severe criticism from the OSCE and CE: ultimately both states loosened their restrictions to accommodate international norms.[32] At the same time, German officials consulted informally with the Baltic governments on the terms and procedures of the Russian withdrawal from Germany in order to help them develop successful policies toward Russia.[33]

Central aspects of Russia's strategy were immediately apparent. In bilateral discussions, it had a substantial advantage because of its power and the force of the status quo. The Baltic states had far greater stakes in the negotiations: if things went wrong, Russian security was not at risk, but for the Baltics their very survival as independent sovereign countries could be at stake. Russian negotiating positions and the government's publicly stated positions took full advantage of the situation, and did not refrain from strong demands and threats to leave the troops in place if Russian concerns were not addressed.[34]

But Russia did not try to dominate the Baltics only through bilateral weight. Its overall approach was more subtle, as it sought multilateral involvement and tried to bring to bear principles from international institutions to favor its arguments on the minorities issues. This is discussed in detail in Chapter 6. To accomplish these ends, Russian officials hoped to use the interests of other states in the region in a broad array of issues including transportation, economic development, and environmental concerns to make the Baltics willing to see a stake in multilateral cooperation. In addition, Russian plans were to link this specific issue more generally to OSCE principles regarding human and minority rights.

Lithuania and Russia reached agreement on the withdrawal in September 1992, and it was completed in August 1993. Latvia and Russia did not reach agreement until April 1994, and Estonia and Russia not until July 1994: both withdrawals were accomplished by 31 August 1994.[35] Thus, while the Russian withdrawal from the Baltics was successful, it was more contentious and troubling that that from Germany, and succeeded under different circumstances and for different reasons.

---

32. Elaine M. Holoboff, "National Security in the Baltic States: Rolling Back the Bridgehead," in *State Building and Military Power in Russia and the New States of Eurasia*, ed. Bruce Parrott (Armonk, N.Y.: M. E. Sharpe, 1995), pp. 111–133.
33. German interview 15.
34. Russian interview 22.
35. Holoboff, "National Security in the Baltic States," pp. 113–114.

INSTITUTIONS AND SECURITY COOPERATION

Why did Germany and Russia successfully cooperate in this issue of fundamental security concern? This was a case of security cooperation, and not merely the implementation of an unproblematic policy. That the withdrawal was ultimately and on balance in the interests of both is not sufficient to explain it, for two reasons. First, German officials and politicians at no time took success of the withdrawal for granted. They were concerned about its progress and put considerable time and effort into the enterprise. At several points government ministers became involved in working through problems: attention at the highest level is a good indication that obstacles were not taken lightly. Second, the Yeltsin government suffered substantial domestic costs for living up to the agreement, on issues of particular vulnerability for the government: the large economic costs that the end of the cold war and economic reform were imposing on Russia, a weakened and resentful military that increasingly played a role in politics, and nationalist cries about Russia's diminished great power status. Although in the end these did not prove great enough to lead the Yeltsin government to violate its commitment, Russian domestic politics made the withdrawal a difficult political decision.

The success of the withdrawal itself raises two questions. First, why was it successful at all? Second, why was Russia not able to change the terms of the agreement when it became more costly to carry out? The Baltic case demonstrates a Russia willing to use its power and the sometimes implicit, sometimes explicit, threat simply not to move to press for the conditions it wanted. Why did this not happen with of the withdrawal from Germany?

The answer to the first question does not require an institutionalist framework; it can be answered by a straightforward realist account of power and interests. In terms of a secure balance of power, Russia simply did not need to deploy such a huge military force in Europe. Germany was committed to no more than 370,000 troops, and the reduction of American forces in Europe was already under way. One Russian official (11) linked the reason for Russian willingness to withdraw its forces directly to German-Russian balance by noting that were Germany not to live up to that commitment, the Russian government would retaliate by stopping its withdrawal. Other officials were less explicit on that point, but the importance of a general reduction in forces in Europe in Russian calculations was consistent in all my interviews. Furthermore, the WGF was arguably a military liability rather than an asset: although highly capable and well equipped, it had no direct logistical support linking it to the Russian homeland and no compensating echelon of Russian allies to bridge the distance. Russian officials and politicians did not express any confidence or place any faith in the importance of the WGF as a fighting force. As long as we need to withdraw our troops from Germany anyway, one politician (31) said, we may as well do so in the context of an international treaty that supports our role as a dependable partner with good intentions.

Just as important, the political benefits for Russian-German relations arising from a successful and cooperative operation in this central security area were clearly in Russian national security interests. Russian officials and politicians consistently raised the prospects of positive long-term military, political, and (not least) economic relations in discussions about the troop withdrawal, and especially why it continued despite the rising costs. This hope was consistent throughout the government and across the political spectrum.

In addition to these reasons, a realist explanation based on a benign security dilemma is consistent with the outcome in this case. As explained in Chapter 3, the overall context of security assessments was one of low threat and the limited value of military forces for dealing with security relations in Europe, particularly Russian relations with Germany. Because both Germany and Russia had an interest in the withdrawal and because withdrawal posed no security threat to either state, concern about being exploited was not an obstacle to cooperation. Suspicions about intentions and offensive military capabilities would have created substantial obstacles to German-Russian cooperation. Officials in both countries consistently attributed success to the importance of the overall context of a cooperative European security environment and continuing vigilance about intentions and capabilities. This was true for thinking about the implications of the withdrawal even after it was accomplished: one Russian politician (55) said that because the withdrawal of troops had changed the European geopolitical situation "we have to watch German behavior."

Yet although this case does not disconfirm a realist explanation, it does show its indeterminancy. It is true that the balance of power was favorable to cooperation and military withdrawal, but that favorable balance of power was in large measure a result of conditions created by multilateral cooperation supported by international institutions. At the most basic level, German membership in NATO anchored its interests and power, which in the words of one German official (19) limits Russian military options: "Without NATO, this whole process would not have been so favorable in the end." To the extent that Russia chose to cooperate because the risks of intransigence were made clear by Germany's alliance commitments even after the cold war, the institution of NATO undergirded German-Russian security cooperation.

Similarly, although it is true that German and Russian officials spoke about the troop withdrawal operation in terms that demonstrated the causal importance of a benign security dilemma, German and Russian assessments of these benign conditions and their ability to signal credibly depended upon institutions. Officials in both countries rarely talked about the withdrawal without reference to the CFE treaty and the environment of military transparency created by institutions and agreements, including the OSCE. German officials repeatedly praised the value of European security institutions for enhancing transparency and encouraging Russia to participate in confidence-building practices oriented toward defensive military capabilities and cooperative security. "We have civilized them," one said (15). Insofar as Russian confidence about German intentions and capabilities was a function of Germany's integration in international institutions and its consistent commitment to multilateral security policies within them, a strict realist explanation cannot account for the outcome.

Furthermore, Russian officials consistently said that the importance of Russia's reputation and the need to reassure other European countries were the main reasons why Russia lived up to the agreement despite its costs. Politicians from different parties said that the withdrawal from Germany was necessary to improve Russian prestige abroad and change the perception of Russian intentions in central Europe. Withdrawing Russian troops from Germany and the Baltics in accordance with agreements was meant to demonstrate that Russia is a reliable partner and that it has benign intentions.[36] Beyond relations with Germany, the withdrawal was seen as a foundation for building cooperative relations in Europe.[37] Said an official (49): "Russia's withdrawal of troops from Germany and the Baltics according to the previous agreements demonstrates that Russia is a reliable partner and that it wants to build normal relations without special claims. Russian policy is consistent if judged by the final results." Some went further and explicitly linked Russia's concern for its credibility on this issue to western commitments: "Russia has a right to say—we followed all our commitments even knowing what domestic problems we create for ourselves," said one (51). "Now it is the West's turn to respond by meeting their commitment to Russian reforms." Similarly, a Duma deputy (53) said: "The Russian withdrawal of

---

36. Russian interviews 59 and 68.
37. Russian interviews 9, 55, and 61.

troops on time was an important signal that Russia has a faithful attitude toward western Europe and the Baltics. We need to use this as much as possible—we made a concession to you, now help us in economic terms."

Thus while we cannot conclude that institutions were a necessary condition for eventual withdrawal, they nevertheless had an independent effect on the outcome in two ways. First, they mitigated any regional or bilateral security dilemma that might have shaken Russian confidence in the wisdom of the policy. Second, they increased the benefits of a successful withdrawal to Russia, not merely because of the financial "reparations" paid by Germany, but because Russian security officials and politicians saw that living up to the specific rules, commitments, and procedures had a positive impact on Russia's reputation and its ability to claim reciprocal cooperation from other western and European countries.

In the absence of the institutions, uncertainty about intentions and capabilities would have made cooperation more risky, and Russia would not have been able to point to this major achievement as a signal of its positive intentions and good behavior. Although the mere fact of a withdrawal without an explicit treaty would have been a positive sign of Russian intentions, it would not have had the impact that fulfillment of an explicit international commitment did, because the treaty made it easy to judge Russian behavior and motivations. Asked whether the precise terms of the treaty and agreement were really seen as significant, a German official (17) said that the government paid careful attention to strict adherence to the terms and timing. These rules made it clear that the withdrawal was being accomplished despite all its difficulties not only on time, but ahead of schedule: "We see this as a sign of their intentions." Compare this to the murkiness surrounding Russia's intentions and even its behavior during the withdrawal from the Baltics.

When we turn to the second question—why did Russia fail to get a better bargain in the end with Germany as it was able to do in the Baltics?—the evidence is not consistent with a realist answer. First of all, the optimistic realist approach does not explain the outcome because it does not make determinate predictions: knowing anything about the security dilemma does not help us to understand why Germany succeeded in resisting Russian demands. Optimistic realism also says little about cooperation problems other than those characterized by an underlying collaboration issue. The obstacles to cooperation raised by the increased expenses of the withdrawal, the Russian-Ukrainian disputes, and the German-Russian disputes about the sale of WGF property and the costs of environmental damage were those of a coordination or bargaining game: the problem was whether and how the bargain might shift.

But we can derive a prediction from realist theory: the more powerful state will get the bargain it wants.[38] German power explains German success, and Baltic weakness explains Baltic failure to resist Russian demands. There are several problems with this assessment, however.

First, Germany was not strictly more powerful in this issue area than Russia, since Russia still had a much larger military capability. Germany was more powerful than the Baltics, to be sure, but the relevant relationship would be that between Germany and Russia. If one includes Germany's NATO alliance in the balance, then arguably the German side was more powerful. The importance of Germany's alliance ties played a role in the cooperative resolution of the troop withdrawal, according to the German officials involved. But even those who brought up NATO and the allied presence in Berlin as a factor to explain the successful withdrawal did so in the context of the overall success, not in connection with German success in resisting changes in the bargain. Furthermore, including NATO forces is somewhat ad hoc, since NATO was not party to the troop withdrawal. To the extent that allied western forces figured in the issue, it was by virtue of the specific provision in the 2 + 4 agreement, which linked their presence in Berlin to Russian troop presence and thus created a link through institutional means. Even this was symbolic, rather than substantive: the western allied forces were not a fighting force, but a "signal" to the Russians, according to a German military officer (19).

Second, if Germany was more powerful, why was *it* not able to get a new and better deal? If realist approaches to bargaining are right, then Germany should have pressed its power advantages to improve the deal once the terms of the original agreement were brought into question. But this did not happen; although Germany did achieve an accelerated withdrawal, it came at the price of more assistance. Since the Russian withdrawal was already well ahead of schedule at the time Kohl made the offer in December 1992, one can even question whether the extra payment was necessary. A German official (31) explained the increased payment in terms of getting more money into Russian hands to ease the housing problems and to give Yeltsin something he could use against his critics at home, not in terms of German pressure brought to bear against vulnerable Russians. Nor did Russian officials complain in late 1992 or 1993 about German pressure.

---

38. See Stephen D. Krasner, "Global Communications and National Power: Life on the Pareto Frontier," *World Politics* 43 (April 1991): 336–356.

Most important, an explanation based on preponderant German power does not accord in the slightest with the reasons both German and Russian officials gave for the resilience of the original deal. In their estimation, the most important reasons for the shape of the outcome lie in the agreement itself. I explicitly asked German officials why the Russians were not able to use their presence as leverage for getting better deals. The WGF in 1991 and 1992 pressed repeatedly for German assistance on several issues and Russian officials told me of the government's complaints and expectations that Germany would be of more help on the core problems.

German officials consistently gave the same explanation, the basic theme of which was well summarized by one (19): "I must say, whatever is written down, the Russians will abide by it." The treaty made the Soviet Union solely responsible for the withdrawal of the WGF, and since Russia had declared itself the sole continuing successor state to the Soviet Union with regard to Soviet forces stationed abroad, it was Russia's responsibility to oversee the withdrawal. On disputes over where to place the housing, officials replied that the agreement left it to the Soviet side to decide where to build the housing and Germany had undertaken no responsibility for those issues. Why did Germany not have to pay more for the withdrawal once expenses began to mount? Because the financial arrangements were calculated to move Soviet personnel and equipment to the Soviet borders: if Russia wants to move equipment and personnel further east because the Soviet Union has broken apart, that is their choice and their responsibility, one official (17) said. Another (15) said, "This was very well calculated and we will not change the payments." The transition agreement, he added, specifically provides that the financing as agreed upon is final, so this is a legal bilateral document. Several officials pointed out that the wording of the 1990 agreements had been very careful to specify that the German payments were a "contribution," not an obligation to cover the entire expense.[39]

When asked why Russia, although perhaps on shaky legal grounds, did not nevertheless use its military presence for bargaining leverage, German officials again referred to the 1990 treaty and agreement. The withdrawal *treaty* was carefully written to separate the issue of the Soviet Union's obligation to withdraw from the *agreement* covering the financial arrangements. That is, one official (15) concluded, the Russian government is obligated to accomplish the withdrawal even if the apartments are not built and the property is not sold. Of course, he added, it is

39. German interviews 15, 17, and 19.

our obligation to fulfill the terms of the financial agreement, and it is in our interests for the housing to be built and the property to be sold. But there is no linkage, he insisted, and the Russians know that. One German officer (19) said that despite the housing difficulties raised by General Burlakov there was no attempt by the WGF to delay the withdrawal, "because there is no link between the building of housing and the timing of withdrawal of troops within the treaty."

Discussions with Russian officials also revealed that the agreement itself was taken quite seriously. I asked one foreign ministry official (24) in an office overseeing the withdrawal about the costs and difficulties of implementation, and whether the refusal of the German government to adapt its policies on the withdrawal to these new circumstances did not threaten the agreement. No, he answered, because the Russian government does not see Germany as to blame for the difficulties which have arisen. We have accepted the position that disputes with other countries do not involve Germany, he said, and that Russia is solely responsible for the withdrawal. He acknowledged that the financial issues were creating problems, "but these are fully a matter of discussion, not conflict." Another (11) complained that it had become apparent that the German financing did not even begin to cover the costs of the withdrawal, but when asked whether this would be a reason to suspend the operation, he said that he could not imagine that the Russian government would take such a step. As the issues and demands that arose were shown to be inconsistent with the treaty, the Russian government gradually gave way to German positions. One foreign ministry official (26) said, "We have signed this international treaty and we will abide by it, despite the hardships."

As explained earlier, some modest changes were made during the withdrawal operation, the most important of which was an earlier completion date in exchange for an additional German contribution to the housing program. German officials were aware that intransigence and complete inflexibility could risk long-term relations and might not be in German interests if it created more hardships for Russia and the WGF. One German official (15) said that the two sides had been able to cooperate because of the basic agreements, but then also because of the ability to negotiate further and more specific agreements under this "roof." Those changes that were made, however, were within the structure of the basic agreements and consistent with the agreements' principles. German officials would not budge on that, and Russian officials came to agree.

The value of the treaty in establishing the status quo for Germany was apparent in those changes which were effected as well. One German official (44) had told me before December 1992 that Kohl would bring to

Moscow something "small"—perhaps DM 1 billion—as a gesture to help Yeltsin for something like more apartments for the troops since "that is a key pressure point, and it really would be in our own interests to give money for that." The Russians received only half that amount, indicating that the previous agreements gave the German government an advantage in the bargaining, since it was the Russians who were trying to move the agreement away from an established status quo.

That is, the treaty served as a focal point for bargaining once the conditions that had been the context for the original agreement were shaken. If, for example, the agreements had specified that Germany would pay for the total cost of the withdrawal including the movement of WGF forces to their ultimate new bases, my evidence suggests that Russian officials would have been able to wrest more financial resources and concessions from Germany because the latter stuck to the letter of the agreement.

Although we can only speculate on the counterfactual, the completely different conditions of Russian bargaining with the Baltic states over the terms of the withdrawal are indirect evidence that the German-Russian treaty did serve as a significant focal point for the eventual outcome. Baltic leaders had no preexisting bilateral international treaty to rely upon. They did appeal to international norms and principles, especially OSCE rules that troops could be stationed abroad only with the host country's approval. But they spent most of the period from 1991 from 1994 try to *negotiate* the withdrawal, rather than implement an agreement. As a consequence, Russian officials were far more successful in raising issues and demands that were at least as tenuously related to the issue at hand as the demands they made upon the German government. The protection of Russian minorities had nothing to do with Russian forces or bases, and there was no particular reason why the Baltic states should have had to pay for the privilege of removing military forces that had occupied their countries for over fifty years. At least in the German case, the matter of German guilt and reparations for World War II made for a plausible link: in the case of the Baltics it was quite absurd. Yet once there were withdrawal agreements with the three Baltic states, the Russian government did live up to them.

So institutions did matter in this case: they contributed to the broader European context of a relatively benign security dilemma, and they reduced uncertainty about German and Russian intentions, which reinforced Russia's decision to implement the 1990 agreements. The 1990 agreements themselves did not cause the withdrawal, but they sustained the operation through a period in which the costs to Russia mounted severely and in which the Yeltsin government was increasingly vulnerable on the domestic front.

VARIATION IN SECURITY PROBLEMS AND INSTITUTIONAL FORMS

This brings us to the next set of analytical questions: what were the underlying obstacles to cooperation in this case, and did institutional rules and procedures provide German and Russian decision makers with the necessary and appropriate instruments for overcoming them? In Chapter 2, I argued that collaboration, coordination, transparency, and linkage are all fundamentally different kinds of obstacles, requiring different institutional solutions. If institutions matter, then the choice of institutions should matter as well.

The problem of Russian troop withdrawal was not one of collaboration, though at first glance it might look like a Prisoner's Dilemma in which each party has an incentive to defect from implementing the agreement. It was not a collaboration problem because neither side hoped to break the agreement while the other continued to abide by it. The course of the withdrawal was not threatened by misperception which might lead to a cycle of defensive and retaliatory acts of noncooperation because officials in both countries were confident that the other side's intentions were not exploitative. Rather than raising suspicions and fears that an end to the cooperative withdrawal lurked around the corner, officials and politicians in both countries assured me that it was in the other's interests to continue.

That said, we should note that the treaty and the agreement were structured to deal with the threat of defection, and their provisions met the conditions institutionalists have long identified as necessary for overcoming Prisoner's Dilemmas.[40] Provisions for monitoring and verification were extensive and detailed, and carried out to the letter. The operation as a whole was broken up into yearly, quarterly, and monthly plans, which made it easy to monitor and verify. The payment system was designed to release the credits and loans throughout the course of the operation, rather than in large lump sums. A full payment up front might have reduced the incentive to the WGF to abide so strictly by the

40. Robert M. Axelrod and Robert O. Keohane, "Achieving Cooperation under Anarchy: Strategies and Institutions," in *Cooperation under Anarchy*, ed. Kenneth A. Oye (Princeton: Princeton University Press, 1986).

rules, and withholding payment until the end, one German politician (60) said, would have made it difficult for the WGF to see the tangible benefits early on.

Nonetheless, although this system had put in place the mechanisms necessary for overcoming collaboration problems, by 1992 it functioned more to maintain transparency than to create disincentives against defection. To a far greater degree, German and Russian officials discussed these procedures in terms of transparency and confidence-building rather than those of checking for cheating. Indeed, the one German official who used the term "cheating" in connection with the monitoring (15) quickly added that the concern was not that the Russians intended to "cheat" in military terms, but rather "we are worried that they will get the money when they have not earned it."

These views demonstrate one of the advantages of monitoring and verification systems: when properly designed, they are especially valuable for overcoming the *mix* of collaboration and transparency problems which analysts have identified as lying at the core of the security dilemma. Monitoring and verification systems are difficult to negotiate and onerous to implement and sustain, but the greater effort and expense are worth the investment because the cost of being exploited can be national survival. Although inefficient in cases where states really do not intend to exploit one another, monitoring and verification systems, because of their value for transparency and reducing uncertainty as well, may be necessary conditions for security cooperation.

The most significant obstacle to cooperation in this case was the constellation of changes arising from the demise of the Soviet Union which fundamentally shook the original terms of the deal. The possibility that they were no longer "on the Pareto frontier,"[41] led to difficult negotiations on modifications to the original agreement. The situation posed the risk of indefinite delay in achieving the withdrawal since the issues that arose cut to the heart of Russian capacity and willingness to carry on. But as institutional theory predicts, Germany and Russia escaped an endless cycle of claims and counterclaims because the terms and conditions of the original agreement served as a focal point. Although the Russians would have preferred to shift the substance of German-Russian mutual cooperation to a new equilibrium where the costs to Russia were lower, the existing equilibrium remained for Russia better than no agreement at all. As institutional theory predicts, when multiple

41. Krasner, "Global Communications and National Power."

deals are possible, the one that players will choose is the one reinforced by an institution.

Yet, although a status quo and focal point, the original deal was not rigid and immovable. Had this been the case, my interviews indicate that the course of German-Russian relations would have been more negative because of the substantial costs Russia faced and its potential resentment of German intransigence. The value of the treaty and the agreements was not only their precise terms, but the rules and procedures they established for solving the problems of the withdrawal. The 1990 agreements were firm in establishing the terms, but they did not merely establish fixed principles: they established agreed-upon structures in which further bargaining and negotiation could take place. The presence of these structures increased the incentives to the Russian side of staying within the existing agreement and seeking to shift the deal to reduce its costs. Although in the end the deal did not shift enough, the process of negotiation and adjustment enabled Russian officials to emphasize the joint nature of German-Russian cooperation, especially to domestic Russian audiences.

The fourth obstacle to mutual security cooperation introduced in Chapter 2 can be thought of as disincentive problems, in which either one side has an interest in unconditional cooperation or one side has no interest in cooperation. This creates an incentive to use institutions for linkage: to make cooperation in the issue area a condition for cooperation in other issue areas.

Clearly, these kinds of dynamics pervaded the issue of the troop withdrawal. Germany desperately wished to rid itself of all occupying military forces, especially those of a Russia with an unknown future. This raised the prospect that Germany would pay Russia or accede to its demands regardless of Russian behavior in effecting the withdrawal. On the Russian side, the mounting costs of the operation raised the possibility that the balance of costs and benefits had shifted to the point where Russia would defect.

Some linkage through institutions played a role in sustaining German-Russian cooperation, as the discussion in this chapter has shown. Of course, the 1990 agreements established a basic linkage by offering German financial assistance for the withdrawal. Although according to the treaty Russia was obligated to accomplish the withdrawal regardless of German actions, the agreement on German financing depended on a withdrawal. Furthermore, the form of the payments—to the WGF directly and for military housing—created an immediate and direct linkage for the Russian military.

[97]

Strictly speaking, however, institutions played no role in the most important linkage issue of all: Russia's willingness to cooperate in the withdrawal in order to establish its reputation as a worthy and reliable partner and in order to develop positive relations with western countries in the interests of substantial assistance for its program of economic reforms. There was no official institutionally created connection between Russian cooperation in this issue and the broader context of political and economic relations. There was certainly a link, because Germany was an important member of all the most significant international institutions that would play a role in the other issues which concerned Russian decision makers. Nevertheless, it would be a stretch to attribute this crucial linkage for Russian calculations directly to international institutions. What linkage existed was informal, diffuse, and part of the broader context of interstate relations, so we really cannot attribute the importance of Russia's concern for its reputation and its hopes for western reciprocity to an institutional effect.

INSTITUTIONAL EFFECTIVENESS

Finally, why were the 1990 treaty and agreement effective as institutions in the case of withdrawal of formerly Soviet forces from Germany? In Chapter 2, I proposed that institutions will be effective for two reasons: because their form meets required functions, and because they exist as part of a network of institutions which states can rely upon as backup. Three conditions were crucial for the ultimate effectiveness of institutions in this case: the dramatically changed circumstances under which Russia would have to accomplish the withdrawal, Russia's stake in its reputation and the prospects for broader cooperation with the west, and German and Russian confidence about intentions and military balances, which mitigated potential obstacles arising from the security dilemma. The question then is whether the relationship of institutional form and function and the layering of institutions contributed to successful management of these conditions.

The evidence is mixed on the first factor, institutional form and function. The structure of the agreements as both resilient focal points and adaptable bargaining forums was crucial to their effectiveness in sustaining German-Russian cooperation. Thus we can conclude that institutional form was important for the successful operation of bargaining. However, the distinction between collaboration and transparency did not require different institutional forms. Indeed, this case suggests that institutions may need to address both types of obstacle at the same time.

[98]

Finally, it also demonstrates that institutional linkages are not crucial for successful and effective security cooperation, because the agreements did not provide for explicit or formal linkages. Indeed, German officials argued that it was the absence of rigid linkages that made for successful bargaining.

This case does constitute strong support for the effectiveness of layered or embedded institutions. German and Russian officials and politicians consistently pointed to the importance of the overall security environment and the network of institutional mechanisms that contributed to transparency and stable defensive military balances. The set of effective institutions went far beyond the actual withdrawal treaty and agreement, and included Germany's ultimate reliance on NATO as well as Russia's hopes for the system of international economic assistance and cooperation embodied in western economic institutions. In the end, Germany and Russia successfully cooperated because of a favorable balance of power and a benign security dilemma, both of which depended in large measure on the interlocking sets of multilateral and bilateral institutions in which the two countries negotiated.

[5]

Balances and Military Forces

Although the Russian troop withdrawal from Germany affected the regional balance of military capabilities, it was ultimately a bilateral issue. Another set of military issues important in the aftermath of the cold war were multilateral in nature. They concerned the Conventional Forces in Europe Treaty, the disposition of Soviet nuclear forces, the development of the "Eurocorps," and the question of an "out-of-area" role for German military forces.

BALANCE OF CONVENTIONAL MILITARY FORCES

The Conventional Forces in Europe (CFE) Treaty was a follow-on to the failed Mutual and Balanced Force Reduction talks.[1] Bilateral negotiations between NATO and the Warsaw Pact began in 1989, with the ob-

---

1. "CFE treaty" refers to the Treaty on Conventional Armed Forces in Europe, signed in Paris on 19 November 1990 by the member states of NATO and the Warsaw Pact. It is also known among officials as "CFE1" because the treaty included a commitment to negotiate further measures to reduce the risk of war in Europe. On 10 July 1992, the CFE parties signed the "Concluding Act of the Negotiation on Personnel Strength of Conventional Armed Forces in Europe" a politically binding agreement to limit the number of military personnel known as "CFE1A." Unlike the CFE treaty, in which the overall numerical limits are bilateral (that is, specified for NATO and the Warsaw Pact), the numerical limits of CFE1A are given for each country individually, as a party to the agreement. The CFE1A personnel limits are listed in the first column of Table 1 (no overall limit is listed since none was agreed upon). As of mid-1998, negotiations continue on a second treaty to reduce conventional forces further multilaterally, without any reference to overall limits based upon NATO and the now-defunct Warsaw Pact: the draft treaty under discussion is known as "CFE2."

jective of achieving lower levels of offensive military forces in Europe, along with a more stable defensive balance of forces. The treaty was signed on 19 November 1990 and entered provisionally into force on 17 July 1992. The original parties to it were the sixteen members of NATO and the seven members of the Warsaw Pact. The precise numbers changed with German unification (which eliminated the GDR) and the Soviet demise (whereby Russia, Belarus, Ukraine, Kazakhstan, Moldova, Armenia, Azerbaijan, and Georgia became parties to the treaty).[2]

The treaty imposed three important legal obligations.[3] First, it placed overall limits on the conventional military forces—tanks, armored combat vehicles (ACV), artillery, attack helicopters, and combat aircraft—of the two sides in the "Atlantic-to-the-Urals" region (see Table 1). Country limits within these were left to each side to agree upon. The treaty has regional sublimits in four zones, which are roughly concentric territories: Zone 4 is the smallest, Zone 3 includes all of Zone 4 plus a second echelon of territory, and so on. The objective was to limit military equipment most closely in the probable cold war battleground at the heart of Europe (see map). As one moves from Zone 1 to Zone 4, the treaty allows progressively smaller amounts of equipment. In addition, the treaty designated a special territory known as the "flanks" which are the territories in Zone 1 but not in Zone 2. Special limits were placed on military equipment in the flanks, which in turn created a new problem after the Soviet breakup (this problem is discussed below). In addition to limiting equipment in active units, the treaty placed limits on storage within the treaty area. It explicitly commits its signers to observe a principle of "sufficiency" in armed forces. No party to the treaty may hold more than 30 percent of the total allowed in the ATTU region.

The second obligation was that signers would reduce equipment levels to treaty limits no later than forty months after the treaty came into force, that is, by November 1995. Furthermore, the covered military equipment—"Treaty Limited Equipment" or TLE—had to be gotten rid of in a manner prescribed by the treaty, primarily destruction. A limited amount of equipment could be converted to noncombat use or "cascaded" to other parties to the treaty as long as overall limits were met.

---

2. The number of parties further increased when Czechoslovakia split in 1992. The Baltic states were excluded from the treaty in the fall of 1991 because they refused to accede as Soviet successor states holding that their inclusion in the Soviet Union had always been illegal. Although in principle their exclusion from the territory covered by the treaty could have been a problematic precedent, in practice the case was seen as unique.

3. In addition to my own interviews, this discussion draws on Richard A. Falkenrath, *Shaping Europe's Military Order: The Origins and Consequences of the CFE Treaty* (Cambridge: MIT Press, 1995).

Table 1. Conventional Forces in Europe Treaty limits

	Personnel	Tanks	ACVs	Artillery	Combat aircraft	Attack helicopters
Overall for each side:	XXXXXX	20,000	30,000	20,000	6,800	2,000
Former Warsaw Pact: [a]						
Armenia	32,682	220	220	285	100	50
Azerbaijan	70,000	220	220	285	100	50
Belarus	100,000	1,800	2,600	1,615	260	80
Bulgaria	104,000	1,475	2,000	1,750	235	67
Czech Republic	93,333	957	1,367	767	230	50
Georgia	40,000	220	220	285	100	50
Hungary	100,000	835	1,700	810	180	108
Moldova	20,000	210	210	250	50	50
Poland	234,000	1,730	2,150	1,610	460	130
Romania	230,248	1,375	2,100	1,475	430	120
Russia	1,450,000	6,400	11,480	6,415	3,450	890
Slovakia	46,667	478	683	383	115	25
Ukraine	450,000	4,080	5,050	4,040	1,090	330
NATO:						
Belgium	70,000	334	1,099	320	232	46
Canada	10,660	77	277	38	90	13
Denmark	39,000	353	316	553	106	12
France	325,000	1,306	3,820	1,292	800	352
Germany	345,000	4,166	3,446	2,705	900	306
Greece	158,621	1,735	2,534	1,878	650	18
Italy	315,000	1,348	3,339	1,955	650	142
Netherlands	80,000	743	1,080	607	230	69
Norway	32,000	170	225	527	100	0
Portugal	75,000	300	430	450	160	26
Spain	300,000	794	1,588	1,310	310	71
Turkey	530,000	2,795	3,120	3,523	750	43
United Kingdom	260,000	1,015	3,176	636	900	384
United States	250,000	4,006	5,372	2,492	784	518

Source: The Military Balance 1995–1996 (London: International Institute for Strategic Studies, 1996).
[a] Kazakhstan is technically included in the CFE treaty, since a portion of its most western territory lies west of the Urals. However, the Kazakhstan government has pledged not to deploy any CFE TLE in that extremely small portion of its territory.

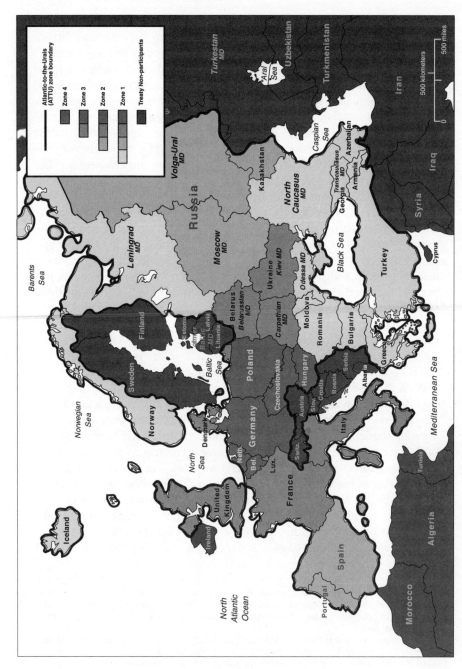

Territory under the Conventional Forces in Europe Treaty showing regional sublimits. The flank zones are Zone 1 minus Zone 2. *Note:* "MD" stands for "military district." *Source:* U.S. Government, On-Site Inspection Agency

Reduction of TLE was subject to unrestricted on-site verification. In addition, the treaty specified time periods within the forty months during which percentages of each country's reduction liability had to be met.

Finally, the treaty obligated the parties to comply with and participate in an extensive and elaborate verification system. On the day before the treaty was signed in 1990, all participants declared their holdings of TLE, thus establishing their reduction liability.[4] Each treaty signer has a "passive quota," the number of on-site inspection missions it must accept each year. A country's passive quota is determined by its number of "objects of verification" (OOV); an OOV is a military unit containing TLE. During the treaty implementation period, the passive quota for a country was set at levels varying from 10 to 20 percent of its OOVs. After November 1995, each country's passive quota is set at 15 percent of its OOVs. Therefore, roughly speaking, the more TLE a country has and the more dispersed its TLE, the more inspection missions it must accept. Each state has the right to conduct as many inspection missions as it must accept. In addition, the treaty provides for "challenge inspections" beyond the yearly inspections of OOVs. Although challenge inspections are voluntary and may be refused, they provide a backup means to check that a country is not circumventing the treaty by hiding TLEs in military units that have not been designated as OOVs. Although verification is the right and responsibility of each treaty party individually, NATO coordinates verification for its members.[5]

With the end of the cold war, two issues complicated the treaty. First was the question of whether it still made any military sense at all. The purpose was to reduce the capacity to launch offensive military operations by reducing combat equipment and limiting ability to mass forces. With the end of the cold war and consequent reductions in military budgets, these forces were being reduced anyway. Furthermore, with the dismantling of the Soviet bloc and Soviet military withdrawal from central Europe, the threat of offensive conventional warfare dissipated. The treaty was going to be very costly to implement. German sources estimated the costs of meeting Germany's arms control reduction obligations at DM 7.8 billion; Russian sources estimated that the costs would

4. In addition, the treaty obligates members to provide information on military equipment not limited by the treaty, command structures of forces in the region, changes in TLE and command structure, and other details regarding the status and deployment of their conventional forces.

5. German interview 9. Coordinated verification helps ensure comprehensive coverage, given that each country is required to accept only its number of passive quota missions. "It is not possible for everyone to go inspect the paratroop unit at the Kremlin; someone has to go to Bulgaria," the official explained.

be some 5 percent of the Russian military budget.[6] It was reasonable to ask why the treaty remained necessary.

The second issue was how the Soviet allocations were to be distributed given that eight countries occupied formerly Soviet territory covered by the treaty. In some cases treaty subregions (and thus sublimits) were split among multiple countries, making allocation even more difficult. For example, TLE in the limited Soviet "flanks" would have to be split among Moldova, Ukraine, Russia, Georgia, Armenia, and Azerbaijan. Since several of these countries were in conflict with one another and all were suspicious of others' intentions, this unexpected need for further arms control negotiations would have to be met under difficult conditions. In order for the treaty to enter into force and for implementation to begin, all the Soviet successor states covered by it would have to ratify it, and to do so they would have to agree on their allotments.

Concern for the balance of military power played an important role in the delay. Well aware of Russia's questionable acceptance of its sovereignty and independence, Ukraine sought an allocation that would support its defense and deterrence capabilities against Russia.[7] Ukraine's position was that countries should be allocated TLE commensurate with equipment actually deployed on their territory. This would have given Ukraine TLE roughly equivalent to Russia's within the ATTU area, because Soviet military forces had been forward deployed for war in Europe. Generally speaking, defensive forces need not match those of the offense for success, so at least in theory Ukraine was demanding more than it needed. Russia's position was that each former Soviet state should receive a TLE allocation based on population and territory. This formulation would clearly benefit Russia, since it would result in Russian TLE holdings over twice those of Ukraine, the only former Soviet treaty member whose allocation would be substantial.[8] The Russian government (not only the Russian army) took these balances quite seriously. The smaller new states were also concerned about the effects of their TLE allocations on military balances. The object of their concern was not so much Russia, however (since under no possible allocation scenario would they be able to defend against Russia in any event), as it

---

6. "Kaum Spielraum für Einsparungen," *Süddeutsche Zeitung*, 6 May 1992, p. 6; Russian interview 18.

7. Interview with official, Ukrainian Ministry of Defense, Kiev, July 1992.

8. For details on the Russian proposals, see an interview with General K. Kobets, "Generaly ishchut puti razdela vooruzhennoi moshchi byvshevo soyuza," *Izvestiya*, 13 February 1992.

was one another. This was particularly true of Armenia and Azerbaijan, which were at the time at war.

The impasse continued for some time and threatened to delay the treaty's anticipated entry into force in July 1992. Intensive diplomatic activity from January through May 1992 focused on pressuring the CIS states to agree and removing obstacles to agreement. Through the "High Level Working Group" (HLWG) and North Atlantic Cooperation Council (NACC)—both newly created structures affiliated with NATO—all parties to the treaty were able to meet to discuss solutions. Both Russian and German officials said that these institutions played a crucial role in allaying concerns of the former Soviet republics about their security as it related to military balances and CFE limits, and that the forum provided material assistance which led to the ultimate agreement. One German official (27) said, "NACC was instrumental in bringing the CFE treaty into force." Another (12) explained that Ukraine's insistence that it must have equipment that matched Russia's in numbers in order to prevent attack inspired a series of discussions and seminars on the requirements for defensive operations in which western military experts showed how defensive forces can prevail even if they hold less equipment and fewer troops. Another official (29) said that NACC played a role as "a forum for political dialogue," aiding the CIS states by explaining the treaty, offering training in verification procedures and preparing inspection teams, developing assessment processes for data collected, and even providing personal computers. Then the governments can explain to their domestic audiences the importance of the security system as a whole for relations among the members states, he added. The value of NACC, according to German officials, was that it was a comprehensive, political, and flexible forum. One official (9) said that the organization was particularly effective and important because all the CFE member states were in it and it met intensively in early 1992 so "there was no way to escape it." Another (63) was even more blunt about the role of NACC in getting intra-CIS agreement: "In NACC, we could do demarches, have them here, and hit them over the head."

According to Russian officials and politicians, NACC played an important role in relations and negotiations among the CIS states. They acknowledged that all the former Soviet republics were worried about military balances and this created obstacles to agreement, especially since war raged in the southern Caucasus and they fear reassertion of control by Moscow. One political adviser (19) said that NACC had proved itself useful "by teaching the other former Soviet republics about defensive defense and their military requirements in a way that the other republics would not have accepted or trusted coming from Russians." An official

in the foreign ministry said in April 1992 that the government was anticipating problems, but that the objective was to get agreement at the CIS
summit in Tashkent in mid-May. Asked if that was reasonable, he
pointed out that there would be a NACC meeting on 6 May immediately
preceding the CIS meeting, and a CFE meeting in Oslo in June, so with
these two constraints, the former republics should be able to come to an
agreement. When pressed on whether there could be agreement with
conflicts in the former Soviet Union beginning to emerge, he said, "Well,
they [all the republics] took on all the obligations: they understand that
this is the development of a forum for the future." Another Russian foreign ministry official (6), asked later in the year to explain the successful
agreement, offered NACC's influence as the reason. Probably the most
important thing for ultimate agreement was to sit at the same table, but
Ukraine and Russia have trouble with that, he observed. NACC's role
was to be a "forum where we are forced to cooperate." Another official
(46) emphasized the practical assistance that NACC contributed through
seminars on military doctrines and special courses for OSCE countries at
the NATO school in Oberammergau and the NATO Academy in Italy.
These were valuable in particular, he said, for bringing Russian military
officers to NATO seminars.

Finally, in May 1992 at the CIS meeting in Tashkent, the eight countries agreed upon the apportionment of TLE (see Table 2). Georgia was
not a member of the CIS, so it sent a special representative to approve the
allocation. The agreement was clearly a compromise between the Russian
and Ukrainian initial demands. It is noteworthy for codifying a Russian-
Ukrainian balance that preserves defensive advantages, and for establishing equal entitlements among the countries of the Transcaucasus.

Once the CIS allocation problem had been solved, a new difficulty
emerged. Since the treaty's limits and subregions had been negotiated
on the assumption of an intact Soviet Union that no longer existed, the
implications of its provisions did not always match the realities of Russia's security situation. In particular, the flank zones became a clear
problem. Although official Russian requests for review of the flank limits became public in 1993,[9] the issues were clear in 1992.

The problem was twofold. First, it was becoming clear that Russia's
most important military security problems would lie to the south, not to
its west. The flank zone limits—acceptable given planning for war in

9. Richard A. Falkenrath, "The CFE Flank Dispute: Waiting in the Wings," *International
Security* 19 (Spring 1995): 118-144.

Table 2. Tashkent Agreement on CFE allocations for the former Soviet Union, May 1992

	Total FSU	Total for Russia	Total for Ukraine	Total in region 4.2[a]	Of which for:		
					Russia	Ukraine	Belarus
Tanks	13,150	6,400	4,080	10,300	5,100	3,400	1,800
ACV	20,000	11,480	5,050	17,400	10,100	4,700	2,600
Artillery	13,175	6,415	4,040	9,500	4,735	3,150	1,615
Combat aircraft	5,150	3,450	1,090	—	—	—	260
Attack helicopters	1,500	890	330	—	—	—	80

	Total in flanks	Russia	Ukraine	Of which for:			
				Moldova	Georgia	Armenia	Azerbaijan
Tanks	2,850	1,300	680	210	220	220	220
ACV	2,600	1,380	350	210	220	220	220
Artillery	3,675	1,680	890	250	285	285	285
Combat aircraft	—	—	—	50	100	100	100
Attack helicopters	—	—	—	50	50	50	50

Source: "Tablitsa raspredeleniya ODVT mezhdu gosudarstvami SNG i Gruziey."
[a] Region 4.2 includes portions of Russia, Ukraine, Belarus, and Kazakhstan.

central Europe—constrained Russia's capacity to deploy and develop forces to meet these new conditions.[10]

Second, the flank zones included the Caucasus to the south and the Leningrad military district to the north. This had made sense given the assumption of conventional war against NATO, where flank forces from north and south could support offensive operations against a single enemy. But after the cold war, it made little sense to include these widely separated military districts under the same equipment limit, since tanks in the north could hardly be used to support operations in the south. Russia's basic complaint on the flanks issue was that it wished to be able to hold more troops in the southern part of the flank without reducing troops in the northern portion. Russian defense officials asked for some 400 tanks, 2,400 ACVs, and 800 artillery pieces above the flank sublimits.[11]

The CFE treaty was deeply unpopular in large segments of the Russian security establishment. The Soviet military had actively opposed it, and both the Russian military and nationalist politicians criticized the treaty.[12] The "flank limits" became the particular target of Russian military complaints. The Russian military also criticized the CFE treaty in light of NATO expansion when it argued that since the expansion would cause states to change sides, NATO's treaty limits would be exceeded and the military balance shaken.[13]

Although in public German policy supported the existing treaty, in private discussions German officials agreed that Russian complaints were legitimate. Both because of the end of the cold war and because of the emergence of regional conflicts to Russia's south, several officials conceded, the flank limits made little contribution to the original purpose of the treaty and were a serious constraint on legitimate Russian military security concerns. They resisted renegotiation of the flank provisions, however, because any such revision would open the entire treaty to renegotiation, which clearly could threaten ratification.

Yet after much complaining and several warnings that Russia might abrogate the treaty,[14] intensive negotiations achieved an agreement that

10. For an early public discussion of Russian concern, see Lt. Col. V. Mukhin, "Voina v zakavkaze i Pridnyestrovye tolko nachinayetsya," *Nezavisimaya gazeta*, 26 June 1992, p. 1.

11. *The Military Balance, 1995–1996* (London: International Institute for Strategic Studies, 1996), p. 104.

12. Douglas L. Clarke, "The Russian Military and the CFE Treaty," *RFE/RL Research Report* 2, no. 42 (22 October 1993): 38–43.

13. Russian interview 58. "Moscow Claims Expanded NATO Threatens CFE Treaty," *RFE/RL Daily Report*, no. 138 (22 July 1994); "General Staff Warns against NATO Enlargement," *Jamestown Foundation Monitor* (electronic version), vol. 2, no. 14 (18 July 1996).

14. Falkenrath, "The CFE Flank Dispute," pp. 121–123.

preserved the treaty's overall structure but accommodated the flank problem. Several revisions (which did not require that the treaty undergo reratification) were agreed upon at the first CFE review conference, which took place 15–31 May 1996. Several territorial districts were temporarily removed from inclusion in the flanks, the amount of equipment that could deployed in the flanks was temporarily increased, and Russia was permitted to seek renegotiation of the Tashkent flank quotas with its neighbors.[15] In return, Russia agreed to allow more inspections in the flanks. Russia had substantially complied with the CFE limits by the November 1995 deadline. Although in technical violation of the treaty in November 1995 because it had not met its required numbers and held 700 more TLE than allowed,[16] Russia was still in substantial fulfillment of its commitment, which required a total reduction of some 15,000 TLE. Only Germany came close to Russia in terms of TLE reduction liability under the treaty, at nearly 11,000 pieces.[17]

Soviet Nuclear Weapons

The political breakup of the Soviet Union meant the dissolution of the Soviet army. Although this was a long and complex process, that the formerly Soviet conventional military would be drastically reduced was clear in 1992. Although the potential for instability and increased uncer-

---

15. "Outflanked: Conventional Forces in Europe," *Economist*, 8 June 1996, p. 52. The excluded territories were Pskov, Volgograd, Astrakhan, and much of Rostov. The effective limits were increased retroactively to 1,897 tanks, 4,397 ACVs, and 2,422 artillery pieces. As of 31 May 1996 the allowed numbers would come down to 1,800, 3,700, and 2,400 respectively. Georgia has since agreed to give some of its flank quota to Russia. In late 1997, Armenia rescinded its grant of some of its TLE to Russia.

16. Sarah Walkling, "CFE Treaty Final Cuts Implemented: Progress Made on 'Flank Dispute'," *Arms Control Today* 25 (December 1995–January 1996): 22–23; *The Military Balance, 1995–1996*, p. 105.

17. The large German reduction liability was primarily a result of unification, which had made former GDR Nationale Volksarmee (NVA) forces part of the Bundeswehr. The Bundeswehr took over not only all NVA personnel and equipment, but also all its facilities and unusual properties such as the Berlin Wall, including its defensive systems. The Bundeswehr's inheritance proved to be quite a problem. The NVA had been designed and equipped to be independent of the government and civilian economy, so it turned out that it had its own electrical power plant in east Berlin. The Bundeswehr did not need the electricity the plant produced, an official (18) told me, so it was shut down. The next day the command in Berlin got a call from the government of a town near Rostock on the Baltic Sea; the power plant was also the sole source of electricity for the entire town, and it had been cut off. So the Bundeswehr had to operate the plant solely for that town—at a financial loss—until the town could be put on another electricity grid.

tainty caused concern, for the most part the end of bipolar military confrontation was seen as positive for European security.

The implications of the Soviet demise for nuclear balances and uncertainties were equally important and in many respects more complicated. Unlike the case of conventional weapons, no allocation of the nuclear arsenal among the Soviet successor states would contribute to security and stability.[18] German and Russian decision makers—along with a virtually unanimous international consensus—believed that the only acceptable outcome was for Russia to be the sole Soviet nuclear successor state.

This was a problem, because Soviet nuclear weapons were deployed throughout the country's territory. Tactical nuclear weapons had been deployed in all republics except Tajikistan and Kyrgystan. The Soviet military began to withdraw these to the Russian republic in 1991, and with the exception of some remaining forces in Belarus and Ukraine all tactical weapons had been moved by the time of the Soviet breakup. The withdrawal was suspended for a time in early 1992 when Ukraine demanded guarantees that the weapons were being destroyed and that Ukraine would play a role in future agreements and arrangements for nuclear disarmament. After considerable western pressure including united public criticism of Ukraine at a NACC meeting in April, Ukraine resumed the transfer in mid-April. The United States had guaranteed assistance in supervising the destruction, and Russia agreed to both a joint CIS commission to oversee weapons destruction and Ukrainian participation in future START discussions.[19] The transfer of tactical nuclear weapons from Ukraine was completed on 5 May 1992 and from Belarus on 28 April 1992.

That left Soviet strategic nuclear weapons deployed in Russia, Ukraine, Belarus, and Kazakhstan.[20] The international community recognized all the states of the former Soviet Union in principle as successor states, on the condition that all states except Russia become nonnuclear states under the NPT regime. The most important effort to limit the

18. Although, for a dissenting view see John Mearsheimer, "The Case for a Ukrainian Nuclear Deterrent," *Foreign Affairs* 72 (Summer 1993): 50–67.

19. Russian interview 10; "Ukraine bringt Atomwaffen nach Rußland," *Süddeutsche Zeitung*, 18 April 1992, p. 8.

20. For an early and insightful analysis of the problem, see Kurt M. Campbell, Ashton B. Carter, Steven E. Miller, and Charles A. Zraket, *Soviet Nuclear Fission: Control of the Nuclear Arsenal in a Disintegrating Soviet Union*, CSIA Studies in International Security no. 1 (Cambridge, Mass.: Center for Science and International Affairs, 1991). In December 1991, deployments of nuclear weapons outside the Russian Federation were: in Ukraine 130 6-warhead SS-19 ICBMs, 46 10-warhead SS-24 ICBMs, and 40 strategic bombers; in Belarus 54 single warhead SS-25 ICBMs; and in Kazakhstan 104 10-warhead SS-18 ICBMs and 21 strategic bombers.

transfer of certain weapons and capabilities, the regime based on the 1968 Treaty on the Nonproliferation of Nuclear Weapons also involves the International Atomic Energy Agency and the Nuclear Suppliers Group. The regime makes available nuclear technology for energy and research to nonnuclear weapons states, but on the condition of inspections, safeguards, and limits on the more weapons-usable aspects of the technology. A cold war institution, the NPT was nonetheless an east-west cooperative venture. Although far from universally praised, the nuclear weapons and technology control regime was seen as valuable after the cold war because the conditions that made nuclear proliferation a danger still existed. In 1995 the NPT was extended indefinitely by its signatories.[21]

This arrangement appeared unproblematic at the time. The CIS agreements had placed nuclear weapons under CIS command, and officials assumed that that meant Russian command.[22] Ukraine agreed to send all strategic nuclear weapons to Russia by the end of 1994, and Belarus by 1996–1997. Both Belarus and Ukraine publicly committed to joining the NPT as nonnuclear weapons states. Furthermore, Ukraine's strong anti-nuclear stand was well known: before independence, the Ukrainian parliament had voted to affirm that the country would be nuclear-free, and that it would adhere to the NPT. Kazakhstan's leadership had always been ambivalent about such a commitment, however, and had not made similarly clear pledges.[23]

The single-successor solution to the question of the post-Soviet nuclear balance was thrown into doubt when in February 1992 Ukrainian President Kravchuk questioned the wisdom of sending nuclear weapons deployed in Ukraine to Russia. The disposition of Soviet military forces became a political issue and a bargaining chip among the former Soviet states. In part, Ukraine intended to gain leverage in bargaining with Russia, but it also aimed to gain attention and leverage in relations with the west and (especially) the United States. As one Russian politician (5) said about the sudden attention U.S. Secretary of State James Baker paid to Ukraine and Kazakhstan in the spring of 1992, "They asked themselves 'what do we have to attract this attention—a strong human rights record, economic strength? No; of course, it is the nuclear weapons!'"

---

21. On the NPT review conference, see International Institute for Strategic Studies, *Strategic Survey: 1995–1996* (London: IISS, 1996), pp. 58–60. On regimes for export control, see *Proliferation and Export Controls: An Analysis of Sensitive Technologies and Countries of Concern* (London: Deltac, 1995).

22. German interviews 24 and 43.

23. Russian interview 46.

In addition to the transfer of nuclear weapons to Russia, the START I treaty became a problem when Ukraine, Kazakhstan, and Belarus insisted on being parties to the treaty on the grounds that many of the weapons it targeted for elimination were on their territory. After intensive negotiations, those countries along with the United States and Russia signed a protocol in Lisbon on 23 May 1992 recognizing them as parties to the treaty with obligations to implement its terms. The protocol also, however, provided for the further commitment by the three to join the NPT as nonnuclear weapons states.

Kazakhstan ratified START I in July 1992, the United States in October 1992, Russia in November 1992, and Belarus in February 1993. Russian ratification, however, was made conditional on ratification by the other three CIS nuclear states and by their entry into the NPT as nonnuclear weapons states. Ukraine refused to ratify the agreement, since relations with Russia had taken an adversarial turn with political conflicts over the Black Sea Fleet, possible secession of the Crimean peninsula from Ukraine, Russian suspensions of natural gas supplies to Ukraine, and the emergence of nationalist domestic politics in both countries. START ratification became both a political bargaining chip and a genuine Ukrainian security concern, since it was at least unusual and perhaps unprecedented for a country willingly to give up important military forces, and even worse send them to its potential adversary.

Nevertheless, Ukraine had made international commitments to do just that, and the west saw their fulfillment as a security priority. Western involvement in the issue was therefore intense, consistent, and at high levels from the very beginning. The U.S. program for "cooperative threat reduction" created by the Nunn-Lugar Act of 1991 funded not only conversion and technical assistance programs similar to those of other western countries and the EU, but targeted destruction of Soviet strategic nuclear weapons. American diplomacy with Russia and Ukraine often focused on this issue.[24]

The programs and the diplomacy paid off. In January 1994, the United States, Ukraine, and Russia reached agreement: Russia would provide Ukraine with fuel for its nuclear reactors in exchange for the weapons material, and both the United States and Russia pledged that they would guarantee Ukrainian security once the START I treaty came into force

---

24. "USA bieten diplomatische Garantien," *Süddeutsche Zeitung*, 30 April 1992, p. 12; "Bush und Krawtschuk über Start-Vertrag einig," *Frankfurter Allgemeine Zeitung*, 8 May 1992, p. 7.

and Ukraine became member of the NPT. In February 1994, Ukraine removed the conditions it had imposed on its original ratification in November 1993, and in December 1994 it acceded to the NPT as a nonnuclear weapon state. START I then came into effect: all nuclear weapons had been removed from Kazakhstan by April 1995, and all from Ukraine by June 1996.[25] Belarus claimed delays in its withdrawal program were due to financial difficulties, but the removal was accomplished by 1997.

Denuclearization of the Soviet successor states and the continued reduction in nuclear weapons through START I and START II were core international security issues for Germany and Russia in the post–cold war period. The matter was not one of particular importance in bilateral relations, but part of the larger context of security concerns. Germany and Russia successfully cooperated in this issue area, but German cooperation came as part of western cooperation, clearly led by the United States. Neither German nor Russian decision makers saw any particular role for the bilateral relationship to play in the problem. Indeed, when they discussed this issue, German officials and politicians most often spoke of American programs and diplomacy, although they agreed with and supported American leadership on this issue.[26] Russian officials were similarly focused in these discussions on the United States. One foreign ministry official (38) attributed this to "our mentality of Russia as Great Power." This is reinforced by popular sentiment, he said, which may not know much about specific agreements but supports U.S.-Russian negotiations and meetings.

Despite the small German role, however, several aspects of this case are important for understanding German-Russian relations and security cooperation. First, although Germany did not play a direct role in post-Soviet denuclearization, this was not because German security interests were unaffected. German officials were deeply concerned about the problems that emerged in early 1992, and very much involved in developing policies and strategies to addresses those problems. While Germany was not directly involved in negotiations on START I, it actively participated in convincing Ukraine that the west's commitment to the NPT and nonproliferation regime was serious and consequential. One foreign office official (58) said, "Our position is clear—Ukraine, Kazakhstan, and Belarus cannot under any circumstances be considered nuclear

---

25. Ustina Markus, "Nuclear Weapons Removed from Ukraine," *OMRI Analytical Brief* (electronic version), vol. 1, no. 153 (7 June 1996).

26. For public evidence of German support for American leadership on this issue, see the comments by German Defense Minister Volker Rühe in "'Die deutsche Wacht am Amur,'" *Der Spiegel*, 3 February 1992, pp. 30–32.

weapons states." German politicians, in particular, saw the prevention of post-Soviet nuclear proliferation as a priority. This view was consistent across the political spectrum, from an SPD politician (16) who listed instability and nuclear proliferation as the two greatest threats to German security, to a CDU politician (60) who called Ukrainian bargaining on this issue "use of military means to pressure us." At meetings between German and Ukrainian officials, the issue of nuclear nonproliferation was consistently raised.[27]

Any direct German role in the issue, however, was precluded by Germany's status as a nonnuclear weapons state. An official directly involved in arms control policy (20) said, "Pressing Ukraine to abide by international obligations on nuclear weapons is the responsibility of the U.S., Great Britain, and France." Another (27) said, "Germany is not in any way involved in nuclear weapons: we are not and do not want to be a nuclear weapons state." Part of the reason why Germany did not play a leading role, he said, was the government's determination to demonstrate to its neighbors that it has no interest or involvement in nuclear weapons. In other nuclear issues Germany can be directly involved, he added, such as nuclear reactor safety, disposal, and conversion.

Germany also was not directly involved because its economic and alliance ties in the west mean that German interests were met through cooperation with its allies, particularly the United States. Arms control policies are always coordinated among the allies, one official (20) said, and given America's status as a nuclear power it is entirely appropriate that the issue be managed by the United States, with our consultation and cooperation. Thus, western multilateralism played an important role in the success of security cooperation in the problem of post-Soviet nuclear weapons proliferation.

German Military Forces

Contemporary Germany remains shaped by its history as the violent aggressor of World War II. That history has had profound effects on many aspects of German life and politics, and an especially direct influence on Germany's position as a modern military power. Germany was permitted to rearm only in connection with its accession to NATO in 1954, and a prohibition on the use of military forces outside the NATO alliance

27. German interview 52.

area was enshrined in the German constitution. By integrating the German military into alliance structures and limiting its territorial reach, the postwar generation intended to prevent future German aggression and reassure Germany's neighbors that such an act could not be repeated. These constraints played a leading role in the acceptance of German unification.

The post–cold war world challenged this equilibrium in two ways. First, responses to military threats to Europe would not be confined to traditional missions of defense against regular armies on the European continent alone. The Persian Gulf War and conflicts in southern Africa and southeast Asia which drew western involvement highlighted the limitations on Germany's status as a full-fledged member of the western alliance. Second, German policymakers determined that, although unification had been achieved and accepted on the basis of European integration as it stood in 1990, the only way to ensure future German multilateral cooperation across all issues *and* to assure Germany's neighbors was to "deepen" integration. This was accomplished in most spheres through the European Union. In the military sphere, the main avenue of deepening integration was to be the creation of a French-German "Eurocorps."

The Eurocorps arose from a bilateral agreement in 1990 to create a joint brigade, and the initiative was revived by Kohl and French President François Mitterrand in response to conflict in southeastern Europe in 1991. The Eurocorps would, supporters argued, serve the purpose of European integration—which was built upon the German-French relationship as core, as the European Economic Community had been—and develop flexible military capabilities for dealing with new post–cold war military realities, such as the need for peacekeeping and humanitarian intervention.[28]

At a French-German summit in May 1992, Kohl and Mitterrand agreed to establish the joint force. The headquarters is located in Strasbourg, and the main components are the French 5th Armored Division and the German 10th Armored Division. The Eurocorps was open to participation from other countries, and Spain (a brigade), Luxembourg (a battalion), and Belgium (a division) assigned forces to it in 1993–94. In November 1995 the Eurocorps was declared operational and capable of action for defense, humanitarian missions, and crisis operations, with 45,000 troops.

---

28. Christoph Bertram, "Das Korps der guten Hoffnung," *Die Zeit*, 29 May 1992, p. 3.

Originally meant to put in place an enhanced European military cooperation capability in anticipation and in advance of the reduction in American military forces in Europe, the agreement also had more subtle specific purposes. On the French side, one of them was to supplant and get around NATO. The German side had a directly opposite aim: to draw France into NATO cooperation. Thus, Germany's official position was that the Eurocorps would be subordinated to NATO. In 1992 after the agreement in principle was announced, there was some public disagreement between French and German officials on this issue. Eventually, the German position won out, and the Eurocorps was to be subordinated to NATO in case of military conflict.[29]

Military integration through the Eurocorps did not settle matters, however. The emergence of new types of conflicts after the cold war which seemed to require new approaches created other dilemmas for Germany. First, these conflicts required new military instruments: namely, peacekeeping, peace enforcement, and humanitarian intervention. Second, these conflicts required operations outside of the NATO area. German defense and political officials had assumed that its constitution prevented Germany from deploying military forces beyond NATO territory. Beginning in 1991 this consensus began to break down. Although some held to the strict interpretation, others argued that German military forces could operate out-of-area as UN peacekeeping forces (the position of the SPD), still others that German military forces could operate in combat missions as long as such missions were under UN mandate (FDP); the Kohl government's position was that German out-of-area missions had to be limited to multilateral operations, but that these would not necessarily require an explicit UN Security Council resolution. Further complicating matters was the question of whether any of these variants required a change in the German Constitution of 1949.

When war in Yugoslavia broke out in 1991 and worsened in 1992, the issue became even more important in Germany. German policymakers sought multilateral cooperation to cope with the conflict, but officially continued to rule out German military contributions. This position had caused a considerable problem in allied relations during the Gulf War in 1990–91, when the allied perception was that Germany would benefit from the defeat of Iraqi aggression, but that Germany was not willing to put its own citizens at risk. German officials also quickly learned that without the capacity or willingness to offer military forces for peace operations, they had little credibility or say in how the operations would be

29. For a discussion, see "Bonn will künftiges deutsch-französisches Korps der Kontrolle des NATO-Oberbefehlshabers unterstellen," *Süddeutsche Zeitung*, 27 May 1992, p. 1.

conducted. Yugoslavia was especially problematic: Germany after all, had been the leading country pressing for recognition of Croatia and Slovenia, perceived in many quarters to be one of the major contributing factors to the war. Having appeared to help cause the war, Germany now claimed that it could do nothing in the way of effective military action to help end it. In July 1992, Germany sent a destroyer to aid in the sanctions mission against Serbia, but the ship's orders did not permit combat action. Even so, the SPD did not accept the government's position on the legality of the mission, and brought suit against the government in the Federal Constitutional Court. In July 1994 the court ruled that the constitution did not preclude out-of-area operations under international multilateral agreement if the Bundestag gave its approval in each case. Under these terms, German forces have participated in the NATO mission in the former Yugoslavia.[30]

The question here is whether these changes in German military capabilities inspired fear, distrust, or a balancing response from Russia. The answer is an unequivocal no. I found German officials, in fact, to be far more worried about the implications of the removal of constraints on Germany's military operations than were Russians. Russian officials said Germany has the right to participate in peacekeeping as an independent state and normal country, and that its doing so does not violate any German-Russian treaty. As to the Eurocorps, officials and politicians thought it posed no threat, and one joked that it would keep the Germans and French so occupied in working things out between themselves that they could not pose a threat to others.[31] Liberal and moderate officials said they were concerned that the corps could develop into a link between military and political-economic European institutions, but none saw its existence as an enhancement of Germany military capabilities that would affect Russian calculations.[32] Only two officials I spoke with expressed concern about such a development. One (12) was concerned that it could mean the rise of a French-German military role in Europe overshadowing that of the United States and NATO, while another (27) feared that French-German cooperation would strengthen the security aspect of the EU, a problem from the Russian point of view because Russian is unlikely to become a member.

There were, however, two important conditions for this sanguine evaluation of the Eurocorps and out-of-area developments. First, Rus-

---

30. For an argument that these changes mean less than they might appear to, see Franz-Josef Meiers, "Germany: The Reluctant Power," *Survival* 37 (Autumn 1995): 82–103.

31. Russian interviews 12, 33, and 40.

32. Russian interviews 41 and 42.

sian officials said that German military missions would be acceptable only if Germany did not act unilaterally; such missions had to be undertaken strictly in cooperation with international or European institutions. One official (12) said that German military missions were not a problem and "more an issue is the process than who does what." Another (10) said that the multilateral structures could be either UN, OSCE, or NATO, as long as any operations were in accordance with UN rules and procedures. A politician (31) explained that German participation in peacekeeping operations would be in Russian interests if it was conducted jointly with other countries in accordance with UN rules, and therefore the government would have no objections.

The second condition was that Germany could not participate in any such missions on formerly Soviet soil (actually, at least two Russian officials slipped and said "Russian territory," then corrected themselves when I asked if they meant the Russian Federation—they actually meant the former Soviet Union). This was true not only for Germany, however, but for any western multilateral force, whether UN, OSCE, or NATO.

On balance, these issues were not very important, and I would not want to imply more than a marginal role for multilateral structures in Russian acceptance of change in German military capacity. Nevertheless, it is worth noting these issues precisely because they were *not* particularly important: Germany was emerging from the special constraints meant to ensure that it could not again unleash the sort of destruction it had dealt out earlier in the century. Given that Russia was one of Germany's greatest victims in World War II and given the importance of historical memory in Russia, it is significant that the loosening of these constraints was met with calm, indifference, and even support. To the extent that Russians believed multilateral processes and rules made an active German military role beyond its borders acceptable and even desirable, institutions were quite significant in this area of security concerns and the balance of military power.

INSTITUTIONS AND SECURITY COOPERATION

In all three issues examined in this chapter, Germany and Russia were involved in successful multilateral security cooperation. In the case of conventional military forces, cooperation was substantial and far from certain, since it entailed ratifying and implementing a treaty that created new problems, and conducting additional negotiations under difficult circumstances. Countries were able to cooperate, but not because cooperation was easy or obviously in their interest. The countries of the former Soviet Union were highly suspicious of and threatened by one another. This case is quite a strong test of institutionalist predictions, because relative gains concerns were not absent and the usefulness of military force by no means ruled out. The security dilemma was not obviously benign, and countries were worried about one another's capabilities and intentions. Therefore, neither realism nor optimistic realism can explain successful cooperation in this instance.

The strategic arms case likewise was one of cooperation, and not merely the straightforward pursuit of national interests. Ukraine's interests in maintaining a nuclear capability were clear and strengthened over time, and German and Russian officials took those interests and Ukrainian intent quite seriously. Furthermore, while in this case cooperation primarily consisted of implementing commitments already made, it also entailed some new negotiations as well, including the complex and drawn-out provisions for START ratification. This case is not, however, a direct test of the role of institutions in German-Russian relations, because German and Russian interests were compatible. The problems of cooperation, that is, were not between Germany and Russia, but between the west and Russia on the one hand, and Ukraine on the other.

The same cannot be said about loosened restraints on Germany's military forces through the Eurocorps and out-of-area missions. Realist theories expect that states will seek to balance shifts in military capability. Although the change in German military capacity was limited, nonetheless Russia showed little concern and did not try to balance against Germany's enhanced military options. This cannot be explained within the realist framework.

Did institutions matter? That is, did they play an independent causal role? The result in the conventional forces case is clear: institutions played an independent role in enabling twenty-seven countries, Germany and Russia among them, to cooperate. The rules and procedures of the treaty sustained cooperation by providing information and the system of verification and monitoring. Furthermore, the evidence shows that the larger network of European institutions played a role in the successful agreement at Tashkent. The technical assistance and consultations made possible under the NATO umbrella through the HLWGs and NACC, in conjunction with reinforcing principles of defense sufficiency, were important in the bargaining and calculations of Russian policymakers. Russian officials concluded they were very important for reducing uncertainty about the effects of policy choices (reduce offensive forces) on outcomes (stability and defensive capabilities) for other post-

Soviet leaderships wary of Russian intentions and military balances. Far from resisting these institutions for the assurances it gave Russia's wary neighbors, Russian officials made use of the assurance mechanisms.

Moreover, the case provides clear evidence that institutional rules matter and do constrain policies even in a state's military affairs. German officials took the rules of the CFE treaty so seriously that Germany's plans to begin destruction of its equipment stocks by mid-1992 were at risk if there was delay in ratification. According to the treaty, none of the members could begin to destroy TLE until the treaty came into effect in order to prevent changes in the numbers on national reduction liabilities. Germany in 1992 was very eager to begin destruction, especially of the useless forces inherited from the GDR. But the United States and other allies refused to bend the rules to allow Germany to begin.[33] Defense Minister Volker Rühe said in May 1992 that Germany needed ratification as soon as possible in order to begin the process, observing that it would be "an irony of history" if an arms control treaty prevented German disarmament.[34]

Russian officials also believed that the rules themselves mattered and were constraining, which is why they spent so much time and energy pressing for compromise on the flanks limits. Russian officials consistently spoke of the treaty in terms of its effect on Russian policies. One politician noted the contrast between negotiating the split up of Soviet conventional forces in Europe and the unsuccessful and quite acrimonious discussions over dividing the Black Sea Fleet, and observed that at least one important difference in the two cases was the fact that the latter was not subject to an international treaty, so Russia and Ukraine faced only each other in negotiations.[35] A political adviser (5) offered the same comparison, and added that this was true despite the fact that the conventional military balance had far more real military meaning than the Black Sea Fleet, which he dismissed as "a fleet in an aquarium."

The treaty made a difference because it already existed, and neither German nor Russian officials wanted to lose what had been achieved. They knew that the increased complexity and uncertainty of the post–cold war world might well make renegotiation impossible. A German official told me that there was quick and easy agreement in principle in January 1992 that the CFE treaty should not be amended or renegotiated because that would reopen issues that had been previously

33. German interview 2.
34. "Rühe besorgt über Abrüstung," *Frankfurter Allgemeine Zeitung*, 4 May 1992, p. 4.
35. Russian interview 33. Russia and Ukraine finally agreed on dividing the fleet in May 1997.

settled, allowing new disputes among the former Soviet states to delay or even prevent ratification. He went on to express strong doubt that a CFE2 treaty could be achieved, precisely because issues of military balances and defensive defense are more difficult with multiple parties. A Russian official (27) said that the key issues in future conventional arms control discussions should be qualitative differences and balances, but that he doubted any agreements could be achieved given the large number of states and the multiple issues that would have to be involved.

German officials expressed this view in particular with reference to Russian complaints about the flanks limits. For example, an agreement based on the old bilateral order may not match today's realities, said one (29), but we cannot reopen the treaty for renegotiation because we will never achieve an agreement among many states. He gave a concrete example of the difference: because the bilateral approach was no longer possible, the CFE1A agreement on troop limits was a weaker, merely politically binding agreement in which each state unilaterally declared its troop ceilings.

That is, officials believed that under conditions current in 1992, the CFE agreement could not have been achieved. This view has extremely important implications for our assessment of the independent effects of international institutions. John Mearsheimer, for example, has argued that while we may observe institutions, they are merely reflections of power and interests: that is, states would behave substantially the same and make the same choices of security strategies without the institutions.[36] My evidence does not support this hypothesis: both Russian and German officials were convinced that the treaty could not have been achieved in 1992, *and* this belief led them to a more determined set of policies to see the treaty ratified and implemented. If institutions are merely a reflection of power and interests, a new treaty could have easily been negotiated from scratch in 1992. The fact that the officials interviewed were absolutely convinced that this was not so is strong support for institutionalist hypotheses on security cooperation.

In the nuclear case, however, international institutions were neither directly nor primarily important. The problems were successfully overcome because the issue was of high salience to the two nuclear superpowers, and those two countries used high-level diplomacy to seek a solution. Furthermore, American economic resources played the leading role in creating incentives for Ukrainian cooperation and in mitigating

---

36. John J. Mearsheimer, "The False Promise of International Institutions," *International Security* 19 (Winter 1994/95): 5-49.

the costs of denuclearization. One political adviser, asked about possible Russian complaints about western interference in this issue, said western "interference" helped. The United States took a very firm position and told Ukraine that this was an issue of cooperation with the west, he said, and "then it was solved in a week."[37] Although that view was less equivocal than most, Russian officials were consistent in viewing American and western pressure on Ukraine in positive terms. Thus, power and interests are sufficient to explain both Ukrainian compliance in this case and German and Russian policies.

On the issue of Germany's enhanced military missions, the independent causal effect of institutions in leading both Germany and Russia from unilateral balancing behavior is clear. German officials could not and would not contemplate any missions for German military forces beyond German territory outside the bounds of multilateral structures, agreements, and institutions. One reason was that the German public would simply not allow it, so any unilateral policy was unsustainable, but equally important was the ongoing recognition that Germany must constantly assure its neighbors that it is not threat to them. The best way to convey that assurance, both officials and politicians said, is through integration and commitment to multilateral action.[38] And as this chapter has shown, Russian acceptance of, and virtual indifference to, these developments in German military options were contingent on the role of institutions as instruments preventing unilateral action.

So institutions clearly mattered in two of the three cases examined in this chapter. In response to greater uncertainty about intentions and capabilities in the aftermath of German unification and the breakup of the Soviet Union, neither German nor Russian officials fell back upon simple strategies of balancing. Although calculations about the balance of power were important to their concerns about conventional and nuclear forces, as we would expect, the availability of institutions facilitated multilateral cooperative security policies.

Variation in Security Problems and Institutional Forms

This brings us to the next hypothesis: Did institutional rules and procedures provide German and Russian decision makers with the instruments for overcoming the obstacles to cooperation? What was the nature

---

37. Russian interview 18. A political analyst (41) was similarly unequivocal: "Baker solved the nuclear problems with Ukraine. The political situation in Kiev is very soft, they are very much influenced by the U.S. and its political stands."
38. German interviews 16, 30, 45, and 60.

of those obstacles (collaboration, coordination, transparency, or linkage) and did variation in the problems matter to German and Russian officials in their choice of strategies?

The underlying problem in arms control is usually that of collaboration: the parties would like to cooperate if others do, but would prefer to exploit others if possible and hold more arms. This would appear to have been true in both the conventional and nuclear arms cases. However, reality was more complicated.

The conventional arms control problem was not one of collaboration although the treaty was designed to limit the capacity of NATO and the Warsaw Pact to conduct large-scale offensive military operations in the heart of Europe. From the western point of view, this task was accomplished on the political level by the demise of the Soviet Union and on the operational level by the reduction and retreat of the Russian military from central Europe. From the Russian point of view (assuming an improbable western intention to attack Russia), such an attack would have to cross Poland and Belarus. Thus, the purpose for which the CFE treaty was designed was largely irrelevant by 1992, and certainly not a top priority. In this regard, this case does not support the hypothesis that there is a strong relationship between institutional form and function: the CFE treaty was designed to overcome problems characteristic of Prisoner's Dilemma, but neither German nor Russian officials saw collaboration problems as an obstacle to multilateral cooperation.

Traditional arms control was not irrelevant after 1991: a few Germans and most Russians spoke of the value of CFE in terms of establishing balanced military forces, having guaranteed monitoring systems, and ensuring an advanced warning system that enables members to respond to violations. A German foreign office official (43) said that democratization in Russia (and in Ukraine) is "not unchangeable." The military balance still matters, he said, and the treaty is one part of that balance. Another German official (29) observed that in a sensible and open world, states might choose lower levels of forces. But given instability, historical memories, and multiple neighbors with different capabilities, states are inclined to build more conventional forces than they need. The process of consultation, he concluded, permits states to assess their military requirements more reasonably because the processes are regular and ongoing and involve all states which could be affected.

The importance of traditional arms control aspects of the treaty was a consistent theme in my discussions with Russian officials. A Russian politician (33) was clearly still thinking in terms of balance and traditional arms control when he explained how the purpose of CFE had changed: "Its goal is no longer to achieve parity between two opposing sides, but to achieve a stable and secure balance of conventional weapons in Europe while reducing their number." A Russian general (30) said, "It is not possible to underestimate its military-technical meaning. The system of verification is very important, as are the limits on tanks." Asked whether the limits actually changed Russian military planning beyond what would have been done without the treaty, he insisted that they did because they changed the balance of military forces in Europe. The reduced numbers created logistical and doctrinal changes: our way of thinking about how to organize units has to be re-worked, he said, because some Russian units would lose 80 percent of their tanks. But in the end, he said, we accept these changes and constraints because they are consistent with new conditions and security requirements and "in order to fulfill our obligations: it is a political act with military material." He thus confirmed a view expressed to me by a Russian foreign ministry official (24) that the CFE helps translate political security concepts into military reality: the Soviet military never permitted the development of defensive sufficiency, he said, but the defensive orientation of military forces made necessary by CFE limits will force the development and implementation of these concepts.

Furthermore, Russian officials valued the CFE treaty and CFE1A negotiations for their role in military balance within the former Soviet Union. One official (27) said that the limits on western countries were useful, but not nearly as important as the constraints on the military forces of Russia's new neighbors since any military threats to Russia's security will arise from them. A foreign ministry official (16) told me that the most important purpose of the treaty was to prevent an arms race among the CIS states. Another official (27) told me that Russia intended to use its verification and observation rights more to keep an eye on its former Soviet and WTO allies than against NATO. Another said early in 1992 that Russia sought 7,000–8,000 tanks and wanted Ukraine to receive 3,000 (the remaining allocation to be distributed among the other former Soviet states). I pointed out that Russia's preference would give it over a 2–1 balance, which seemed to indicate intentions to be able to carry out an offensive. He dismissed that, saying that Russia has more territory to cover, while Ukraine could concentrate its attention only on Russia.[39] Coming from a civilian in the foreign ministry who was generally supportive of reform, this is an indication of how serious was the concern to limit the military assets of Russia's new neighbors. Another concern in

39. Russian interview 10. It is interesting that the Tashkent Agreement less than one month later gave Russia about 6,000 tanks and Ukraine about 4,000.

negotiating with Ukraine was that, with the splitting up of the Soviet army, the best-equipped and best-trained troops happened to end up in Belarus and Ukraine because they had been forward-deployed during the cold war.[40] So although Russian officials did not want western interference in Russian security affairs, they did want western participation in security affairs when that encouraged the former Soviet republics to abide by international commitments to reduce and limit arms.

The CFE treaty was important because it served a purpose more significant than dealing with collaboration problems as a result of the breakup of the Soviet Union. Providing transparency and information in the face of increased uncertainty—and its dangerous effects on potential security dilemmas in Europe—became the treaty's most important purpose, according to German and Russian officials. The CFE treaty was important for security cooperation because it was "portable": verification and monitoring systems could serve both collaboration problems and transparency problems.[41] In commenting on the role of NACC in solving problems of mistrust and competition among the CIS states, one German official (63) said, "An instrument for east-west balance turned out to be a very good instrument for this new problem."

Germans and Russians consistently dismissed the view that the problem of conventional arms in Europe was the fear of being exploited, as in collaboration problems. A few years ago arms control was meant to take the confrontational element out of east-west relations and add cooperation to a basically adversarial relationship, a German foreign office official (2) said. "Now, since there are no adversaries for us in Europe, arms control has the function of creating order, stability, and predictability." When asked about the balance of forces created by the treaty, another (27) replied that the CFE numbers were not particularly important because many countries were planning smaller armies than the treaty allowed. Did this now make arms control irrelevant, I asked? No, he said, now it is clear that it is as important as before if not more so, because of instability and uncertainty: "The verification system is crucial for European stability." On German support for the CFE1A agreement another German official (2) said, "If the CIS leaders put their signatures to such a document it would have an ordering impact on the situation in Europe: the agreement creates a new point of orientation." Even the Russian

---

40. Russian interviews 15, 17, and 18.

41. For introduction and development of the concept of "portability" see Celeste A. Wallander and Robert O. Keohane, "Risk, Threat, and Security Institutions," in *Imperfect Unions: Security Institutions in Time and Space*, ed. Helga Haftendorn, Robert O. Keohane, and Celeste A. Wallander (Oxford: Oxford University Press, forthcoming).

politician (33) whom I earlier cited as having spoken of the treaty in balancing and traditional terms added, "The significant advantages afforded by qualitative differences in equipment make transparency through arms control and verification procedures all the more important for European security."

That is, the purpose and value of the CFE treaty after 1991 lay in assurance and transparency as well as in the traditional arms control function of constraining competition. Rather than checking on the behavior and force deployments of countries suspected of aggressive intentions, or monitoring in order to prevent cheating, Germany and Russia put considerable effort into ratification and implementation because they feared that uncertainty and instability could lead to conflicts. Increased complexity and uncertainty made the CFE treaty more valuable rather than something to escape, but not for the reasons for which the institution was designed. One Russian foreign ministry official (23) said that the treaty was important because even if bilateral relations can be maintained in good order, maintaining stability and reducing the risks of conflict require discussion and agreement among multiple countries. This cannot be accomplished bilaterally, he said, but requires multilateral treaties like CFE and structures like OSCE. We need to know what our neighbors intend, said a Russian politician (31), and arms control agreements such as CFE are important because "ratification is a sign of intention."

Indeed, some officials objected quite strongly when I posed questions of numbers and monitoring procedures. When I asked whether the monitoring procedures should not be modified to allow the CIS states a larger number of inspections among themselves since that is where the greatest threats and risks seem to lie, one German official (29) told me that I was thinking too much along military lines, "reconnaissance thinking." The main thing about these verification procedures is not military information, he said. The main thing is the system of confidence-building. "I do not think the Moldovans care whether Russia has 11,200 or 11,300 tanks. But they are concerned with getting themselves and the others in a system of cooperation and peaceful resolution of conflicts. The idea is not to give general staffs data so they can plan campaigns, but to achieve transparency." A Russian official (6) made a similar observation when I asked whether one reason for Russian commitment to the CFE treaty was to constrain the Bundeswehr. He told me that in asking the question in this manner I was thinking too much in technical military terms: that the real value of the CFE treaty was the political process and the political transparency it afforded.

[127]

In contrast, the problem in nuclear arms control was more clearly that of the temptation to defect. Nuclear nonproliferation poses the problem that states will develop nuclear weapons to match others: if one state has nuclear weapons the next will want them, and then the next. The nonproliferation system was designed to prevent a spiral of nuclear arming by preserving a status quo in which nonnuclear states would forgo the capability in exchange for access to commercial nuclear technology. The system was reinforced by a treaty an elaborate system of safeguards and inspections implemented by the International Atomic Energy Agency. For states that might be tempted, the system was meant either to deny access to nuclear technology or to create strong incentives for compliance by linking non-weapons status to commercial access. With the breakup of the Soviet Union, the idea was to maintain the system by keeping only Russia as a nuclear weapons state and by recognizing the other Soviet successors only if they would preserve the status quo.

Thus, the institutional structure was designed to solve both collaboration and linkage problems. Ukraine's policy, however, threatened to disrupt the status quo and therefore spark the unraveling of the nonproliferation solution. The problem was that the system was not designed to overcome fundamental fears about national security, such as Ukraine held—not without reason—with respect to Russia. Exhortations as to principle and promises of aid and good will from the west paled in comparison to concerns about national survival; for this reason direct and high-level American efforts and clear American attention to Ukraine's security concerns were needed.

The potential obstacle to multilateral cooperation in the case of enhanced German military options and reach was the need for transparency about German intentions. Neither German nor Russian officials believed that Germany sought the Eurocorps or out-of-area capabilities in order to launch unilateral operations or exploit its neighbors. But German officials knew that its neighbors could be insecure if Germany emerged from cold war restrictions on its military capabilities without reassurance and transparency about German intentions. Therefore, the German government never questioned the need to develop those capabilities through international institutions and integration. Reliance always first on institutions, said one official (35), is simply a basic assumption of our security policy "because it is in German interests to show that we are not interested in becoming more powerful." Similarly, it is striking that Russian officials, who were not concerned about German intentions, did not seek a more direct role in constraining or overseeing German military developments, but were content with the quite simple and

[128]

minimal features of the Eurocorps, WEU, OSCE, and UN which provided transparency about German intentions and capabilities.

INSTITUTIONAL EFFECTIVENESS

Comparison of these three cases enables us to evaluate hypotheses about institutional effectiveness because of the variation in outcomes. Were institutions more effective in the cases of conventional arms control and German missions than in that of strategic nuclear weapons because there was a better fit of institutional function and underlying problem, and because in the first two instances there was a broader set of institutional linkages which supported cooperation?

The results here are quite strong in support of institutional hypotheses. The case of German military missions supports both hypotheses. Transparency was needed to make cooperation in this area possible, and transparency was readily available in multiple institutions for political and military security open to Germany. Furthermore, the interlocking nature of these institutions was important, because it provided Russia multiple sources for monitoring Germany's benign intentions as it developed its military capabilities.

Similarly, the CFE was effective because it provided very clear rules about limitations and reductions which withstood the system-shattering end of the cold war. More important, the very stringent system of monitoring and verification, designed to operate in a situation of bipolar competition and mistrust, was easily adaptable and quite useful for the far less stringent demands of transparency, assurance, and confidence-building ushered in by the shift from "threats" to "risks."

At the same time, the effectiveness of the CFE treaty for German and Russian cooperation resulted from the broader set of security problems and institutions. The stakes were greater than merely the CFE itself. Officials in both countries told me that the CFE was important because it was a link, a "bridge,"[42] and part of the process of developing a post–cold war European security system. One German official (43) said that "the CFE process must not be jeopardized" because it creates continuity for the future. It binds Germany and the west, he said, "but especially the inexperienced countries of the east and the former Soviet republics into the mentality of negotiations, so that they learn how these

---

42. Russian interview 12.

things are done." In this way, he said, they will learn to be part of a process and share information about capabilities and intentions: they will not feel threatened by other states. Other concerned officials said CFE ratification was needed for progress on other confidence-building measures, such as the Open Skies Treaty signed in March 1992. Especially important, one official (29) said, was agreement in time for the July 1992 Helsinki summit and the development of the OSCE: "An entry into force of the CFE would open this cooperative security system." Another (43) said that although arms control must change and adapt, we "cannot lose the process of interaction, the way of thinking, the rules of consultation."

Russian officials also linked the CFE to development of confidence-building measures and institutionalization of the OSCE. One (6) said, "We are interested in convincing neighbors that there are no surprises awaiting them." One foreign ministry official (27) said that the Russian government considered it important to ratify the CFE treaty, abide by its limits, and make progress in future conventional force negotiations "or you [the west] will simply not believe us anymore." He went on to explain that the CFE embeds Russia in an active, high-profile multilateral effort that maintains its status as a major international player: the treaty is evidence to the Russian public that Russia is disarming not because it is weak, but because it is living up to mutual commitments that enhance Russian security by gaining arms reductions by other countries as well. One political adviser (18) said, "It is for us not an issue of security, but of being a member of the civilized international system."

Both German and Russian officials raised another linkage that made CFE ratification significant: its connection to follow-on negotiations on a CFE1A agreement on troop limits. The linkage was important in general for reasons related to transparency, assurance, and confidence-building. But both Russian and German officials had specific and direct concerns as well. For the Russians, a CFE1A agreement was desirable for domestic political consumption and to bolster the legitimacy of the Yeltsin government's claims to be providing for Russian security in a responsible manner. One Russian official (16) pointed out that the prospects for further German force reductions depended on CFE follow-on agreements: to the degree that Russia had a positive assessment of the low German threat, it was based partly on Germany's commitment to limit its conventional forces, therefore Russia has an interest in ratification of the treaty. A successful CFE1A agreement was also important to Russian officials as a justification for Russian troop levels. "Since we are going to reduce anyway" to 1.5 million soldiers, another official (24) said, we may as well get all the other European countries to reduce through an international commitment. Far from deeming them "interference," Russian officials privately welcomed the CFE constraints as a way to justify Russia's security policies. One said he did not view efforts to ratify and implement the CFE and CFE1A as interference because

> it is in our interests to demilitarize ourselves, the other republics, and Europe. It is in our interests to reduce military expenses, and to have others reduce in the bargain. And it is in our interests to have a reduced army. . . . The reason for CFE is that to follow a path of unilateral military reductions would be difficult for the new democracies to explain or sustain.[43]

German commitment to the CFE treaty also was partly a function of its linkage to a CFE1A agreement. For the Germans, achievement of a multilateral CFE1A agreement was crucial because Germany was the only country in Europe which had made an international commitment to limit its forces. As part of the agreement on unification, Germany had committed itself to a limit of 370,000 military personnel. At the time, however, German officials were uneasy about the commitment because it perpetuated Germany's status as a special case and implied that in this respect it was less than sovereign. German concerns about this asymmetric limit were not military but entirely political. Several officials and politicians said that the importance of the treaty was to continue the CFE process, which had to be accomplished in order to rid Germany of this special status. One politician said it would be "very awkward" for the German government if a CFE1A agreement were not reached because "we have made our advance payment on the reduction in the expectation that the others will follow."[44]

Before assessing whether institutions were ineffective in the case of Soviet strategic nuclear weapons for reasons predicted by institutional theory, we should note that institutions did do two things that supported security cooperation. First, institutions served to link cooperation in this issue area to other political and economic issues in which the post-Soviet states, especially Ukraine, were interested. One German politician (60) said that the nuclear weapons issue could not be solved merely by traditional diplomacy and required large and consistent economic incentives, which means you need the coordinated policies and

---

43. Russian interview 27. I asked an adviser to the Supreme Soviet (19) the same question about western "interference"; he said that he did not see that the United States was really all that concerned about observing the independence of CIS states.

44. German interview 52. In 1992 Germany reduced its troop limit to 345,000 in the CFE1A agreement.

substantial resources available only though multilateral cooperation. This was a consistent theme in German discussions, and one I take up in greater detail in Chapter 7. Even Russian officials, who were inclined to focus on the U.S. role in this case, told me that it was the size, but, most important, the consistency and the comprehensiveness, of an economic assistance package which would create incentives for Ukraine's compliance with its international commitments.[45] At stake were not merely good relations between Ukraine and the United States, but the potential package of G–7 support which Ukraine sought. The context of multilateral international involvement through institutions such as the NPT and the G–7 makes it easier for leaders in the post-Soviet countries to accept their commitments, one foreign ministry official (23) said, "because then it is not a matter of giving in to one powerful state."

The second role of institutions was the force of principles and norms in creating clear expectations about acceptable behavior and violation of the rules. Russia held an enormous advantage because it was playing by the rules, while Ukraine risked breaking some of the most important ones. German and Russian decision makers took the rules and structures of the NPT seriously and consistently cited the regime as a important and influential factor in managing the problem of post-Soviet nuclear instability and uncertainty. Once, when I began a question by saying that Russia "is seen as" the sole Soviet nuclear successor state, a German official (28) interrupted to insist that it was not merely *seen* as such, but "it simply *is* the successor state," and that this was reinforced by the NPT. As with the CFE treaty, a German official pointed out that any change in the nuclear status of a Soviet successor state other than Russia would require a change in the NPT, which might undermine the nonproliferation system if countries like India considered the basic rules and principles open for discussion.[46] The basic prohibition of the NPT regime against an increase in the number of nuclear powers was important in establishing a consistent and principled policy denying nuclear weapons status to the Soviet successor states. One Russian official (37) pointed out that Russia had to concede Soviet property to the other Soviet successor states, but in the case of nuclear weapons, the nuclear nonproliferation regime supported Russian claims to sole ownership. While the principle

---

45. Russian interviews 7 and 37.

46. German interview 57. In May 1998 India and Pakistan tested nuclear weapons. In doing so, they severely undermined the nonproliferation regime, although the fact that both had nuclear weapons was well known. The reason for their decisions appears to be their mutual distrust and regional insecurity, not any questions about the nuclear status of the Soviet successor states.

alone could not have effected the outcome, it was an important instrument of German and Russian security policy.

It is important to point out the limited role of the NPT not because it supports institutional hypotheses, but because it does not. An elaborate system had been designed to alter the incentives and opportunities facing a potential proliferator, and that system was linked to multilateral political and economic institutions such as the G–7, which promised substantial benefits for cooperative behavior. Yet the availability of appropriate and layered institutions was not sufficient reason for successful cooperation. The limited effectiveness of institutions in this case given the overwhelming importance of American and Russian interests and power makes clear the limits of institutional effects in security relations. No institution can guarantee the national survival of a state, so such institutions are unlikely to be created. The nuclear nonproliferation regime entailed no such guarantee. When a country such as Ukraine fears for its national survival, it will seek unilateral capability, such as nuclear weapons, or important allies, such as the United States. Institutions support and define balance, they do not replace it.

Thus the explanation for successful security cooperation in two of the three military cases is entirely inconsistent with realist predictions about security relations after the cold war. Multilateral security cooperation was achieved in conventional arms reductions and in changing German military capacities despite very serious obstacles and completely altered conditions. In the case of nuclear weapons, neorealist expectations are supported, because cooperation was the result of the power, interests, and attention of the United States and Russia. Although institutions played a role in supporting the cooperative outcome in this case, they were secondary and clearly insufficient alone.

More generally, the end of the cold war did not lead German and Russian officials to seek to escape the constraints of institutions forged under bipolarity; to the contrary the value of existing institutions increased. Officials and politicians were aware of the dynamics of unstable military balances under conditions of increased uncertainty which could lead to conflict and arms races, as realist theories predict. But German and Russian officials were not helpless in the face of such possibilities, and instead were able to rely upon existing international institutions to reduce uncertainty and rationally to choose self-interested strategies of security cooperation.

[6]

Threats, Risks, and Conflicts in Europe and the Former Soviet Union

In this chapter, I return to the distinction between "risk" and "threat" discussed in Chapter 3, but with a different focus. Security entails not merely military forces, but the what, where, and how of potential conflicts in which those forces might be used. German and Russian officials faced many scenarios that might have involved their countries in regional conflicts or affected their security indirectly through the pressures of refugees and migration.

REGIONAL CONFLICTS

The end of the cold war brought demands for separate states or redefinition of international borders. In July 1990 the Slovenian and Croatian republics declared sovereignty and called for a Yugoslav confederation; in June 1991, they declared their independence. The federal Yugoslav army tried to block Slovenian independence, but failed and withdrew with EC mediation and peacekeeping. In Croatia, the military situation was more complex because of the territorial concentration of Serbs in the Krajina region. Fighting between the Croatian military and police and local Serb militias led to Yugoslav army intervention on the side of the Serbs. In December 1991 the EC decided to recognize Slovenia and Croatia as independent countries in the hope this might deter Serbian military action by internationalizing the war. A cease-fire was achieved in January 1992, and UN peacekeeping forces (UNPROFOR) were sent to disputed territories in Croatia. Conflict had also broken out in Bosnia-Herzegovina, so in April 1992 the international community recognized Bosnia in the hope that act would have the same effect. It did not, and the war in Bosnia escalated.[1]

The period until signing of the Dayton Peace Accord in December 1995 (accompanied by IFOR, a NATO-led large-scale military deployment) exhibited a mix of political and military intervention, and of peacekeeping and peace enforcement. The UN never committed itself entirely to the position that Serbian forces were an aggressor, although it imposed trade sanctions on Serbia in May 1992. Intervention, when it came in July 1992 and expanded after the London conference in August of that year, took the form of humanitarian assistance and placed UN personnel in the midst of the fighting without authorization to use force to implement their mission. Similarly, UN resolutions establishing no-fly zones and safe havens never carried clear enforcement mechanisms and were not consistently implemented. Efforts to assist in political negotiations were consistent, centering first around the Vance-Owen Plan developed in January 1993 and then, after April 1994, on a plan worked out by the Contact Group (composed of the United States, Britain, Germany, France, and Russia). But these plans foundered on the reality of nearly continuous fighting by all parties, irreconcilable political demands, and the lack of commitment to enforcement.

Conditions changed gradually when in response to Serbian attacks on Sarajevo and other "safe areas," NATO (with UN authorization) launched air attacks in reprisal for the first time in February 1994. With this precedent, and with successful Croatian and Bosnian government military offensives in 1995, the military situation altered. When Serbian artillery shelled a Sarajevo market once again in August 1995, NATO conducted a two-week air campaign until Serbian forces agreed to withdraw and begin negotiations. Combined with substantial Serbian territorial losses, these made for the conditions leading to the Dayton Peace Accord, which governs Bosnia into 1998.

Russian policy supported the claims of ethnic Serbs and the republic of Serbia, but Russia also sought conflict resolution. It supported the UN arms embargo, sanctions against Serbia, deployment of UNPROFOR, and other multilateral measures. Under the OSCE's "consensus minus one" procedure adopted in January 1992, an OSCE member could no longer veto a decision against itself if all the other members were in

---

1. Susan L. Woodward, *Balkan Tragedy: Chaos and Dissolution and the Cold War* (Washington, D.C.: Brookings Institution, 1995); Misha Glenny, *The Fall of Yugoslavia: The Third Balkan War* (London: Penguin, 1992); Michael Libal, *Limits of Persuasion: Germany and the Yugoslav Crisis, 1991–1992* (Westport, Conn.: Praeger, 1997).

agreement on the sanction; therefore, the decision to deny Serbia Yugoslavia's seat in the OSCE could have been vetoed if any other OSCE member chose to support Serbia. Russia was reluctant to vote against Serbia on this issue, but it was not alone: France and Romania also refused at first. When in early 1992 France was persuaded to change its intended vote, Russia then also quickly changed its policy and voted for exclusion. "The French were the key," said a high-level German official (45) who had been involved in the negotiations with Russia on this decision, "because had they not gone, neither would the others. France would have served as the cover for Russia and Russia did not mind being closely aligned with France. Only because France ultimately did not hold out did Romania and then Russia give in. Russia did not want to take the blame itself." Russian officials disputed the idea that Russia's policy was purely tactical, but conceded that the prospect of standing alone against all the other OSCE members and undermining this first use of the mechanism, which, as one (6) said, "is part of the strengthening of the CSCE which we have sought," was made more difficult after France had changed its vote.

I did not find much concern with Yugoslavia and Serbia per se within the Russian government. When I asked one official (38) what role Yugoslavia played in Russian policy he said, "It is a catastrophe for all those peoples, but it is a good lesson for us, as the president and his aides now work hard to find compromises on disputes with Ukraine, Moldova, and Georgia." Official Russian government policy statements consistently defended the Serbian perspective, but just as consistently supported multilateral conflict resolution and criticized all unilateral attempts to exploit the other parties.[2] Outside official circles, analysts were consistent in the view that the issues of Yugoslavia and Serbia were not in themselves important for Russian foreign policy. To the extent that the issue of Russian policy on Serbia mattered, it was not because of the foreign policy stakes or interests, but rather because of domestic politics and the emergence of a conservative and nationalist opposition to the government which seeks to use the issue to achieve support. "Support for Serbia," said one analyst (41), "is an internal matter." Politicians did pay more attention to the issue, with views in support of Serbia lining up predictably along the nationalist-liberal spectrum. But this was rhetoric, with only a marginal effect on substantive policy.

2. See "Londonskaya konferentsiya po byvshei Yugoslavii," *Diplomaticheskiy vestnik*, no. 17–18 (15–30 September 1992), p. 8; "Rossiya i problema Yugoslavskogo uregulirovaniya," *Diplomaticheskiy vestnik*, no. 9–10 (May 1993), pp. 21–25.

Russian views of German policies on the Yugoslavian conflicts were mixed. On the one hand, none thought Germany sought to expand its power or intervene. On the other hand, Russian officials thought Germany's push for recognition of Slovenia and Croatia contributed to the conflict, raising unpleasant memories of German policies in the Balkans in World War II. One official with generally positive views of Germany's role in Europe (40) said, "We cannot and we may not forget Germany in Yugoslavia in World War II." A political figure (21) said that Germany had made a mistake in this instance, "but we helped with the mistake and so did the U.S. in the process of how we recognized them." More a matter of concern was that European countries not take sides and not intervene competitively in support of favored parties, and instead work for a joint policy of compromise and political settlement.[3] Although criticizing German recognition of Croatia and Slovenia, a Russian politician (31) said, "The answer is not just to support the other side, but to end the problems." As the issue of external military intervention became important, Russian officials made clear that any German involvement in former Yugoslavian territory must be through multilateral channels, and that German combat forces could not be deployed, even under multilateral control.

Official German policy saw no possibility of preserving a single Yugoslavia given the hostile actions of the Serbian government, directly and clandestinely through local armed Serbian groups in Croatia and Bosnia. Germany favored international recognition of the constituent republics as states in the hope that the Serbian government could thereby be pressured to accept international norms and be deterred from what would then be an international, not merely a civil, war.[4]

German policy was preoccupied with geopolitical reality: "Yugoslavia," one official (12) said, "is *very* close." Conflict in Europe was startling for German security officials, who believed war no longer to be a legitimate instrument of security policy. As one (45) put it, "This common view and understanding have been thrown away by the Serbs, which is one of the reasons that the Europeans have been so shocked by their action. It is such a complete break with this common basis."

German policy was also based upon the principle that the rigid distinction between international and "internal" matters could no longer be sustained. Policymakers viewed the question of Croatia and Slovenia even

---

3. Russian interview 26.
4. For a detailed explanation of official German policy, see Libal, *Limits of Persuasion*, esp. chaps. 5–9.

within Yugoslavia as a matter for international security and OSCE principles, such as prohibiting the changing of borders by force. In Europe, one (35) said, "the argument that it is an internal matter is not accepted anymore."

Yugoslavia was also important for German officials as a warning. Said one (20), "We have faced that we will have a number of these situations; the task is to control and cope with emerging crises, get a ceasefire, get the sides talking, find resolution mechanisms. We cannot avoid the Yugoslavias, but we can be managing them." A politician (25) offered a similar view, saying, "We had the fantasy of creating peacekeeping forces after the conflicts rather than before, but we cannot wait to do things after the fighting has begun."

Germany's Yugoslavia policy in 1992 was focused not only on trying to stop the fighting in Bosnia, but on preventing the spillover. These were especially important problems because any potential conflicts in Macedonia or Kosovo could easily involve Greece, a NATO member. Conflict in the Vojvodina region of Serbia in turn had the potential for spillover to Hungary, moving conflict out of the Balkans and closer to central Europe. Worried as we may be about the fighting within the former Yugoslavia, one official (59) said, a greater crisis is possible if the conflict spreads.

German views of Russian intentions and policy in these conflicts recognized that Russia did not have a truly direct stake in the struggle and was not an unqualified supporter of Serbia. The problems in Yugoslavia, one official (40) said, are not due to Russian policies, and the reason for Russia's greater support for Serbia was that it feared for its own status as the successor state to the Soviet Union. The Russian government's preferred outcomes, policies, and solutions often differed from those of Germany, but as another official (45) told me, so do those of the United States, France, and Britain. More important, he said, was the fundamental common interest in stopping the fighting and achieving a workable long-term solution; no one is trying to exploit the conflict for national gain.

Potential conflicts in central and eastern Europe also occupied the attention of German and Russian security officials. Romania and Hungary had competing territorial claims, as did Ukraine and Poland; very substantial Hungarian minorities lived in Romania. In 1992, the Czech Republic and Slovakia agreed peacefully to split apart. A potential German-Czech dispute over the formerly German territory of the Sudetenland and expulsion of ethnic Germans after World War II was settled in 1996 after protracted negotiations. Germany and the Czech Republic signed an agreement in which both countries acknowledged their border and apologized for past harm.

In the former Soviet Union, potential regional conflicts took several forms: non-Russian national groups struggled with historical legacies and claims to territory; the substantial numbers of Russian settlers throughout the Russian and Soviet empires were now minorities in other countries; and Russia attempted to achieve influence over its neighbors through political, economic, and even military pressure. These incompatible demands for autonomy, ethnically based rights, and political power created the potential for military conflict in and near Europe.

The most important potential conflict in the former Soviet Union was that between Russia and Ukraine. Russians tend not to see Ukraine as a distinct ethnicity and culture. They therefore find Ukraine's detachment from Russia unacceptable. Concrete conflicts of interest also were a problem. Some 11 million ethnic Russians live in Ukraine and make up 22 percent of that country's population, concentrated primarily in its eastern regions. However, Ukraine's citizenship laws were progressive, defined in civic, not ethnic, terms. This avoided discrimination that could have been a pretext for Russian intervention.[5]

In addition, the important and geopolitically significant territory of the Crimean peninsula—which included the Black Sea port of Sevastopol and the naval base of the Soviet Black Sea Fleet—had historically been part of Russia, but in 1954 had been ceded to Ukraine. Ukrainian policies toward military personnel of ethnic Russian origin were sensitive to the need to be nondiscriminatory, and allowed officers to remain in Ukrainian service as long as they took an oath of loyalty and became Ukrainian citizens.[6] This policy helped, but did not solve the problem of the Black Sea Fleet, because that asset constituted a major portion of Russia's conventional naval capability and presence. Division of the fleet, ownership of Sevastopol, and Russian recognition of Ukraine's sovereignty and borders were finally settled by treaty in May 1997.[7]

Compounding the political sources of antagonism was the fact that Russia and Ukraine were the two most powerful Soviet successor states,

---

5. Interview with official, Committee on Nationality Questions of the Council of Ministers, Kiev, July 1992. See also Susan Stewart, "Ukraine's Policies toward Its Ethnic Minorities," *RFE/RL Research Report*, vol. 2, no. 36 (10 September 1993): 55–62.

6. Interview with officer, department on personnel, Ministry of Defense, Kiev, July 1992.

7. Further complicating matters is the concentration of ethnic Russians in Crimea and the separatist leaning of the local government there. Andrew Wilson, "Crimea's Political Cauldron," *RFE/RL Research Report*, vol. 2, no. 45 (12 November 1993): 1–8.

meaning that any active conflict between them might bring about substantial war. As one Russian official (11) said early in 1992, "The biggest danger is Russian-Ukrainian conflict: if that starts, then the Croatian-Serbian conflict is a children's war." A German official (12) observed, "Such a conflict would be such a catastrophe that everything we have accomplished in Europe would be lost. . . . The prospect is so terrible and we could do so little." Another German official (24) said of such a scenario, "We would be back to square one." Was the government thinking about this contingency? "Of course we are thinking about it, but you cannot plan it out and say now that we would defend Ukraine against a threat or attack by Russia."

In the Baltic states, matters were about as complicated politically, ethnically, and territorially as in Ukraine, although the imbalance of power between Russia and the Baltic states gave conflicts there a different cast. Ethnic Russians were 30 percent of the population in Estonia, 33 percent in Latvia, and 9 percent in Lithuania. In Estonia and Latvia, a large portion of the ethnic Russians were active or retired Soviet military officers and their families. Lithuania had an inclusive definition of citizenship similar to Ukraine's, but Estonia and Latvia chose highly restrictive definitions and regulations. When protection of the 25 million Russians living in the countries of the former Soviet Union became an important issue in Russian policies, conflicts with Estonia and Latvia were bound to arise. Furthermore, in addition to the problem of Russian military forces stationed in the Baltic states, some territorial disputes between Russia and the Baltic countries remained. Only in February 1997 did Russia and Latvia settle their disagreement on territorial demarcation; as of summer 1998 Russia and Estonia had not done so.

One of the most peculiar remnants of central Europe's complicated ethnic and territorial history was an issue that directly involved Germany and Russia. Kaliningrad is a region (*oblast'*) of Russia which lies east of Poland and northwest of Lithuania, and is therefore isolated from the rest of the Russian Federation. At the same time, the city Kaliningrad is the old German Baltic city of Königsberg, formerly located in East Prussia, territory lost by Germany after World War II. When problems arose in 1992 with proposals to recreate the Volga republic, Kaliningrad was mentioned as a potential ethnic German republic. Furthermore, as an important port, Kaliningrad could support Russian trade, especially with Europe. But the region causes unique problems. It became packed with Russian soldiers withdrawn from formerly Soviet-occupied territories, east and west. Any hint of a special German interest in it raises fears about Germany's general interests in historically German territory. The German government, however, ruled out any territorial claims or special political and economic relations which would cause suspicion, and the Russian government knew little would come of the potential associa-tion.[8]

Political disputes with Ukraine and the Baltics based on territory, eth-nicity, and military forces were potentially serious, but they did not es-calate into armed conflict. Other post-Soviet disagreements of a similar origin did escalate. In Moldova ethnic Russians lived in a section of the country east of the Dniestr River (thus the self-proclaimed name of Pri-dniestrovye, or Transdniestr). Claiming to defend themselves against Moldova's intentions to merge with Romania, local Russians created their own militia which in late 1991 and early 1992 moved to gain control of towns and villages. In March 1992 the Moldovan government mobi-lized its military to suppress the conflict, but its forces were inferior to those of the "militia," which was supplied and supported by the old So-viet 14th Army. In April 1992, President Yeltsin subordinated the 14th Army to Russian command, and soon thereafter the 14th Army directly intervened, shelling Moldovan forces in Bendery and threatening the capital Chisinau. In July 1992, Yeltsin and Moldovan President Mircea Snegur signed a bilateral agreement establishing a peacekeeping force composed of Russian, Moldovan, and Transdniestr forces and establish-ing a negotiation process.[9] A long-term political settlement has not been reached, although Russia has promised to withdraw the Russian re-mains of the 14th Army from Moldova. A Russian promise to live up to this commitment was one of the conditions for its Council of Europe membership in 1995, and the OSCE has been involved in negotiation on a political settlement. As of August 1998, Russian forces have not been withdrawn, and Moldovan-Transdniestr differences have not been re-solved.

Other conflicts in the former Soviet Union lie within post-Soviet states or between non-Russian post-Soviet states. The conflict in Tajikistan began in March 1992 as a civil war among regional groups,[10] and had es-calated to full-scale internal war by that summer. In September 1992 a multilateral peacekeeping CIS force was constituted under the Tashkent Treaty on Collective Security, although in practice it is dominated by

8. German interview 43; Russian interviews 24 and 61.
9. On the Moldovan conflict and Russian intervention, see Stuart J. Kaufmann, "Spiral-ing to Ethnic War: Elites, Masses, and Moscow in Moldova's Civil War," *International Secu-rity* 21 (Fall 1996): 108–138.
10. On the regional—rather than religious or ethnic—basis of identity and political cleavages throughout Central Asia, see Pauline Jones Luong, "Ethno-Politics and Institu-tional Design: Explaining the Establishment of Electoral Systems in Post-Soviet Central Asia" (Ph.D. diss., Harvard University, 1997).

Russian military forces. The conflict has not been solved, though large-scale fighting has ended.

In Georgia two intrastate disputes escalated to war. A separatist movement in South Ossetia (seeking to join North Ossetia in the Russian Federation) was stabilized in July 1992 with a trilateral agreement and deployment of Russian, Georgian, and South Ossetian peacekeeping troops. More serious was the separatist war in Abkhazia. After the region declared its independence in August 1992, Georgian military forces entered the regional capital, Sukhumi. In the ensuing conflict, small Abkhazian forces defeated and drove out the numerically superior Georgian forces. The Abkhazian forces benefited not only from Russian supplies and training, but from direct Russian military planning and support, especially from combat aircraft and helicopters.[11] Russia used Georgia's vulnerability to force Georgian concessions, including joining the CIS and permitting Russian military bases. In May 1994 the parties signed a ceasefire agreement that provided for a CIS peacekeeping force (which in practice has been entirely Russian) monitored by UN observers.

The conflict in Nagorno-Karabakh was rooted in separatism, but also had an interstate dimension. The population of this autonomous region of Azerbaijan is Armenian. Armed conflict between the local population—aided by Armenia—and the Azeri government began in 1988. In February 1992 remaining Russian forces were withdrawn, and various Russian government proposals advanced for UN and CIS peace operations. In December 1994 the parties agreed upon an OSCE peacekeeping force, but this has never been implemented. Instead, actual OSCE involvement has been limited to observer missions and mediation under the active nine-member "Minsk group," which was convened under a German initiative in 1992. In mid-1998 a settlement remains impossible because the territory demands independence and Azerbaijan refuses to consider that outcome.

German officials paid attention to these conflicts, but they were not a high priority. One official (43), asked whether the government was concerned about war in Nagorno-Karabakh or Moldova, said of course there was concern, but primarily about the problem of the great powers getting involved on competing sides. He explained that no one believed

---

11. Catherine Dale, "The Case of Abkhazia (Georgia)," in *Peacekeeping and the Role of Russia in Eurasia*, ed. Lena Jonson and Clive Archer (Boulder, Colo.: Westview, 1996), pp. 121–137; Dmitri Trofimov, "The Conflict in Abkhazia: Roots and Main Driving Forces," in *Crisis Management in the CIS: Whither Russia?*, ed. Hans-Georg Ehrhart, Anna Kreikemeyer, and Andrei Zagorski (Baden-Baden: Nomos, 1995), pp. 75–90.

these conflicts to be rooted in unbridled Russian aggression, and thus they were risks to be managed rather than threats to be countered. Another German official (45) said, "We do not see any potential aggressors in Europe. Yes, we still face Nagorno-Karabakh, Moldova, Kosovo, Macedonia. But these are not traditional forms of political-military confrontation." German politicians also were not concerned about threats, but rather about risks. One (16) said that the main worry is instability in the CIS and "the incapacity of the existing structures in those countries to handle tensions and change and social interests, which means a chance of them exploding." Said another politician (25): "The leverage of the west is limited in the CIS, and is even less than it is in the former Yugoslavia. The only influence of the west is to make sure this devolution occurs in a peaceful way, with respect for borders, and respect for minority rights. But to stop the process is senseless: you cannot stop it." German politicians were more directly concerned about proper German involvement. We cannot take sides in disputes, said one analyst (52), and must refer to multilateral forums for settlement.

The Yeltsin government's public attention to partnership with the west coexisted with a growing focus on conflicts and instability in the former Soviet Union as Russia's primary security problem, and this entirely new geopolitical situation was a source of national interests different from the west's. One otherwise reformist official (40) argued that the leaders of these now independent countries were going to have to limit their nationalism if they expected to have good relations with Russia because of the potential for local and ethnic conflicts. A political adviser (19) referred critically to the post-Soviet states' "euphoria of sovereignization" and said that security must be based on military forces, not mere declarations of independence. Relations with former Soviet republics became a point of dispute between the Yeltsin leadership and the Supreme Soviet very early.

Even in the foreign ministry, views on the former Soviet Union were aptly summarized by an official (38) who said, "It is difficult for Russia to recognize these republics as sovereign." I found no evidence of any intention by the Russian government simply to reacquire these territories: the reality was more complex. Because of the presence of Russian minorities, the historical scope of the Russian empire, the practical integration (however artificial) of the Soviet republics, and the active problem of militarized conflicts, Russia was inevitably going to be involved in the affairs of these countries.

Russian views of CIS conflicts also had a strategic military element, in that the rupturing of a unified and comprehensive defense system had increased the difficulty of controlling military conflict in the region. A

Russian defense official (30) said that Russian involvement in Moldova and Georgia had been more direct than in Tajikistan because Moldova and Georgia were not at that time members of the CIS, so the Tashkent Treaty on Collective Security, which provided for multilateral peace-keeping, could not be operative. Not an option in his repertoire, however, was Russian indifference to the course of military conflict in these regions because of their relation to Russian territory and security.

Many Russian officials and politicians believed that German participation in any kind of policy in CIS conflicts, ranging from purely political conflict prevention to more directly military peacekeeping would be acceptable as long as it were to be effected through international organizations such as the UN or OSCE. One official (40) gave his positive assessment of German involvement, but added that this was not an actual issue because the real constraint on German participation was the domestic legal and political limit on German involvement outside the NATO area. As another official (6) put it, Russia is ready for European interest in solving problems in the former Soviet Union, because this is in our interests as well. But there is a difference, he said, between Germany's working through multilateral means and its getting involved in order to develop a special role and political influence in these countries. Russian sensitivities on this varied, being greatest about German influence at Russian expense in countries such as Ukraine, and most tolerant of German involvement in political disputes and issues in Estonia, Latvia, and Lithuania.[12]

In summary, German and Russian officials for the most part believed these conflicts and crises to be central security problems, and consistently saw them in terms of risks and instability, not threats and aggression. None of the conflicts escalated to region-wide war or drew the major powers in on competing sides—as so often has been the case in European history with disastrous consequences. In several cases multilateral cooperation did contribute to containing and even preventing conflict (as in Macedonia and Ossetia), and in others it may be contributing to conflict resolution (as in Bosnia). Nonetheless, on balance multilateral security cooperation failed in its most stringent tests: war in the former Yugoslavia, where effective action came late if at all, and conflicts in the former Soviet Union, where Russia acted largely alone and pursued its interests without much reference to the policies of countries such as Germany.

12. Russian interviews 21, 22, and 61.

REFUGEES AND MIGRATION

Regional conflicts also have implications for national and international security because they can spark refugee and migration problems.[13] Some 25 million Russians lived outside the territory of Russia in the former Soviet Union. By 1993, Russia had 2 million registered displaced persons and probably some 1–2 million unregistered migrants. Nor has the problem disappeared: in 1996 Russia took in another 375,000 migrants from other former Soviet states.[14]

Russia sought to stem the tide through direct pressure on its neighbors, intervention in post-Soviet conflicts, and appeals to the international community. The problem has diverse causes. In countries such as Ukraine, Estonia, and Latvia, ethnic Russians wished to stay, even if that meant adopting local citizenship or remaining foreign residents. In these cases, problems of migration were caused by discrimination, and the solution was for post-Soviet states to adopt nondiscriminatory citizenship, employment, and social welfare laws. But in other cases, primarily in Central Asia and the Caucasus, the causes were armed conflicts. Here the solution was prevention and resolution of the internal and regional conflicts. The Russian government wanted to prevent a mass influx of Russians claiming citizenship and protection at a time of economic hardship, and as a consequence it defined this problem as a core security issue.[15]

In its unusually high vulnerability to migration and refugees, Germany had much in common with Russia. Germany's geographical location and liberal asylum laws made it a special magnet for refugees, particularly from Romania and the former Yugoslavia, but also from conflicts in the former Soviet Union. In 1992 alone, 500,000 people from

---

13. See Myron Weiner, "Bad Neighbors, Bad Neighborhoods: An Inquiry into the Causes of Refugee Flows," *International Security* 21 (Summer 1996): 5–42; Alan Dowty and Gil Loescher, "Refugee Flows as Grounds for International Action," *International Security* 21 (Summer 1996): 43–71; Barry R. Posen, "Military Responses to Refugee Disasters," *International Security* 21 (Summer 1996): 72–111.

14. Sheila Marnie and Wendy Slater, "Russia's Refugees," *RFE/RL Research Report*, vol. 2, no. 37 (17 September 1993): 46–53; David Filipov, "Russia Population Declining; Aging, Ailing Society Seen," *Boston Globe*, 28 February 1997, pp. A1, A10.

15. "Rasporyazheniye prezidenta Rossiyskoi Federatsii o voprosakh zashchity prav i interesov rossiyskikh grazhdan za predelami Rossiyskoi Federatsii," *Diplomaticheskiy vestnik*, no. 1–2 (January 1993), p. 8; "Iz brifinga zamestitelya ministra innostrannykh del RF V.I. Churkina, 24 avgusta," *Diplomaticheskiy vestnik*, no 17–18 (September 1993), pp. 32–35. Russian interviews 5, 12, and 38. On Russian military doctrine at the time, see "Osnovnyye polozheniya voyennoy doktriny rossiiskoy federatsii," internal Russian government document, 1993, 34 pp.

Yugoslavia entered Germany and were granted status as political refugees.[16] This, along with an upsurge in violence against foreigners in Germany, led to a change in Germany's laws in July to restrict the terms under which asylum would be granted. Much of the pressure for the reform came from the *Land* governments, which bore the brunt of providing for refugees.[17] German attempts to revise asylum laws on a European basis were not successful.[18] Furthermore, the experience with Balkan refugees raised the priority of post-Soviet disputes in German security policy. German officials feared that conflicts, discrimination against ethnic minorities, and economic deprivation in the former Soviet Union would be sources of further pressures on German borders.

In addition to asylum seekers from formerly communist countries, Germany faced immigration pressures from Russian citizens of ethnic German heritage. In 1992, some 2 million people of German descent lived in the former Soviet Union. By 1996, 1.7 million ethnic Germans had moved to Germany, most coming from the former Soviet Union.[19] The presence of so many ethnic Germans in formerly Soviet territories was a historical artifact: German immigration had been encouraged by Catherine the Great. In 1924 an autonomous Volga republic had been created where ethnic Germans were concentrated, but in 1941 Stalin had deemed these citizens a threat to the Soviet Union, dissolved the republic, and deported them to Siberia and Central Asia. With political liberalization in the late Soviet years, many *Aussiedler* (resettlers) began to emigrate, utilizing the "right of return." German law guaranteed citizenship to any ethnic German who returned to the Federal Republic.

After the breakup of the Soviet Union and facing an uncertain and possibly threatening political and economic future, these ex-Soviet citi-

---

16. "Asylbewerberzahlen für Juli 1992," *Presse- und Informationsamt Bulletin*, 7 August 1992 (no. 88), p. 843; "Bonn Favors Tighter Rules on Asylum for Refugees," *International Herald Tribune*, 14 October 1992, p. 1. Romania was the origin of the second largest group of asylum seekers in Germany in 1992, numbering more than 60,000. "Abkommen mit Rumänien erleichtert Abschiebung," *Frankfurter Allgemeine Zeitung*, 18 September 1992, p. 1. When the ceasefire in Bosnia took effect, the pressure of asylum seekers from the former Yugoslavia decreased. "'Seasonal' Rise in Asylum Applications, Ministry Reports," *The Week in Germany*, 14 February 1997, p. 2.

17. Calls for a more effective German and European foreign policy to deal with the conflict at its source became a topic of heated Bundestag debate. See for example "Deutscher Bundestag—12. Wahlperiode—113. Sitzung, Bonn, Donnerstag, den 15. Oktober 1992," pp. 9571–9580.

18. "Mehrheit für Änderung des Asylrechts," *Frankfurter Allgemeine Zeitung*, 12 September 1992, p. 4; "Bonn Seeks Help on Refugees," *International Herald Tribune*, 14 September 1992, p. 1. Foreign Minister Klaus Kinkel was quoted in the latter article as telling the closed meeting "Our political stability is in danger," and "we cannot do everything alone."

19. "Bonn to Aid Integration of Resettlers," *The Week in Germany*, 14 February 1997, p. 2.

zens had two options. The first was simple emigration to Germany; the second a more limited "return" to the Volga area, aiming to establish an autonomous republic or region and preserve German language and culture. An autonomous republic was more appealing than emigration to many ethnic Germans who had extensive family contacts in the former Soviet Union. On a visit to Germany in November 1991, Yeltsin promised to restore the autonomous German republic in the Volga region. The German government, relieved to reduce the chances of a mass emigration, offered economic support for the policy—some DM 200 million.[20]

In early 1992, however, Yeltsin reneged on this offer because of protests by local residents who feared they would be displaced or discriminated against. In March he issued orders for the creation of German "areas" rather than the legally distinct status of an autonomous republic.[21] This step ameliorated Yeltsin's domestic problems, but caused consternation in Germany, where it undermined the government's hopes of limiting the influx of resettlers. In April Yeltsin promised a "step-by-step" program to create a homeland for Russian Germans, but German officials privately admitted that no autonomous republic would be created and resigned themselves to the fact that the resettlers would come. Said one official, the Russians "have to try because of all the money Chancellor Kohl is dangling in front of them," which means they will gather together a few thousand Germans and create a "Potemkin Volga-German village," but nothing will really be accomplished.[22] Another official noted that the German government accepted that there would be no republic but could not publicly say it was not pursuing the issue any longer, "because they [German Russians] would be here tomorrow."[23]

20. F. Stephen Larrabee, "Moscow and the German Questions," in *The Germans and Their Neighbors*, ed. Dirk Verheyen and Christian Soe (Boulder, Colo.: Westview, 1993), pp. 201–229, esp. p. 223; Wolfgang Schlör, "German Security Policy," *Adelphi Paper* no. 277 (London: International Institute for Security Studies, 1993), pp. 51–52.

21. Russian interview 24. For the creation of German areas, see "O neotlozhnykh merakh po reabilitatsii rossiyskikh nemtsev," Presidential decree, 2 March 1992.

22. German interview 43. He saw little chance the tide could be stemmed quickly enough to sustain a viable political, economic, and cultural community in Russia, "so in four years, there will be no more problem." The rate of influx was 200,000 per year by 1993, although by 1996 the figure for the total of registered resettlers from the east was closer to 170,000. "Numbers of New Asylum-Seekers and Ethnic German Resettlers Continue to Drop," *The Week in Germany*, 19 July 1996, p. 4.

23. German interview 31 (my insert). In addition, the German government was being pressured not to prevent resettlement. I discussed this with representatives of the Landsmannschaft der Deutschen aus Rußland e. V., which was involved in government lobbying and public information through their publication "Volk auf dem Weg." They spoke little German, so we spoke in Russian.

What we are looking for now, he said, is a process of slowing down the rate of emigration, making their return to Germany more orderly, but knowing German policy will not prevent eventual return.

INSTITUTIONS AND SECURITY COOPERATION

The record of multilateral security cooperation in these cases is very complex. The wars in Yugoslavia were neither prevented nor managed well despite multilateral involvement including the UN, the EU, the OSCE, and NATO. In important cases in the former Soviet Union, including Tajikistan, Georgia, Nagorno-Karabakh, and Moldova, virtually unrestricted warfare raged for some time. Furthermore, not only did political conflicts become militarized in these instances, but Russia often pursued its national interests unilaterally and initially with little deference to the principles, norms, and rules of international institutions.

In addition, as feared by officials in both countries, conflicts in the former Yugoslavia and the former Soviet Union generated thousands of refugees, which Germany and Russia coped with primarily though unilateral or bilateral means. More effective than multilateral cooperation was the change in Germany's asylum laws and bilateral negotiations.[24] Russia was also largely ineffective in stemming the flow of ethnic Russians away from conflicts and harsh living conditions in much of the former Soviet Union. The problem of the mass emigration of post-Soviet citizens of German ethnic background was not solved by active multilateral cooperation: Germany simply accepted them.

The record on conflict prevention and resolution does show some positive outcomes, however. Early and active UN and OSCE involvement managed the real risk of spillover to Macedonia. In other cases, including Russian disputes with the Baltic states and Ukraine, serious political tensions over political, ethnic, and even military issues did not result in armed conflict. Little migration stemmed from Estonia, Latvia, Lithuania, and Ukraine, because all four states have adopted nondiscriminatory citizenship and residency laws. In Ukraine and Lithuania, these laws were adopted readily and early; in Estonia and Latvia the outcome was delayed. Both the latter states came under considerable pressure not only from Russia, but from European states, the OSCE, the EU, and the

---

24. "Schutz für die deutsche Minderheit," *Süddeutsche Zeitung*, 22 April 1992, p. 2; "Projekte für die Rumäniendeutschen," *Frankfurter Allgemeine Zeitung*, 16 May 1992, p. 4; "Abkommen mit Rumänien erleichtert Abschiebung," *Frankfurter Allgemeine Zeitung*, 18 September 1992, p. 1.

UN. As late as April 1997, the OSCE High Commissioner on National Minorities criticized Latvia's naturalization procedures as "too complicated" while approving Estonia's procedures.[25]

Is this variation in security cooperation explained by national interests, with conflict where interests were opposed precluding jointly acceptable cooperative outcomes? Sometimes yes: both Armenia and Azerbaijan sought the territory of Nagorno-Karabakh, leaving no room for compromise. But in nearly all the cases, interests were not so purely conflictual that deals could not be struck. In most disputes, interests were highly competitive, bargaining was hard-fought, and distributional issues were important. We cannot say, however, that all the parties *wanted* conflict above settlement. In many instances, security cooperation was possible and institutions should have supported cooperative security strategies.

Were these failures due to the unilateral exercise of German and Russian power and interests? Failure to cooperate often had causes predicted by realism. Failure of multilateral cooperation in conflicts in the former Soviet Union was largely due to Russia's assertion of its power, interests, and prerogatives, compounded by the fact that western countries (including Germany) demonstrated no great interest in becoming involved. Insofar as conflicts in the former Soviet Union were managed by "spheres of influence" and balance of power, these cases fit realist expectations. German officials and politicians evinced no interest in intervening over Russian objections. One (46) said it was fortunate that the former Soviet republics had not asked for NATO's help in conflict resolution because it would not have been forthcoming. Russian officials knew this. A politician (33) said he had no objections to OSCE and UN involvement in these conflicts, but did not think it would happen, since "Europe has its own questions, and needs to deal also with those problems, not ours." Another (5) did not wish to speculate about Russian preferences on international involvement because it was not a "practical question," and asked "Do you want to become involved?" An official (12) said that OSCE mediation was welcome and might be effective, but he did not see prospects for intervention because it was "expensive, uncertain, and dangerous." Another said, "Yes, UN troops could be even in Moldova," but saw no likelihood that such a mission would be created.[26]

---

25. *RFE/RL Newsline* (electronic version), vol. 1, no. 6, Part II (8 April 1997); *RFE/RL Newsline* (electronic version), vol. 1, no. 9, Part II (11 April 1997).

26. Russian interview 37. Another foreign ministry official (10) thought UN peacekeeping possible in Nagorno-Karabakh, but not in Moldova because of the presence of the 14th Army, which was under Russian command.

But realism does not so easily explain the variation in cooperation that did occur. While the major powers (Russia, the United States, Germany, Britain, and France) failed to prevent or solve conflicts, they did succeed in avoiding competitive intervention and conflict escalation. German and Russian officials—aware that competitive intervention in smaller conflicts had often been the source of war among the great powers throughout European history—feared competitive intervention and escalation of crises and instability in Europe as much as the conflicts themselves. A Russian official (37) said despite real conflicting views, "We have at the same time managed to avoid the mistake of intervening unilaterally for individual advantage outside the UN and other consultation mechanisms." Said one German official (56) of conflicts in Yugoslavia and in the former Soviet Union: "I think that the most remarkable thing is that there is not Great Power competition on one side or another, although we do not notice it because it is now so normal. This is not a chess game: that thinking is something from the nineteenth century. We simply cannot afford those games now."

Post–cold war uncertainty and instability simply did not result in conflict among the great powers or in attempts to manage conflicts through balancing, partly because of historical memory, but also because institutions were available. Although those institutions were not always effective, German and Russian officials sought to use them precisely because the nature of risks and uncertainty in security relations made the employment of force or unilateral measures ineffective. When one German official (16) listed as Germany's security problems regional conflicts, instability, refugees, and proliferation, I observed that these did not sound like traditional threats to security. He continued:

> Exactly—that is how we come to international institutions. Instability does not stay in the east where it arises, but comes to western Europe as well, with the refugees of Yugoslavia the visible evidence of the danger of instability. The central security problem of Europe is how to solve the problem of conflicts, and this requires institutions.

Despite the failings of multilateral cooperation through institutions, German officials never seriously considered falling back upon unilateral or balancing strategies, such as arming Croatia. Of course there are problems in adapting existing mechanisms to these new security situations, said one German official (35), but the greater danger is that with conflicts and failures, countries and their governments get the impression that multilateral cooperation does not work, "and then your mind is set toward national solutions."

Institutions mattered because they could support the option of consultation rather than competitive balancing. Further, while Russia's policies in the "near abroad" were hardly a model of multilateral cooperation, both power and institutions played a role in strategies. In the case of Russian minorities, Russia certainly used its power to pressure Estonia and Latvia. But at the same time, Russian strategies sought to get institutions such as the OSCE, the Council of Europe, and the Baltic Sea Council involved in disputes.[27] A Russian official (22) explained the government's strategy to "contribute to democratic institutions in the former Soviet republics" by involving multilateral institutions in support of democratic and human rights. He showed me the government's talking points for an upcoming OSCE meeting, which had near the top of the agenda efforts to get members to agree to send missions to investigate the problem of Baltic citizenship. At the same time, of course, Russia was pressuring the Baltics through a slow pace of troop withdrawals and escalating political rhetoric about Russian national interests. Nevertheless, Russia employed these political security institutions to push Estonia and Latvia to abide by norms and principles on citizenship and minority rights, and as a strategy to involve other countries for leverage in an area where the Russian government believed its demands were legitimate and supported by institutional norms. The strategy has worked in keeping the OSCE involved in pressing Latvia and Estonia to change their discriminatory citizenship laws.

Similarly, institutions have not been irrelevant to Russian intervention and peace operations in the former Soviet Union. Russia was not constrained by institutions in its interventions in Moldova and Georgia, but the Russian government sought at different times OSCE, UN, and CIS involvement in these conflicts. In Tajikistan, South Ossetia, and Abkhazia, UN and OSCE missions oversee Russian or CIS peace operations. In each of these cases, the Russian government sought to use the legitimacy (and sometimes the instruments) of international institutions to support its security interests. In Tajikistan, the CIS force operates under the collective security provisions of the Tashkent Treaty which permits intervention against aggression. Multilateral, though Russian-led, peace

---

27. See official Russian statements and proposals in "Zasedaniye SMID SBSE v Prag," *Diplomaticheskiy vestnik*, no. 4–5 (29 February–15 March 1992), pp. 39–47; "Khelsinki i vstrecha glav gosudarstv i pravitelstov gosudarstv-uchastnikov SBSE, 9–10 iuliya," *Diplomaticheskiy vestnik*, no. 4–5 (29 February–15 March 1992), pp. 14–24; "Zasedaniye SMID SBSE v Stokgolme 14–15 dekabrya memorandum RF o polozhenii russkoyazychnogo naseleniya v Latvii i Estonii," *Diplomaticheskiy vestnik*, no. 1–2 (January 1993), pp. 34–35.

operations in Moldova and Georgia eventually conformed to UN norms.[28]

Why were Russian strategies affected at all by institutions, even if irregularly and weakly? Russia sought the legitimacy and resources of international conflict prevention and management institutions while trying not to be constrained by them. The value of the OSCE to Russian officials was that it was unformed and thus formable: said one official (6), "The CSCE is not really there yet so we can make of it what we will." Russian officials also preferred the OSCE because it is designed for "political" rather than "military" security, as both public official statements and private interviews consistently revealed.[29] The OSCE's preexisting system of political consultation was a considerable asset that Russian officials thought could be called upon. As one (24) said, if aggression is not the main security problem in Europe, European states need "transparency of intentions," and the OSCE is best suited to provide that. On this point, the government and its opponents agreed. The Yeltsin government embraced the preference for political and mutual security developed by Gorbachev's "new thinking," while for conservatives, preference for "political" security was an argument against the extension of NATO. One senior foreign ministry official (11) summed up the evolving compromise view:

> Security begins with an understanding of military relations and requirements, and these must be the basis of Russia's security net. But these are just the basis: the real task of ensuring security now is in the process of negotiation. Although the CSCE was irrelevant to this in the past, as it dealt only with issues of human rights, now it can play such a role as a negotiation forum.

Consequently, from 1991 the Russian government supported measures such as the "consensus-minus-one" formulation and the creation of an OSCE security council and a court of arbitration as ways to increase the effectiveness of the OSCE.[30]

The basic accomplishment of the OSCE in early 1992 from the Russian government's point of view was simply incorporating Russia into a Eu-

---

28. See Celeste A. Wallander, "Conflict Resolution and Peace Operations in the Former Soviet Union: Is There a Role for Security Institutions?" in *The International Dimension of Post-Communist Transitions in Russia and the New States of Eurasia*, ed. Karen Dawisha (Armonk, N.Y.: M. E. Sharpe, 1997).

29. For a typical official statement, see "Vystupleniye A. V. Kozyreva, 30 noyabrya," *Diplomaticheskiy vestnik*, no. 23–24 (December 1993), pp. 41–42.

30. Russian interviews 6, 24, and 26.

ropean security institution, especially as an alternative to NATO. "In this transitional time, what is important is to use existing institutions such as the CSCE for integration and stability," said one official (6). As with the CFE, one major OSCE function was to create an incentive for the other former Soviet republics to observe international norms. Another official (38) said that the republics view Russia with great suspicion and consider its policy to be imperialist. The OSCE is a way to reassure them that their sovereignty and independence are not threatened in dealing with Russia, he argued.

Support for cooperative strategies was clear; faith in their effectiveness varied considerably. To my observation that the OSCE had proved itself quite ineffective in dealing with the conflict in the former Yugoslavia, one official (26) said that was true, but so had all other institutions: "No one has the instruments. So the lesson is that we need to strengthen the CSCE, especially to permit fast decisions." But many others were skeptical. One (36) told me that he considered all these multilateral forums basically irrelevant, and more important for Russian security was bilateral cooperation, especially with Germany. A politician (31) said that he thought the question of which institutions to use did not really matter since "they are all limited because they are from the bipolar era. . . . We should use whatever works. But there is not an existing institution that can deal with these security problems."

Variation in Security Problems and Institutional Forms

Concern about effectiveness suggests that variation in institutional form and function as well as national interests and the balance of power affected German and Russian strategies. The pessimistic realist expectation is that power and interest alone determine choice, but that cannot account for variation in Russian strategies in the CIS or for absence of balancing in Yugoslavia. The optimistic realist expectation is that where the security dilemma is benign, cooperation will be possible. But that does not explain variation either. In *all* these conflicts the problem was a serious security dilemma. The institutional expectation is that variation in the underlying security problems and variation in institutional functions and design mattered.

Russian officials did see a mismatch between problems and instruments. Although Russia sought UN and OSCE legitimacy for CIS or Russian-led operations early on, it did so on terms that conflicted with the standard rules and norms of consent, impartiality, and use of force only in self-defense.[31] Russian officials complained that UN peacekeeping norms prevented effective conflict management. One official (37) said:

> The UN has been effective for many peacekeeping operations, but conflicts in the near abroad may not fit with standard UN practices. These are conflicts on our borders, and it is difficult to explain that we have to wait for agreement from sides which are actively fighting in Tajikistan, Georgia, or Moldova.

A political adviser (5) said of the UN's limits, "The system is not effective once the conflict is under way because it is based upon the sides wanting to abide by a negotiated agreement, which is not always the case." When I asked about the OSCE, he said, "Maybe the system is just too young: the hostile countries are all members of the CSCE." A foreign ministry official (25) said that the problem with UN peacekeeping in the former Soviet Union was not the "principles of peacekeeping," which Russian accepts, but the practical obstacles of expense, consent, and how to form willing and capable multilateral forces. When I asked about UN peacekeeping in former Soviet conflicts, a foreign ministry official (26) in February 1992 saw getting consent from the parties involved as an obstacle.

By late 1992 Russian officials had concluded that any chance for effective cessation of hostilities required military operations beyond self-defense, without the establishment of a ceasefire or granting of consent. Impartiality was abandoned. In October 1992, a CIS "peacekeeping force" was established for Tajikistan, but the forces deployed were primarily Russian and created under the CIS collective security provisions for protecting a member from attack. Similarly, in Moldova the 14th Army acted without any pretense of conformity to multilateral rules of peacekeeping and conflict resolution. Even worse, in Abkhazia Russian military intervention was not even aimed at ceasing hostilities; it exacerbated the conflict and destabilized Georgia for short-term Russian interest.

So it was the combination of Russian military capabilities, Russian preferences, western restraint, and institutional inadequacy which produced increasing reliance on unilateral or CIS-cloaked strategies. I did not find Russian officials eagerly anticipating the gains to be made from these conflicts: I found them largely at a loss as to how to manage them. This was even clearer in Russian conflict management strategies in Yu-

---

31. On these rules and norms, see William J. Durch, ed., *The Evolution of U.N. Peacekeeping* (New York: St. Martin's Press, 1993).

goslavia. Although Russia had imposed sanctions on Serbia, many Russian officials remained uncomfortable characterizing Serbia as the aggressor. One (12) said that for conflict resolution, "a more open process is necessary, with consent and participation of all sides." Another (37) said that the problem of UN involvement in Yugoslavia is that sanctions are not truly effective, helpful, or fair. "It is not an easy case," he said, "where only Belgrade is involved. It is not like the Gulf War."

The failure of multilateral cooperation in conflict management and prevention in Germany's case was even more clearly due to uncertainty about the need for consent or coercion, and to the mismatch of needed resources and institutional rules and capacities. German officials focused on the distinction between conflict situations solvable with consent and transparency—"risks"—versus those requiring some element of coercion—"threats." The inadequacy of existing institutional capacities and constraints on direct western intervention for conflict management in the former Soviet Union therefore led to a German strategy fundamentally similar to Russia's: support for Russian military operations because they were effective and forthcoming, but in the context of UN and OSCE authority and oversight in order to provide legitimacy and transparency and to constrain Russian options. One foreign office official (59) said, "It is better to have them there maintaining ceasefires than just pulling out." Nevertheless, there was a possible contradiction between Russian/CIS conflict management and OSCE principles. Yes, he conceded, "but the idea and what is happening is to bring together CIS peacekeeping and CSCE peacekeeping. The Russians have more military forces than they know what to do with, and it is cheaper to rely upon their forces than to send them in from western Europe."

Would the German government support CIS peacekeeping under OSCE authority—"subcontracting" peacekeeping to the CIS as it were—I asked another official (24)?

> That is the best we can hope. What we really have to fear is a CIS or Russian force that says, to hell with the CSCE, and intervenes on its own. We should use the CSCE instrument and restrain any such action, but we really have very little influence in stopping the Russians if they decide to do something. Through the CSCE, we can at best get some say in how they do this—that it be in accord with CSCE principles.

When I expressed some doubt that Russia would allow institutions such as the OSCE to become involved in CIS conflicts, a politician (25) maintained that there was such a role "in terms of incentives and disincentives. The more Russia is interested in dealing with the west, the more it will be careful."

[155]

The early failure to manage conflict through peacekeeping in the CIS resulted in modification of strategies and institutions. During additional interviews in 1994, Russian officials were generally positive about the degree and form of OSCE and UN monitoring of conflict situations in the former Soviet Union. "Since we ourselves seek to resolve these disputes," said one official (61), "OSCE involvement lessens distrust." UN and OSCE oversight was a practical response, said a German official (70) in 1996, developed under the need to cope with dangerous situations, and its advantage is transparency. The OSCE mission reports were far more detailed than embassy reports and are an independent and multilateral source of transparency and information; "If everyone has the same information, it is much easier to come to consensus."

Because of their role in assurance and transparency, strategies for conflict *prevention* depended on the availability of institutions, and both German and Russian official emphasized reliance upon the OSCE here. Macedonia was an important success, and one that both German and Russian officials pointed to as an example of cooperative conflict prevention made possible by international institutions. One Russian official (23) listed several OSCE procedures and capacities that were particularly well suited to transparency and to creating a system of consultation as part of normal interaction among the members. "These may not help once a conflict has already broken out and countries or factions are fighting," he conceded, "but they are part of a system of transparency of intentions which deals with problems before they have reached that level and avoids the more difficult problems of military intervention, peacekeeping, and conflict management." Similarly, when asked about the poor OSCE record in the Yugoslavian conflicts, a German official (59) answered that he did not agree with the premise of the question, because of OSCE missions in Vojvodina, Kosovo, Skopje, and Sanjak, where conflict had threatened but did not break out.

> We do not have the resources to stop the fighting in Bosnia, but the CSCE does have the resources for preventive diplomacy. The task of these observers is to keep attention high, facilitate communication, and maintain a high profile. These are called "spillover missions"—preventing spillover of conflict. So, the CSCE is as unsuccessful in Bosnia as the other international organizations in the main conflict, but it has a chance in the others.

Another German official (70) pointed out that the OSCE long-term missions focus on things like how to draft laws, set up administrative procedures, and cope with the daily issues "which may not get much press attention, but lie at the root of security conflicts in Europe." It can be efficient to send observers before conflict starts, another German official

(59) said, and the OSCE has always had the legitimacy to be involved in internal affairs. "We accept OSCE involvement," said a Russian official (61), "because we are OSCE members."

So both German and Russian officials believed that the underlying security problems causing regional, ethnic, and local conflicts, along with the related problems of refugees and migration which created problems for Germany and Russia, were those of risk and instability. Officials could not, however, completely rule out aggression or exploitative intentions. Was Yugoslavia the result of mistrust, or Serbian aggression? In Nagorno-Karabakh, was there a political solution short of annexation that Armenia would accept? In Moldova and Abkhazia, would peacekeeping enable a political settlement, or serve as cover for Russian military expansion?

Thus, another obstacle German and Russian officials faced in coping with these conflicts was that no one was absolutely certain what the underlying security problem was, and therefore what kinds of security strategies should be adopted to cope with it. Clear aggression would demand a response of collective security or at least sanctioning of the aggressor, as in the Gulf War of 1990–91. The only institution capable of sanctioning one of its members in such a manner was the UN, primarily through Security Council resolutions and under the authorization of Chapter VII. Alternatively, providing for security against aggression is the main purpose of alliances, which are institutions for collective defense.

But conflict resolution cannot be achieved by taking sides against an aggressor, because in such cases there is no aggressor. Conflicts arising from bargaining disputes, mistrust, security dilemmas, and fear of the future—like most ethnic conflicts[32]—require political intervention to help the disputants come to a mutually acceptable settlement. Such intervention may have military aspects in the form of peacekeeping forces involved with the consent of the disputants, but this does not entail intervening *against* any of them.

Conflict prevention, which more ambitiously aims to avoid the militarization of such political differences in the first place, requires established patterns of consultation and transparency. Rather than institutional mechanisms for sanctioning and defense, and in contrast to those for dispute settlement, assurance is a long-term, constant task that requires regular interactions at relatively low levels and at low costs. It

---

32. David A. Lake and Donald Rothchild, "Containing Fear: The Origins and Management of Ethnic Conflict," *International Security* 21 (Fall 1996): 41–75.

makes sense that institutional mechanisms for transparency will be intensive, yet not terribly constraining. The OSCE is "weak" to encourage active and comprehensive participation; it rules out any sanctioning power or the kind of substantial institutional infrastructure provided by the UN Secretariat.

Therefore, the differences between these different kinds of cooperation problems and the need for the right instruments were at the heart of the responses of German and Russian officials and politicians. The problem was that two kinds of institutions were the most highly developed: military institutions for collective defense such as NATO and political institutions for transparency such as the OSCE. The latter did not have the resources and rules needed for peacekeeping, and the former could not play a peacekeeping role in conflicts in the former Soviet Union because Russia would not allow a military alliance of which it was not a member to do so. Concern for power and who wields it is crucial to the explanation, but the explanation holds only because institutional form—including membership and function—matter.

Although the controversy over NATO enlargement erupted into full public view after 1994, these difficulties were clear during my interviews in 1992. In the immediate aftermath of the cold war Russian officials saw NATO either as no threat to Russian interests or as helpful in a transitional period. Both officials and politicians in 1992 and 1993 were relatively confident that NATO member states did not have aggressive intentions toward Russia, and therefore concrete NATO capacity was not seen as a salient threat. A Russian military official (45) said that NATO as it existed did not concern him and he viewed in positive terms NATO's role in keeping the United States involved in European security and in managing the German question. NATO contributes to stability, he said, because "a balance of forces makes balanced outcomes." Others saw value in NATO as a "stabilizing factor," to keep the United States involved in European security for the medium term, and as a residual constraint on German military power and political intentions.[33] One official (12) pointed out that the new NATO concept focused on new types of dangers and risks, rather than threats, in and out of Europe. Our notion, he said, is the same, or at least similar. Another (40) said that there are no ideological or political bases for problems with NATO, and it contributes to stability in Europe. A foreign ministry official (46) in explaining the distinction between "threats" and "challenges" in Russian secu-

---

33. Russian interviews 17, 24, and 41.

rity doctrine concluded, "Obviously, NATO falls under the challenge category."

Some expected NATO eventually to erode given the absence of threat. One senior official in the foreign ministry (11) said, "In a few years, we will not recognize NATO. Everyone here sees that now. U.S. troops were a deposit on European security, but I do not see that in the future. You see this through NACC: slowly, step by step, the meaning of NATO disappears." A politician (31) assured me that "it will be not too long until NATO turns into a political organization." Furthermore, in 1992 some officials—and President Yeltsin in one public statement—floated the idea of Russian membership in a political NATO.[34] But such ideas became less evident as the year went on, because of the obvious international obstacles and domestic political opposition. A conservative political activist (21) ended this line of questioning with the response "The idea of Russia in NATO is nonsense."

Russian officials also did not see a problem in NATO's having peacekeeping or humanitarian intervention capabilities if such missions were undertaken under the UN and the OSCE. This sponsorship gives the appropriate "legal" and international cast to NATO, and of course Russia would have a vote on (and in the UN, a veto over) any such operations. Above all, one official (6) told me, NATO must not impose any solutions on Russia. NATO actions, an adviser (19) warned me, have internal Russian effects.

But an enlarged NATO, excluding Russia, which was still a military institution *was* a problem in their view. Because enlargement would change NATO's membership without shedding its mission of collective defense, it threatened Russia. Enlargement upsets the balance of power, for institutional reasons. One official (12) said that the "military staffs and forces of NATO are a problem because they limit the development of political approaches to security by focusing on military issues." As long as NATO as a military establishment exists, he said, it has to be dealt with on a military level. Other officials and analysts also told me that NATO's military character focuses attention on military structures and criteria.[35] A foreign ministry official (26) said NATO should be weakened to enhance Russian security, but not because NATO itself is a threat. "It would support the arguments of liberals. Lower military levels and the development of NATO as a political institution is important." An adviser (19) said, "NATO must not believe it extends to the former Warsaw

34. Russian interviews 12 and 23; "Military Alliances: Russia Wants to Join NATO," *Current Digest of the Soviet Press* 43 (29 January 1992), p. 19.
35. Russian interviews 40 and 41.

Pact, because that would undermine the reform process and aid conservatives. You must not create a sense of isolation here." A defense official (30) said it is very important to keep separate the "zone of authority of NATO. In that zone, NATO must solve its own problems. And in the CIS zone, the CIS must solve its problems."

Therefore, it is clear that neither NATO's persistence nor its political evolution inspired a balance response or Russian resistance. What did was the prospect of its enlargement and NATO military operations near Russian borders. But NATO's institutional form and function were crucial to Russian assessments.

German ambivalence about NATO's usefulness for coping with risks rather than threats was also apparent in 1992 and supports institutional hypotheses that variation in form and function matters. The German political elite had contradictory views of NATO's role in the new problems of European security and was deeply ambivalent about whether an how NATO should change. One point was common to all, however: NATO remains crucial for German security because it binds Germany to multilateral security cooperation, reinforces Germany's commitment to democracy and civilian control of the military, and is the primary mechanism for reassuring Germany's European neighbors that it cannot and will not threaten them.

The problem bedeviling Germans was that NATO was not yet an institution with capacities based on consent, negotiations, conflict management, and conflict prevention. NATO's form and function were those of enforcement and collective defense, not neutral peacekeeping and political involvement. This made NATO of very limited usefulness. One German official (20) said in the case of Russian-Ukrainian disputes, "We cannot go in and use institutions as direct instruments to handle and mediate the problem; we have to emphasize political means and processes within the CSCE." The common view was that NATO was for collective defense and "threats," and the OSCE was for conflict prevention. Said an official (31), "The mandate of NATO is to deal with attacks on members, not to deal with Yugoslavia, or conflicts in the CIS." One politician (60) answered in revealing terms when asked if Russia or the other former Soviet republics could join NATO in order to extend the benefits of membership after the cold war: "That would deprive NATO of its function as a security entente and make it another CSCE." For these reasons, while NATO enlargement was beginning to be discussed in 1992, it was far from being German policy. One official (63) said:

> The extension of NATO is not foreseen, since such a move would recreate the split of Europe. Say we were to take in Hungary, what do Romania

and Czechoslovakia see in that? That NATO is taking sides among them. Furthermore, that would mean taking NATO to the border of Russia, and that will not be done. Once you start, either you bring in countries that are democratic and thus bring NATO to the CIS border, which cannot be; or you bring the Russians in. But then you come again to the question of security guarantees—against whom? China? . . . I suppose you could do away with Article 5 of the treaty, but then you would have NACC.

Politicians argued either against NATO's persistence or for its evolution, given its limited capacity for dealing with risks as an exclusive alliance for collective defense. Said one politician (16), "NATO still has a defensive role, but the new security problem of Europe requires a collective security system. . . . this is not NATO." He saw enlargement as part of the process of changing NATO's form in line with new functions. An analyst (14) said that the OSCE is more promising for European security because "if NATO were to develop the capacity to handle risks, then it would become the CSCE, as CSCE's job is to handle risks. NATO is a functioning body without a function. CSCE is not a functioning body, but with a function. Therefore, I expect NATO and CSCE to merge." Another German official (53) praised NATO as "the only stable, still functioning organization," but added "Yugoslavia proved that NATO and other institutions do not have the instruments to cope with the security problems that arise now."

German officials saw the value of NACC as a more comprehensive political security institution, not constrained as NATO was. NACC, said one (31), could not exclude the CIS, "so as not to antagonize them or introduce a new cleavage in Europe." NACC was created, another German official (63) said, because we were concerned about a "security vacuum": once you let in the east Europeans, however, you have to let in the Russians because "the moment you differentiate between good Hungarians and bad Russians, you create new gaps." We wanted, he said, to show that NATO is an open house, that it is "transparent," and that requires inclusive membership. Some hoped that NACC could combine NATO's effectiveness with greater comprehensiveness. "Part of the NACC concept is to spread NATO's stabilization security function, without extending the commitments of NATO's defense," said one (64).

Russian officials thought in similar terms. When I asked a Russian defense ministry official (30) about NATO enlargement as a way to encompass European countries, he answered, "That is NACC's function." A foreign ministry official (12) said that NACC was important for comprehensive security because it included all the countries of the former Warsaw Pact. Its function, he explained, is for discussion of military strategy to facilitate cooperation and understanding. Another foreign ministry official (24) said that "NACC was established to make things flexible," as NATO cannot. Russian officials were less pleased with the creation of Partnership for Peace in 1994, not only because that organization was a thinly disguised way to proceed on NATO enlargement, but because unlike NACC which was multilateral, PfP was bilateral between NATO and each new partner. This format, Russian officials realized, reduced Russian influence at the same time that it enhanced NATO's leverage in dealing with Russia in matters of military cooperation.[36]

In this context, the OSCE's advantage was its comprehensive membership and political character. A German political analyst (52) asked, "Why should we do things in a smaller group when we can do them all together? Why NACC when we have CSCE?" Because of its membership and its institutional form, the OSCE was seen as valuable for transparency, assurance, and conflict prevention. The OSCE had the asset of legitimacy in CIS conflicts. One German official (59) said that the OSCE was far more usable because "NACC does not provide the necessary legitimacy for peacekeeping in the CIS. Furthermore, the notion of NATO forces peacekeeping in the territory of the CIS is not imaginable for the Russians—or for NATO."

Nonetheless, the OSCE did not have the rules and procedures to cope with many sources of risks and instabilities. The organization was strained when the call came to serve as an instrument for overcoming coordination problems and distributional conflict. It was not strong enough: it ruled virtually by consensus, operated through loose and ongoing contacts, and had little in the way of resources or capacities. That made it useful when loose consultations, assurance, and confidence building were called for, but it crippled the institution when real disputes divided its members. In a crisis, one German official (29) said, "the OSCE is a toothless dog."

One important example of how *both* the OSCE's strengths and weaknesses lay in its comprehensive membership and its loose, political form was its limited role in conflicts. The decision to extend OSCE membership to all the post-Soviet states, said one German official (51), was "not to allow blank spots on the map, not to draw a line east of the Polish border, not to say 'okay, they fall into chaos, into the nineteenth century.'" As one politician (34) said, "If you want to influence them you have got to have them at the table. . . . you talk to them and explain, if you want to

36. Russian interviews 53 and 62.

be part of the international community, you have to behave like a member." But this, said another German official (31),

> was from the point of view of the CSCE a disaster. The CSCE now is a European political system—it is too weak to be called a security system. We have come to the conclusion in institution-building that you cannot have your cake and eat it. You have to have either a manageable group of countries with common commitments, or an unwieldy large set of diverse countries.

By 1996, the relative advantages of the OSCE and NATO were clear to the German government. One official (65) said that we must not fail to see the comparative advantage of the OSCE in early warning and preventive diplomacy. If these are successfully taken up by the OSCE, there will be no militarization and no crisis; if the OSCE fails in preventive diplomacy, we can then go to NATO. Another (67) said, the OSCE "is not a military instrument . . . it is like the Concert, to include Russia: but for military security, we strongly prefer NATO." Asked whether experience with the OSCE in 1992 and 1993 was not reason for avoiding it, an official (69) said no:

> The OSCE is the one institution where all are members, and where any of them can raise their security concerns. We need to balance integration with cooperative security for those who are not in NATO or the EU or who are not going to be. This is a division of labor, and comparative advantage, with OSCE responsible for early warning and for post-crisis stability.

This evidence supports the hypothesis that choice of institution and variation in institutional form and function matter. As this discussion has shown, German and Russian officials distinguished among conflicts arising from aggression and deliberate attack (collaboration), crisis bargaining and distributional conflict (coordination), and mistrust and misperception (assurance). In their assessments, coping with these different problems required different institutions with different forms and memberships: aggression requires sanction and retaliation (NATO or UN Chapter VII); crisis bargaining requires negotiations, mediation, and peacekeeping (UN Chapter VI or a reformed OSCE); and misperception requires ongoing transparency and confidence building (the existing OSCE and NACC). This is not to dismiss the role of calculations about power and interest in German and Russian strategies. When I asked one German official (46) why multilateral cooperation appeared to be more effective in Yugoslavia than in the CIS, he attributed it to the authority of the UN in the former case, but then conceded, "We have to be honest here and admit that it also has to do with the difference between Russia and Serbia." But we cannot explain their choice of strategies without understanding institutional variation as well.

INSTITUTIONAL EFFECTIVENESS

The third set of institutional hypotheses addressed the question of institutional effectiveness. Realist approaches lead us to expect that institutions are not independently effective: they matter only where they serve the interests of powerful states (as in pessimistic realism) or when the security dilemma is benign (as in optimistic realism). Institutionalism, I argued, leads us to expect that institutions will be effective where there is a match of security tasks or problems to institutional forms. Institutional theory also predicts effectiveness where multiple, layered institutions capable of coping with diverse security problems protect states against vulnerability or exploitation. Do these institutional hypotheses explain the success and failure of German and Russian officials in relying upon cooperative multilateral security strategies to manage and prevent conflicts, migration, and refugee problems?

It is tempting to conclude that they do, because the evidence shows that German and Russian officials believed that variation in underlying security problems and variation in institutional form and function were important to their choices and a component of the success and failure of their security strategies. Public debates about the distinction between peace enforcement and peacekeeping, the futility of crisis management without peacebuilding, the difference between coercion and consent, and the need to adapt the entire panoply of institutions including the UN, the OSCE, NATO, and the WEU to new and more urgent security problems of risks and instability were reflected consistently and quite genuinely in my private, off-the-record interviews.

Therefore, if institutions with the forms and membership necessary for conflict prevention and management are not available, it is not surprising that cooperation fails. As a German official (66) told me, "We can deter threats, but not risks." And it works both ways: mechanisms for conflict prevention do not support multilateral defense and deterrence. Said one German official (71) looking back in 1996, "Bosnia showed you cannot solve problems just by talk, through diplomacy alone; sometimes you need military means." Another German official (35) said, "Some people have exaggerated hopes. . . . the thinking goes something like: if we have institutions, then we will have peace, and if there is not peace, then the institutions must be a failure. But how can any institution prevent war when one is determined to have it?"

Although in Chapter 5, we saw that an institution created to deal with collaboration problems (the CFE) was valuable for dealing with coordination and assurance problems, here it is clear that the relationship does not work in reverse. Institutions for conflict prevention and transparency such as the OSCE could not cope with threats, nor did that organization have crisis management instruments in 1992. Similarly, strong institutions for coping with threats, such as NATO or the UN under Chapter VII, could not be smoothly adapted to the more political, consent-based, mediation, or transparency-oriented security tasks necessary to cope with risks and instability. We need to understand when institutions designed for some purposes can be adapted to new ones, as in the case of the CFE treaty, and when they cannot, as in the cases discussed in this chapter.

Moreover, although frequent failure to cooperate in preventing and managing conflicts in Europe and the former Soviet Union in the immediate aftermath of the cold war was partially due to problems of institutional form, function, design, and choice, as I expected, another crucial institutional hypothesis is not supported by the evidence. The presence of multiple and layered institutions clearly did not contribute to institutional effectiveness in these cases. That was the hope: one German official (40) spoke of "a net of institutions to catch crises and problems, and the more that happens, the more consultations that go on, the more work that gets done, the tighter the net becomes and the less chance that anything will fall through." Officials thought security was served when multiple institutions were available to cope with different problems that arise. A Russian foreign ministry official (23) used a term I heard often when he said that security problems could be managed through "interlocking institutions."

But the problem with multiple institutions is that their net or interlocking potential was also vulnerable to the opposite problem: failure to rely effectively upon appropriate strategies and institutional support in what a German official (31) dryly called "interblocking institutions." The problem was not that security institutions were not layered, or that a rich network of complementary institutions with forms and memberships to serve a variety of functions did not exist. Europe was awash in institutions. The cases of conflicts and instability do not support the hypothesis that the layering of multiple institutions will increase their effectiveness. The ongoing, long-term, and very political tasks of transparency, information exchange, and assurance were supported by the network of institutions in Europe. However, effectiveness also required

[165]

the sustained and substantial interest of important countries, including the United States and Russia.

Success, as they say, has many fathers (although apparently no mothers). But failure also has many sources, and in this case, failure to prevent and manage deadly conflicts under uncertain and unstable circumstances of multipolarity after the cold war had a parentage of power, interests, and institutions.

[7]

Russian Internal Control and Reform

The most immediate problems in German-Russian security relations were posed neither by military balances nor by conflicts, but by the nature of the Russian state itself. The capacity of the Russian state to control its weapons and technology and to provide acceptable living conditions for its citizens was a matter of national security policy for Russia and Germany. Weak states and failing economies always entail humanitarian concern or limited "spillover" conflicts, but they usually do not pose existential security threats to their neighbors because of their low level of military and technological development. The situation with Russia was entirely different: it had weapons of mass destruction not under secure state control. Therefore, in addition to military forces and conflicts, German-Russian security relations involved the capacity of the Russian state.

Germany has a strong interest in a Russian state that can control dangerous technologies and weapons, and that develops an economy able to avoid social breakdown and explosion. Although individual citizens or firms within Russia may have commercial interests in trade, Russia too has a stake in preventing the unfettered spread of weapons and technologies: they could be used to threaten it. Unless we can emerge from this transition period with a functioning state and economy, said one Russian official (6), the greatest threats to Russian security will come from within.

CONTROL AND EXPORTS

Prevention of nuclear weapons proliferation was a German security priority, and Russian interests in preventing expansion of the number of nuclear weapons states were equally clear.[1] This does not mean, however, that Russia's role in nuclear proliferation is not a matter of concern, because of the possibility that Russia would not be able to control its vast nuclear complex including weapons stocks, fissile material, related nuclear technology, and the scientific and technical personnel who might move abroad for more lucrative opportunities.[2] Although not easy, it is possible to build a nuclear device from material obtained even from civilian nuclear energy installations.[3] If the Russian state could not control its nuclear infrastructure, it might "involuntarily defect" from the nuclear nonproliferation regime: that is, violate the regime without having decided to do so.[4]

Proliferation as lack of state control resulting from Russia's economic problems was a qualitatively different problem from that which had previously plagued the world and which the NPT regime had been designed to address. For this reason the American "Cooperative Threat Reduction" program (known more commonly as Nunn-Lugar) funded measures to provide more secure warhead transportation, assistance for dismantling of weapons and ICBM silos, security for storage facilities, and purchase of uranium for American nuclear energy use.[5]

Germany was not a central player in the issue of strategic nuclear weapons, but it was deeply involved in the issue of proliferation of nu-

---

1. On German policy, see "Die Bedeutung der Rüstungskontrolle als Strategie der Konfliktverhinderung," speech by Foreign Minister Klaus Kinkel, 3 August 1992, in *Presse- und Informationsamt Bulletin*, no. 87, Bonn, 4 August 1992, pp. 829–830; State Secretary Helmut Schäfer of the foreign ministry, reporting to the Bundestag. "Deutscher Bundestag—12. Wahlperiode—77. Sitzung, Bonn, Freitag den 14. Februar 1992," pp. 6404–6406. For an excellent analysis of Russia's nuclear weapons policies, see Nikolai N. Sokov, "Russia's Approach to Deep Reductions of Nuclear Weapons: Opportunities and Problems," Occasional Paper no. 27, Henry L. Stimson Center (Washington, D.C., 1996).

2. The problem was foreseen before the Soviet Union broke apart. See Kurt M. Campbell, Ashton B. Carter, Steven E. Miller, and Charles A. Zraket, *Soviet Nuclear Fission: Control of the Nuclear Arsenal in a Disintegrating Soviet Union*, CSIA Studies in International Security, no. 1 (Cambridge, Mass.: Center for Science and International Affairs, November 1991). For a survey of the issues once they had become reality, see Joachim Krause, ed., *Kernwaffenverbreitung und internationaler Systemwandel* (Baden-Baden: Nomos, 1994).

3. See Graham T. Allison, Owen Cote, Jr., Richard A. Falkenrath, and Steven E. Miller, *Avoiding Nuclear Anarchy: Containing the Threat of Loose Russian Nuclear Weapons and Fissile Material*, CSIA Studies in International Security, no. 12 (Cambridge, Mass.: Center for Science and International Affairs, 1996), especially appendix A and appendix B.

4. George W. Downs and David M. Rocke, *Optimal Imperfection? Domestic Uncertainty and Institutions in International Relations* (Princeton: Princeton University Press, 1995), chap. 5.

5. Allison et al., *Avoiding Nuclear Anarchy*, appendix C; Christoph Bluth, "Arms Control and Nuclear Safety: The National and International Politics of Russia's Nuclear Arsenal," *Government and Opposition* 30 (1995): 510–532, at pp. 525–526.

[168]

clear knowhow and materials. As early as March 1992, incidents of the smuggling of nuclear materials became a major concern for the German government.[6] Germany did not question Russia's commitment to preventing nuclear spread; instead, it questioned Russia's capacity to prevent it. "What the Russian government wants is one thing—the reality is another," said one official (57). So the German government adopted policies to help increase Russia's capacity to control its weapons and technology. These included multilateral technical assistance programs through the EU as well as bilateral cooperation, but also involved more fundamental assistance in reforming Russia's political and economic institutions. Germany pressed for nonproliferation to be a major focus of the G–7 summit which it hosted in Munich in 1992, including a commitment to work on a strengthening of Russian export controls.[7]

Russia's nuclear scientists were themselves a proliferation risk, given the temptation to leave terrible economic prospects at home for the promise of wealth abroad. In March 1992 the United States, Russia, Germany, and Japan created an International Science and Technology Center meant to provide employment and research facilities for ex-Soviet nuclear scientists in the hope that they would not be lured to work for countries pursuing a nuclear weapons capability. Germany ceded its place as a founding member to the EU in July 1992, with the EU stake funded at ECU 20 million (about $25 million).[8] Delays plagued the effort, with the longest arising from Germany's ceding of its seat to the EU. The working languages of the center were to have been English, Russian, German, and Japanese (those of the founding countries). Once the German seat was turned over to the EU, France demanded that French also be a working language, and then other EU countries insisted that if French were to be made one, all the other languages of the EC would

6. German interview 24. All the incidents, this official said, involved materials stolen from civilian installations. "Even the most foolish person knows to stay away from a nuclear warhead." For more details on cases of nuclear smuggling from the former Soviet Union, see Allison et al., *Avoiding Nuclear Anarchy*, pp. 23–28.

7. "Die Sieben in München setzen Hoffnung auf Demokratie und soziale Gerechtigkeit in Osteuropa," *Frankfurter Allgemeine Zeitung*, 8 July 1992, p. 1.

8. "Deutscher Bundestag—12. Wahlperiode—91. Sitzung, Bonn, Donnerstag, den 7 Mai 1992," p. 7531. The original idea was that of James Baker, Andrei Kozyrev, and Hans-Dietrich Genscher, hence it was known as the "KGB initiative" for the initials of their last names. German interview 24. The EU participation in the ISTC came under the general EU program of technical assistance for the former Soviet Union, funding for which at the time stood at ECU 50 million. Other countries' contributions to the ISTC were: United States at $25 million; Japan at $20 million; Sweden at $4 million; Canada at $2.5 million, and Switzerland at $1.5 million.

have to be as well.[9] Despite this squabble, however, there was no evidence that delays had contributed to any cases of "brain drain," and the center was operating by 1993.

Although Russia has sought lucrative sales of arms and technology, when those sales contradicted international rules and norms Russia has acceded to the system. For example, Russian officials ultimately canceled a contract with India in order to comply with the Missile Technology Control Regime, which Russia later joined in 1995. In contrast, Russia has maintained its right to sell nuclear technology to Iran under IAEA procedures. In the case of conventional arms sales, there are no direct restraints, and Russia has a strong interest in the financial and commercial benefits such sales might bring. One government official (37) estimated that the export of Russian arms for air defenses alone could bring in $300 million per year and said wryly that next to energy, arms are Russia's biggest export. Another official (27) said there is a "moral obligation" not to allow weapons to proliferate, but then refused to criticize sales that were legal under international agreement. We need norms and agreements, he said, "but now there are none, and so we cannot follow them." Although some distinction is made between offensive and defensive arms, said another official (46), "of course, Russia tries to export as much as possible."

German interests were not all that different. One official (2) said we do not want to interfere with legitimate activities, and our own arms exporters seek not to be controlled. Even in the EU, he pointed out, where a single market and trade system makes common policy sensible, the members have their own interests.

Another problem that arose was control of military technology through the Coordinating Committee, or CoCom. The CoCom regime was meant to cope with the problems of "dual use" technologies—those that have civilian as well as military uses—and to prevent Soviet bloc countries from obtaining them. CoCom balanced competing commercial and security interests by allowing western countries to agree on restricted technologies and states, yet at the same time providing for trade in restricted technologies among the members states.[10]

CoCom was still in place but under pressure to change. Unless the formerly communist countries including Russia were removed from the proscribed list, they could not purchase the type of high technology

9. German interview 58.
10. For the definitive study, see Michael Mastanduno, *Economic Containment: CoCom and the Politics of East-West Trade* (Ithaca: Cornell University Press, 1992).

trade and investment which would develop their economies. "You tell us you want us to change," said one official, "and to open ourselves to private trade and investment, but then you keep it from us."[11] We need to control technology and arms as CoCom did, said another official (1), "but we have to make progress now in the economic sphere in order to support reforms, and CoCom is an unnecessary obstacle." CoCom is a big problem for us, said another official (44), because we see the greatest potential in trade with western Europe, and that is where CoCom restrictions confront us the most. Nevertheless, the export control system which the Russian government began to develop in 1992 was explicitly modeled on CoCom rules and designed to make Russia eligible for membership. Russian officials believed CoCom's system of export control generally too restrictive, but said it was better to be inside the system than outside.[12]

Germany's view of CoCom was also critical. "CoCom was the tool of the west to destroy the development of the East" and therefore not appropriate any longer, said one official.[13] Like Russian officials, Germans pointed out that CoCom restrictions on trade with formerly communist countries was an obstacle to the more basic priority of reform. "You cannot help these interests by maintaining traditional CoCom controls," said one official "because if we want to offer cooperation, we cannot maintain controls in the traditional way."[14] In addition, Germany and other European countries had interests in trade with the former communist countries, which as target countries were restricted by existing rules.[15] Although at one point Foreign Minister Hans-Dietrich Genscher suggested leaving CoCom, this was never a serious policy option because of the advantages to being a member: intra-CoCom trade is license-free, and in particular membership provided access to the U.S.

11. Russian interview 44. See also "Rußland will Schulden nicht mehr bedienen," *Frankfurter Allgemeine Zeitung*, 1 June 1992, p. 15.

12. Russian interview 46; "Rossiyskiy KOKOM tozhe ne smozhet suschestvovat v otdelno vzyatoy strane," *Kommersant*, 8 June 1992, p. 12. This remained a concern as late as 1996. "Russian Agreement Clears Way for Wassenaar Accord," *OMRI Daily Digest* (electronic version), no. 135 (15 July 1996).

13. German interview 38. See also Economics Minister Jürgen Mölleman's statement in "Cocom-Beschränkung für die GUS erleichtert," *Frankfurter Allgemeine Zeitung*, 4 June 1992, p. 17.

14. German interview 54. He added that Germany had a unique perspective because eastern German trade included fiber optics and military maintenance contracts. Germany was allowed special measures to preserve this trade (not permitted to western German, American, or French firms), which was accepted by CoCom members, or "well, tolerated: it is understood that we have a border with Poland, and still Russian troops in our country."

15. "Europäer erarbeiten eine gemeinsame Ausfuhrliste," *Frankfurter Allgemeine Zeitung*, 13 October 1992, p. 15.

market, which Germany would have lost. We have to compare the benefits of access to the CoCom markets to the benefits of access to the former Soviet bloc, said one official (54), "so nobody really thinks of leaving."

CoCom was disbanded in March 1994, although the members agreed to maintain the lists and system of consultation for an interim period. A successor agreement, the Wassenaar Accord, was achieved in December 1995, and Russia signed in July 1996. The inclusion of Russia and the leverage that the prospect of inclusion created for encouraging and shaping its much improved system of export control are CoCom's enduring post–cold war legacies.

Nuclear Reactors and Safety

The most likely scenario for nuclear danger in Europe was an accident in one of the unsafe nuclear reactors located in eastern Europe and the former Soviet Union. German officials considered the issue of reactor safety comparable to that of nuclear weapons because "explosion of a reactor would be like a bomb."[16] Part of the problem, as with export controls, was the administrative incapacity of the post-Soviet states and economies, but the matter was even more complicated.

There were two types of Soviet nuclear reactors. Pressurized water reactors—known by their cyrillic acronym as VVERs—had been developed by the Soviet Union for nuclear submarine and icebreaker propulsion, and were adapted for civilian energy use. Graphite reactors—RBMKs—had direct weapons and military applications. Although how dangerous and how remediable the installations are varies greatly, the VVER reactors can in principle be retrofitted and brought up to international safety standards. The RBMK reactors cannot be brought up to western safety standards, western governments agreed, and should be shut down. (The Chernobyl nuclear reactor is an RBMK type.) RBMK reactors were important in the Soviet Union, producing 40 percent of the region's electrical energy.

RBMK reactors in Russia present a dilemma: they should be closed because they are dangerous and cannot be fixed, but they will almost certainly not be closed anytime soon, because they are needed for energy.

---

16. German interview 57. For Germany nuclear safety was also a matter of domestic politics and economics. Were there another Chernobyl, said officials, there would be a breakdown in European civilian nuclear power systems, because public support would disappear and western governments would not be able to sustain their programs. German interviews 6, 39, and 47.

Given that the reactors will be run, something must be done to improve their safety, even if they cannot be brought up to western safety standards.

For Russia, shutting down the reactors simply was not an option. Russian officials welcomed international assistance to improve their safety, but not at the price of losing them as a source of energy. Furthermore, there was no question of Russia itself paying for the cost of safety upgrades at a time of radical reform and economic decline. In particular, reactor safety would require western commercial contracts and therefore hard currency payments. Russia would not use its hard currency for this, an official (44) said, at a time when we need it for so many other more important things. International assistance was a necessary condition for reactor safety.

Despite its strong interest in reactor safety upgrades, Germany would not embark on a unilateral assistance program for two reasons. The first was simple cost: Germany could not pay for such safety programs itself, especially given the costs of unification and the government's budget deficit. Bilateral and multilateral technical assistance to improve safety was immediately forthcoming, including the EU Technical Assistance for the CIS (TACIS) program, but this did not entail the necessary financing. Unlike the VVER reactors which could be made commercially viable and in which private investment for safety was possible, the RBMKs required government financing. "It is our main interest that this be financed by the European Community as a whole, as well as the United States, Japan, Canada, and all the major countries," said one German official (57). "No bank is going to spend money on something that has no future."

The second reason was more complicated. Although safety might be improved, the risks of accident would remain very high. States were unwilling individually to "improve" nuclear safety because the state responsible for the work would be liable in international law if the "improved" nuclear reactor nevertheless failed. This is not merely a political liability, German officials said, but legal and financial. Spend millions to improve Chernobyl, one said, and then if it explodes, the German government would be liable for hundreds of millions if not billions in claims by survivors. The European view is that we have to refit these reactors or take them out of service, "but it must be international and co-responsibility—you will not find a country willing to do it alone."[17]

17. German interview 47. There was one exception: Sweden helped upgrade Lithuania's RBMK reactors. But, said this German official, they are taking a huge risk, and are being criticized in the bargain for aiding Lithuania. If an accident occurs, he said, Sweden will be held responsible.

International cooperation was necessary because national policies could not cover this larger problem of liability.

At the G–7 meeting in Munich in 1992, the members agreed to shift policy from reliance on commercial improvements and to give the G–24 (another name for the Organization for Economic Cooperation and Development—OECD) a mandate to create an official program for nuclear safety and a fund of up to $760 million for the effort.[18] However, despite continuing meetings, European Bank for Reconstruction and Development (EBRD) studies, and a series of agreements for international assistance to close Chernobyl (with cost estimates ranging from $300 billion to $600 billion), multilateral cooperation for reactor security in the former Soviet Union has failed.[19] The 1996 Moscow summit on nuclear safety and security affirmed all the good intentions, but solved none of the obstacles to cooperation.

ECONOMIC RELATIONS AND REFORM

The topic of Russian economic reform is vast and complex, and a thorough analysis is well beyond the scope of this project.[20] The issue played a role in German-Russian security relations, however: a democratic, market-oriented, and stable Russia was the objective of German national security policy. In the long run, German officials believed, Russia's reform was necessary for stability.

Reform did not play a direct role in Russia's view of its security relations. Instead, reform was the fundamental objective of government policy which shaped—although it did not determine—all other policy, including foreign and security relations. Economic reform was necessary for Russia's survival as a country and for any hope of future stability, prosperity, and security. Multiple reform plans were possible, and they all entailed difficult trade-offs between other goals and painful reform

18. German interview 57.

19. For a comprehensive analysis of western efforts for nuclear safety in eastern Europe as well as in Russia, see Barbara Connolly and Martin List, "Nuclear Safety in Eastern Europe and the Soviet Union," in *Institutions for Environmental Aid: Pitfalls and Promise*, ed. Robert O. Keohane and Marc A. Levy (Cambridge: MIT Press, 1996).

20. For such analyses, see Anders Aslund, *How Russia Became a Market Economy* (Washington, D.C.: Brookings Institution, 1995); Marshall I. Goldman, *Lost Opportunity: Why Economic Reforms in Russia Have Not Worked* (New York: Norton, 1994); Maxim Boycko, Andrei Shleifer, and Robert Vishny, *Privatizing Russia* (Cambridge: MIT Press, 1995); and Brigitte Granville, *The Success of Russian Economic Reforms* (London: Royal Institute of International Affairs, 1995).

policies. But reform to some kind of a market economy was—and re-mains—the center of Russian government policy.

The question here, then, is how German-Russian relations were af-fected by the tasks of liberalization, stabilization, and privatization.[21] The Russian government freed prices for many goods in January 1992, created a system of retail sales, embarked upon a program of privatizing enterprises and assets owned by the Soviet state, and began the process of making the ruble a convertible and stable currency. Inflation and con-traction of GNP (both of which had actually begun in the late Soviet years) eroded Russian living conditions as goods became more expen-sive and money more difficult to come by.

From 1990 to early 1992, much of western assistance was humanitar-ian, going for food and medical aid: Germany gave some DM 3 billion directly and through the EU.[22] Reform required the creation of market institutions such as private property, protection for private investment, financial and banking regulation, and a system of laws and procedures for free and private international trade. International involvement in this regard entailed primarily technical agencies such as US AID and the EU's TACIS, which provided knowledge and advice on how to create capital markets and laws governing international trade and investment which were compatible with international standards. In addition, Rus-sian officials began a process of negotiation and consultation with the EU, IMF, World Bank, EBRD, and OECD on the requirements and rules for participating in international financial and trade regimes.

The third form of aid for reform in Russia was financial assistance, sometimes in the form of grants, but most often in that of loans. These were of three types: assistance for projects and purchases, such as World Bank loans to create modern communications systems; direct financial assistance, such as IMF loans to be used to enable the government to cover deficits; and debt relief, to delay payments on both Soviet and Rus-sian international debts.

International institutions played a role as a provider of resources, but they also established conditionality.[23] Conditionality is a matter of set-ting criteria so that resources are not wasted, and of creating incentives

21. See Gertrude Schroeder, "The Economic Transformation Process in the Post-Soviet States: The Role of Outside Actors," in *The International Dimension of Post-Communist Transi-tions in Russia and the New States of Eurasia*, ed. Karen Dawisha (Armonk, N.Y.: M. E. Sharpe, 1997), pp. 243–276. Schroeder calls these the "three pillars" of reform, p. 256.

22. "Deutsche Unterstützungsmaßnahmen für den Reformprozeß in der ehemaligen UdSSR und der GUS," internal German government memorandum, May 1992.

23. On aid conditionality, see Joan M. Nelson with Stephanie J. Eglinton, *Encouraging Democracy: What Role for Conditioned Aid?*, Policy Essay no. 4 (Washington, D.C.: Overseas Development Council, 1992).

to get countries such as Russia to adopt difficult reform policies that have long- term benefits but short-term domestic costs. "Good economics is usually bad politics,"[24] and Russia was no exception. In principle, international conditionality can allow governments to adopt policies in the face of domestic political opposition. Said one Russian official (3): "On the one hand, we need international conditions because it is the only civilized way to solve our problems. But on the other, the conditions are not the best ones for our political conditions. In Russian dealings with international organizations, there are simply the social and political limits."

Thus, one of the dimensions of German-Russian relations was creating international leverage and resources for Russian reforms. Russia sought access to the international economic system with its resources, expertise, investment, and free trade. Germany sought to embed Russia in this system because the key to a market economy there, German officials said, is "to bring the former Soviet Union into the world economy."[25] Integration would also serve as leverage for reform and to increase the private and multilateral government assets which could spark Russian development. "It is not just a matter of if you are not good you cannot have the cookie: the conditions for private investment must be created," said a German official (56).

German policy on Russian economic reform evolved during 1992. The emphasis shifted from bilateral assistance to multilateral aid efforts and sources. German officials said repeatedly that Germany could no longer be left to shoulder most of the western burden for Russian reform (I was always given reports showing that Germany alone accounted for some 60 percent of all assistance to the countries of the former Soviet Union as of 1992). The costs of unification were creating problems for the government budget and the German economy. When I asked one official (48) if he was not worried that bringing other countries in through the EU and IMF would diminish German influence in Russia, he was genuinely surprised and puzzled by my question. "It is a question of cooperation and stability in Europe. We do not see economic relations in terms of influence. We are asking for multilateral efforts, we are pushing the French to invest more. If Japan comes in, the luckier we are. It is a huge market, we do not have to worry about whether German companies get the contracts."

---

24. Bartlomiej Kaminski and Zhen Kun Wang, "External Finance, Policy Conditionalities, and Transition from Central Planning," in *The International Dimension of Post-Communist Transition*, ed. Dawisha, pp. 277–296, at p. 294.
25. German interview 48.

The emphasis also shifted to limited international contributions to Russian reform. Chancellor Kohl spoke of "a program of help for self-help," and this also became a theme of the G–7 meeting in Munich, to which Yeltsin was invited.[26] As part of this shift, German officials began to emphasize policies to enhance trade, investment, and technical assistance for structural adjustment of the Russian economy, rather than financial assistance through grants or loans. One manifestation of this shift was that Germany pressed the EU in 1992 to negotiate a free trade regime. The EU-Russia cooperation and partnership agreement finally achieved in June 1994 did not establish free trade as Germany sought, but it did significantly lower trade barriers, with exceptions for textiles, coal, and steel, areas where EU countries feared Russian competition.[27]

But political and financial obstacles to these long-term goals existed in Russia. In political terms, a domestic opposition began to emerge in early 1992 which seized upon the costs of early reform measures to argue for greater government spending, maintenance of industrial subsidies, delayed privatization, and other steps that would undermine the reform package. In April 1992, Yeltsin announced a softening of the reform plan in response to political pressure, deciding, for example, not to free energy prices as called for by the IMF. In financial terms, the Russian government simply did not have the resources to provide for the basic necessities of human life, cut government spending, import foreign technology for modernizing the economy, and meet its international financial obligations all at the same time. In order to be able to implement the reforms necessary for creating a stable ruble, a promising investment climate, and healthy foreign trade without squeezing Russian society beyond its capacity to endure, the government needed foreign financing, and it sought a modification of IMF rules as well. In June 1992, the IMF weakened its requirements in order to provide Russia with 25 percent of its quota even though it had not met the conditions usually required; later tranches were to be conditional on meeting the criteria.[28] In 1993 the IMF created the Systemic Transformation Facility, which disburses loans for currency stabilization purposes under looser terms than usual.[29]

But the IMF was not the only source of pressure on Russian finances. In 1992 Russia owed foreign public and private creditors some $80 billion in Soviet and Russian debt. Germany was the largest creditor, with

26. "Rußland soll 30 Milliarden Mark erhalten," *Süddeutsche Zeitung,* 2 April 1992, p. 1.

27. "Agreement on Partnership and Cooperation," document signed between the European Union and Russia in Corfu on 24 June 1994.

28. "Währungsfond legt Plan für Rußland vor," *Frankfurter Allgemeine Zeitung,* 25 June 1992, p. 15.

29. Kaminski and Wang, "External Finance," pp. 289–292.

DM 40 billion at stake in 1992.[30] Negotiations on deferring this debt were the work of the Paris Club of creditor states. By acting multilaterally, the creditors can prevent debtors from using resources from one country to pay off another. The Paris Club also has the value of increasing the visibility of default: a debtor state defaults against all members and its default is public, undermining the defaulter's credibility. Paris Club negotiations granted Russia repeated and substantial deferrals on paying Soviet and Russian debt, worth billions of dollars each year. Debt rescheduling was essential, because of limited government resources. But since Russian good faith and economic credibility were crucial in western offers to aid reform, the debt issue became a major problem in German-Russian relations. If the financial system breaks down, said one German official (61), then reform stops and trade relations break down: our goal is "to inject stability into financial relations in order to continue trade and capital flows." Russia's interest in the Paris Club was not merely in these payment deferrals. As early as 1992, Russian officials sought membership in the Paris Club to enhance Russia's ability to get repayment of $130–150 billion owed it from Soviet-era loans. In April 1996 Russia reached a long-term agreement with the Paris Club on rescheduling its debt, and in June 1997 at the G–8 summit Russia joined the Paris Club.

These issues of IMF conditions and debt were, however, only instrumental to Russia's fundamental interests in international economic integration through trade. Gaining access to international markets and joining GATT were policymakers' central concerns. Entering GATT, one official (8) said, will be the step that will allow the economy to grow. Russia was working to conform to GATT rules, including reducing tariffs and creating a fair and transparent taxation system. Even a very conservative politician (7) critical of reform and the IMF (calling IMF terms "the plundering of Russia") told me that international trade and investment would not be forthcoming as long as Russian laws were not consistent with GATT. It is no secret, said another politician (33), that trade is

---

30. German interview 36. Part of the reason for this substantial debt was the transfer ruble system used to sustain Council for Mutual Economic Assistance (CMEA) trade. Since the eastern European countries did not have convertible currencies, trade was conducted on the basis of the transfer ruble, which was an artificial accounting system with a negotiated value. At the time of unification and the breakup of the CMEA system, one transfer ruble had the value of 2.34 East German marks. Since the terms of unification generally provided for equivalent values of East German Marks for Deutschmarks, the value of the transfer ruble would be DM 2.34. At the time of unification, the GDR held an account balance of 6.5 billion transfer rubles, or DM 15.2 billion. This debt was then inherited by Russia.

our focus and these issues of debt and fair competition are obstacles we must overcome.

In 1992, the path to GATT membership was clear but not easy, and here Germany and the EU played a role in Russian strategies. "The EC is a way to open our window to GATT," said one official (8), because we are learning the GATT regime and developing in areas such as tariffs, juridical issues, content rules, and licenses. In explaining Russian views on negotiations with the EU, another official (2) said, "We need to fix in the agreement the principles of GATT." A politician (32) explained the importance of the EU agreement as a first step to GATT membership because "European regional economic cooperation is easier, more practical, and has more immediate results for Russia." In discussing the EU-GATT link, another official (44) said that the most difficult provisions in the EU agreement arise because Russia is not yet a member of GATT. This means, he said, that every provision in the agreement not only has to be checked so that it is in conformity with GATT rules for the EU countries, but almost always requires modifications or clarifications of Russian practices to conform to those rules.

Therefore, German and Russian relations and strategies involved multilateral economic and financial institutions as sources of financing and technical assistance. Furthermore, institutions such as GATT and the EU played a role in Russian and German strategies because they established criteria for membership or access to benefits which served as benchmarks and leverage for Russia's reform toward a market economy. The G–7 played a different role, more political than economic, and provided no assistance: although in April 1992 the group announced a package of assistance of $24 billion for Russia, this was not G–7 assistance but a collection of existing bilateral and other multilateral programs. Instead, the G–7 operated as a forum for discussion on Russia and—beginning with Russia's limited inclusion in the 1992 Munich meeting and culminating in its nearly full inclusion in the Denver summit in 1997—as a forum for discussion *with* Russia on matters of reform and integration.

INSTITUTIONS AND SECURITY COOPERATION

Although substantively quite different, in analytical terms the cases in this chapter are strikingly similar. All involve three elements: how to make resources available to Russia in order to get the outcomes all parties sought; how not to give those resources freely in order to use them as leverage for painful and costly structural change; and how to keep the western countries—and most important Germany—joined in a common

[179]

front to sustain the strength and credibility of the western resources and leverage. Cooperation, then, consisted not merely of offering aid or changing the rules to Russia's benefit, but of effecting long-term change at bearable cost.

Did Germany and Russia cooperate? In the case of nuclear control, bilateral and multilateral cooperation has been the rule. Attempts to smuggle nuclear materials have occurred, but these have involved civilian materials in small amounts.[31] For export controls and dual use technologies, Russia has adopted western standards and joined the Wassenaar Accord and the Missile Technology Control Regime (MTCR). Russia has sold nuclear technology to Iran, but under IAEA safeguards. Multilateral cooperation for conventional arms restrictions is limited to transparency measures in the UN and Wassenaar notification procedures, and Russia—along with Germany, the United States, France, and other western countries—continues to pursue the arms trade as a lucrative market in which it is very competitive.

The record of cooperation to make nuclear reactors in the former Soviet Union safe has been poor. At best, one can say that high-level attention and national efforts to improve safety have been consistent, as evidenced by the 1996 Moscow summit on nuclear safety, but these national efforts have not made available substantial international financial resources or achieved a regime governing liability which would allow both governmental and commercial efforts to improve reactor safety. Given the way German officials framed this problem as one of nuclear security with urgent domestic implications, this case counts as a substantial failure of multilateral security cooperation in German-Russian relations.

In evaluating cooperation for economic reform, experts debate whether the west failed to offer the kind of massive financial assistance it should have to speed and ease the transition.[32] Russia failed to implement measures to control inflation early on, did not establish a rational tax code and collection system that can support a reasonable government budget, and allowed inflation to run at 2500 percent in 1992. Social suffering has been severe, GDP declined yearly from 1991 to 1998, millions went unpaid and lost their life savings, and Russian life expectancy declined.[33]

---

31. See Allison et al., *Avoiding Nuclear Anarchy,* for a discussion of these instances.

32. Schroeder, "The Economic Transformation Process," surveys this debate.

33. Murray Feshbach, "The Role of External Assistance on Environmental and Health Policies in Russia," in *The International Dimension of Post-Communist Transitions,* ed. Dawisha, pp. 379–397.

But multilateral efforts had a measure of success with respect to the objectives of Russian and German officials and politicians. Russian inflation was down to 15 percent by 1997, in large measure a result of conformity with IMF targets. Russian foreign trade has grown yearly since 1994 and is increasingly with countries outside the CIS.[34] Officials in 1992 to some extent foresaw the issues, reasons for delay, and limited extent of western assistance. One Russian official (10) said, "Germany is ready to help Russia and ready to develop bilateral economic relations, but the theme is 'self-help.'" Although important obstacles to foreign private investment remain and total amounts are small, there has nonetheless been a steady stream of investment, and even stronger continuing interest. One German official (72) in 1996 noted that Germany had upgraded Russia's risk category for purposes of state credit guarantees as "not a sign of confidence, but of more confidence." The Russian ruble is convertible, and Russia has a functioning securities market. The country renegotiated its foreign debt rather than abrogating it, and in addition to joining the Paris Club as a creditor is in 1998 preparing to join the World Trade Organization (WTO), successor to GATT. German officials considered the Paris Club settlements, the creation and implementation of the IMF standby credit and extended facility program, and negotiations on Russia's entrance into the WTO as important successes of their multilateral policies. The shift to multilateral efforts to increase both "burden-sharing" and the amount of resources available, said one (66), was also clearly successful.

What accounts for the failure and success of German-Russian cooperation in these cases? Problems cannot be explained by a simple absence of common interests. I asked one Russian official (44) whether the delay in achieving an EU-Russia agreement was not due to conflicting interests. "No, it is in the interests of Russia, and in the interests of the EC," he said. Russian officials and politicians gave many examples of common trade interests: Germany lives on our natural gas, said a Russian political adviser (36), and wants to pull the east into western European trade. Said another official (39), commenting on positive Russian views of Germany's efforts to aid Russian reform: "The Germans are good workers, but they are not miracle workers—they cannot just print marks as we print rubles." Another official (3) said that the Russian government did not resent that Germany was the one blocking easy agreement

34. Celeste A. Wallander, "The Economization, Rationalization, and Normalization of Russian Foreign Policy," Policy Brief no. 1, Program on New Approaches to Russian Security (Cambridge, Mass: Davis Center for Russian Studies, 1997).

with the Paris Club on debt, since Russian officials understood that most of the debt was to Germany. "It is easy," he said, "for the U.S. and Japan to argue for softer terms."

Most commonly, officials explained obstacles to control and reform in terms of the incapacity of the Russia state. Perhaps surprisingly, Russian officials recognized that the fundamental obstacle to Russian integration was Russia. "The problem is how fast we can accomplish economic reform," said one (44) when I asked about international obstacles such as debt and trade restrictions. A politician (31) who complained about the lack of foreign investment conceded that a big part of the problem was that of Russian "stateness" and instability. Differences in the markets and conditions of east and west create obstacles, said another politician (33) explaining the slow pace of Russian integration in more reserved terms. An official (3) pointed out that for six months in 1992 no EBRD development aid was disbursed to Russia because Russia had not yet issued a "sovereign guarantee" that the state would be responsible for bad debts. This is aid we need and want, he said, but we cannot issue the guarantee because "what does 'sovereign guarantee' mean now? Who will guarantee? Which government structure will guarantee? For these six months, because of *just* this, no money could be disbursed." Although Russia's international trade was increasingly private in 1992, the lack of a convertible ruble meant that international trade transactions still had to be managed through the state foreign trade bank (Vneshekonombank) which was itself not competent in private market international trade. "Credits are easier to get than to implement because of our economic clumsiness," said one official (39), and while the key to reform may be private investment, "the obstacle to private investment is our own system."

German officials also gave me plenty examples of the inadequacies of the Russian state, ranging from obscure lines of authority to cope with nuclear safety, to bribery, to left-over communist officials now negotiating reform ("They are all the same people in Moscow," one official told me, "with even the same business cards and just 'Soviet Union' crossed out and 'Russia' written in"[35]). Said another (43), "Experience shows that any massive amount of money goes down the drain. . . . The problem is not our unwillingness to pay, but rather their inability to make good use of it."

Do balance-of-power policies, constraints, or incentives explain variation in cooperation for control and reform? I found no evidence that Rus-

---

35. German interview 10. He was right: I have a pile of Soviet business cards altered in the same way from my interviews in 1992, although by 1993 people usually had new ones.

sian or German officials were worried about or affected by balance-of-power factors in choosing whether to cooperate. Failure to cooperate in establishing conventional arms control was not driven in the least by power calculations, but by the pursuit of economic gain. Failure to co-operate for nuclear reactor safety resulted not because the west wanted to keep Russia weak or feared that an improved Russian nuclear industry might somehow threaten the west: quite the opposite. Both Germany and the United States have made improving Russia's nuclear safety a priority, Germany through EU programs and the United States through Nunn-Lugar.

Nor did I find any evidence that successful cooperation for nuclear weapons control, export control, debt negotiations, trade, and reform in general is accounted for by balance-of-power calculations, such as German-Russian collusion to balance the United States. Some Russian officials and politicians did entertain the possibility of strong German economic interests in Russia. "The Germans will in the end dominate the EC," said one official (11), and this is good for Russia because "they have what we need and want." A politician (7) warned that the United States should pay more attention to the opportunities for investment in Russia or German business would reap all the benefits, and another (36) said that Germany sought a generous EU-Russia trade agreement in order to dominate the Russian market as it dominated the EU. But these views were the minority; most Russian officials told me that German interest and influence were elements of Russia's objective of international economic integration, not of any balancing goals.

Even if Germany had had a deliberate policy of using Russian reform to enhance German power at the expense of its western partners, it would have failed for the simple reason that all substantial German programs and policies were multilateral, conducted through the major institutions of the EU, G–7, and IMF. As one German politician (60) said: "I do not want Germany to play a leading role in economic relations—I want others involved. " By 1996 a German official spoke of a G–8 summit to reflect Russia's involvement in political and economic issues.[36]

If not balance-of-power calculations per se, does power itself explain variation in cooperation? This would mean that cooperation failed when the most powerful countries did not seek it, and succeeded when they did. American and German support for efforts to cooperate with Russia to achieve control and reform were clearly important to cooperation. Germany and the United States were the two most important national

---

36. German interviews 67, 71, and 72.

sources of financial and technical assistance to Russia. Without American and German economic power, cooperation for control and reform in Russia would not have been as successful. German officials acknowledged the role of American leadership in making Russian reform a priority, especially in the G–7.[37]

But variation in the success and failure of cooperation is not easily explained by American and German power and preferences. Germany sought an open trade agreement with Russia, but was thwarted by opposition from the other EU members. "The vote was 11 to 1, against," one German official (55) answered wryly when I asked why Germany had failed to achieve the more generous agreement it sought. When I asked why Germany did not then pursue more open trade with Russia, he was genuinely shocked at the thought of adopting a trade policy independent of the EU, even though the EU policy was contrary to the government's assessments of the role of freer trade in Russian security relations. I asked many officials and politicians the same question, and they were unequivocal: "Germany does not have an independent trade policy," one official (3) said. Germany was also constrained in negotiating repayment of the Russian debt: although the budget deficit was a serious matter for the government in 1992 and the amount of payment Germany would have to forgive enormous, German officials ruled out any independent policy to pressure Russia for payment because Germany was constrained to deal with Russia on this issue through the Paris Club.

Even the United States was not always able to translate its economic power into its preferred outcomes. For example, the United States took a very conservative view of the need to preserve the CoCom system of restrictions as it stood. The United States, one German official (54) told me, views CoCom after the cold war like a sheriff who prefers that his town have only one street, right up the middle, so he can stand in one place and make sure that he sees all that happens. Yet the United States did not succeed in preserving the system, which was disbanded in 1994. Elements have been preserved and western countries still cooperate extensively for export control, but the Wassenaar Accord is considerably weaker than CoCom. Power and preferences play a role in explaining cooperation success and failure, but they are insufficient alone.

Did institutions support cooperation, and did cases of failed or uneven cooperation result from the absence of institutions? Missing institu-

---

37. German interview 61. At the same time, he resented how the United States took the lead when Germany had up to then provided the great bulk of assistance resources. "The U.S. practices collective leadership—it leads and then collects payments from us."

tions did play a role here, although not in every failure or delay. Failure to cooperate for conventional arms control, for example, was the straightforward result of a lack of common interests. But in cases where there were common interests, the lack of appropriate institutions did contribute to cooperation failure. Western countries sought cooperation for nuclear reactor safety, but were plagued by the lack of national financial resources to compensate former Soviet countries for dismantling their dangerous facilities. The problem of legal liability in case of an accident was the major obstacle. Despite serious incentives to aid Russia in this area, the German government was not willing to risk making substantial efforts without multilateral commitment and co-responsibility.

In contrast, the preexisting systems for nuclear and technology control supported multilateral cooperation in coping with Russia's instability, integrating it into the systems on terms of the international community, and creating changes in internal Russian procedures and capacities. This is not a problem, one German official (58) said; "Russia is an equal supplier and just another country in the club." Although CoCom itself ended in 1994, its procedures and principles served as the basis for Russia's developing control system, and were adapted for inclusion in the new control regime. Like the CFE treaty, CoCom had been created for a different purpose and maintaining it created substantial problems. But also like the CFE treaty, CoCom had some valuable aspects: the system of controls and information exchange among members was useful to Germany and attractive to Russia. Although both German and Russian officials were clear that they would have preferred to drop the system of restrictions, they wanted to have a system of multilateral cooperation for trade in technology. Therefore, the preexisting regime of multilateral technology controls made it possible to sustain cooperation in this area, although with adaptations.

International institutions were crucial in supporting multilateral cooperation for economic reform. The Paris Club enabled the creditor countries to sustain the principle that Russia must pay its debts to all its creditors, to offer easier terms of repayment than they could have extended individually, and to remain unified among themselves. The IMF was simply a necessary condition for achieving the fundamental requirement of Russian reform, controlling inflation and stabilizing the ruble, without which Russian and German ideas about the role of private investment and trade in the long-term transformation of the Russian economy were meaningless. This policy could not be sustained in any way other than through multilateral cooperation. Germany did not have the financial resources, and, more important, only the IMF had the legitimacy and credibility to implement policies of conditionality for painful Russian reform. Germany's interest in Russian stability and Yeltsin was too direct for Germany to be able credibly to withhold assistance. An official (62) said, "We cannot do without the IMF because as an international body it has more weight, it can speak more frankly than we can. It is a kind of 'cordon sanitaire' between Russia and us." Furthermore, IMF rules come with IMF resources, said another (3): "The IMF has the whip and the carrot, which we do not."

The importance of the international legitimacy of conditionality was reflected in Russian views. It is easier for Russia to accept IMF conditions, said one official (38), since the IMF is an institution and Russia is a member. However, the idea that the IMF would not be subject to political influences was not entirely borne out in my discussions with Russian officials. When I asked one (3) whether the IMF understands Russia, he smiled and said:

> The IMF understands quite well that we have serious problems and cannot strictly follow the standard IMF program. The Russian government understands that it is important to conform—to some degree—to IMF recommendations. And everyone understand that an agreement is essential. . . . It is not a problem of understanding, it is a problem of politics. Speeches about IMF and World Bank independence are not serious, because the G–7 countries are the creditors.

Institutions were important because by 1992 it was clear to the officials involved that multilateral strategies and policies were necessary and bilateral policies woefully inadequate. For German officials, it was a fundamental assumption that these efforts would fail unless they were multilateral, and the most important multilateral efforts would be managed through western international economic institutions. German officials were clear on the country's interest in not coping with Russia alone. Said one (6), "We cannot shoulder the entire burden of assistance on our own and need partners, so multilateralizing is a way to bring the U.S. and other European states into the process." Although multilateral cooperation is costly in terms of delays and compromise, said another official (3), "to do it yourself means you have to have the money for it: for political and financial reasons, there is not much of an alternative." What does the EBRD do that German programs cannot, I asked another official (1)? "The financial needs in the east are so enormous that we are looking for organizations that have enough money to cope, and also so that we are not providing only German money, but rather have burden-sharing in Europe."

But beyond the question of resources, I found German officials convinced that effective international assistance for control and reform required multilateral action because individual deviations would undermine joint efforts. One official (24) pointed out that the actions of any one state can prevent success. "We must work through coordinated measures, and not allow ourselves to be divided by individual concerns." Another (38) said that multilateral efforts were necessary because failure by any one state meant failure of the system as a whole. We told them, he said, "You must control the export of weapons and technology and you cannot leave the decisions to some manager of a company: one cannot just leave these decisions to people who want to make money." Yes, said one politician (16), when you work multilaterally there has to be negotiation and compromise, "but you can do more with multilateral instruments, and that makes it worth the work to compromise and negotiate." Given the Paris Club's principle that debtors cannot not pay one member before the other, "there is no way out of multilateralizing this issue," said a finance ministry official (61). And in much the same way that NATO reassures Germany's neighbors, economic multilateralism also makes sure that Germany does not seek a special relationship with Russia at the expense of other countries. One economic policy official (4) told me: "It is good for Russia to have good relations with all the EC, not just with Germany, and it is good for Germany not to be out in Russia alone. We must try to prevent suspicion about Germany. Work in the EU makes the allies understand what Germany is doing and what it seeks to accomplish."

I found Russian officials to be less committed to multilateral policies in principle, and more to whatever works. One Russian official (62) said that Russia uses both: bilateral relations are simple, but multilateral relations establish Russian influence and presence on a wider basis. Russian reliance on bilateral strategies was sometimes a result of exclusion. One foreign ministry official (50) said, "In relations with Germany we give priority to the bilateral relations because we are not accepted in the institutions." Bilateral relations with Germany were themselves a way to use influence with Germany to join European institutions and become further integrated, said a politician (53). Russian officials were relatively straightforward in saying that Russia sought to use Germany's greater interest in trade and greater fear of instability to pull the west into assisting Russia through international institutions. One official (10) pointed out that this is what happened in the course of German unification: German focus on unification meant it brought NATO guarantees and the G–7 into the process. And given the scope of Russia's problem, Russian officials also saw multilateral approaches as unavoidable. The Paris Club, said one (3), "is an uneasy but useful structure," and there is little to be gained in dealing with the western countries separately because we have to solve all of these problems with all of them.

Therefore, institutions did play an independent role in supporting German and Russian cooperation. Existing nuclear and technology control regimes created stability and incentives for inclusion, while the absence of any nuclear reactor safety regime meant states had no system for liability and co-responsibility. In the economic sphere, multilateral institutions were necessary for the financial resources, rules, and procedures, in support of a reasonable, if far from perfect, path of reform. Even more important, Russia sought to enter an international economic system which required institutional membership to gain access to its resources and opportunities. Institutions were unavoidable given Russia's strategy of seeking international assistance for internal reform.

VARIATION IN SECURITY PROBLEMS AND INSTITUTIONAL FORMS

Did variation in problems affect German and Russian strategies and the role of institutions in them? The obstacles to cooperation in all these cases were linkage problems: how to alter Russia's choice environment to favor otherwise costly policies. For the most part, linkage institutions existed and supported multilateral cooperation in Russian strategies. The most basic and immediate problem the Yeltsin government faced was making the ruble a stable and convertible currency, and as the quintessential linkage institution, the IMF had a major impact on Russian strategies.

But the IMF alone was not enough to effect linkage on all issues. Russia faced an array of international financial institutions that promised resources and participation at the cost of negotiation, compromise, and change. The G–7 coordinated western aid and economic efforts, the Paris Club kept track of debt, the EBRD and the World Bank offered resources for marketization and infrastructure. Because these institutions were linked in their purposes and in their memberships, Russian officials could not hope to exploit German vulnerability for resources and softer deals. These institutions changed Russia's international environment: it was dealing not only with states as partners, but with institutions as the playing field. In the case of nuclear and export controls, integration in the system was related directly to good foreign relations with the west. "In order to be a good member of the club, you have to have export controls," as one German official (38) put it. The advantages of join-ing an export control regime outweighed the difficulties, and this was reinforced by high-level attention and lobbying in G–7–Russian rela-tions.

Germany faced the problem that its overwhelming degree of "expo-sure" and its stake in Russian stability made it open to exploitation by both Russia and its allies. Russia could exploit Germany by demanding resources, and Germany's allies could exploit it by counting on its vital interests to lead it to aid Russia even in the absence of help from others. One German official (37) said, "It is difficult to force Russia to play by the rules, because to squeeze the Russians at this time would be counter to our interests." About Germany's allies, another (10) said that the element of subsidies in trade with Russia by companies in the former GDR did not bring complaints in GATT or the EU because "they are happy to let us pay billions to support trade policy in Rus-sia." Institutions were for Germany the way to avoid Russian pressure and western abandonment.

The prevalence of linkage problems in these cases meant that cooper-ation was most successful given clear international rules, procedures, re-sources, and incentives. Linkage mechanisms were effective. If nothing else, one Russian official (3) said, dealing with the G–7 raises the level of attention and discussion within the Russian government. This is the way we get the president and his staff to read the policy papers we write, he added. If Russia could join CoCom, another official (37) pointed out, it would gain access to those technologies. A German official (55) noted that standards of membership are meaningless without incentives. For example, he said, all the EU can do is offer trade. "If we were very strict on what kind of economy they must have, we would have to come up with the money. Unlike the IMF, which is providing the money after es-tablishing the criteria, we do not have the right."

The value of linkage institutions among the western countries in deal-ing with Russia was not just the simple face of unity; established rules and procedures limited bargaining among the western allies. Delays in establishing the International Technology and Science Center (ITSC), disputes about changing CoCom, diverging views about how generous to be in debt issues, and even about the Russia-EU agreement under ne-gotiation reflected different western preferences. But in none of these cases did diverging western views produce unilateral policies. Only in the matter of nuclear reactor safety was there a failure to narrow the scope of disagreement in order to maintain one basic policy toward Rus-sia. Where institutional rules and procedures did constrain bargaining, successful cooperation was the norm. In meeting these kinds of obstacles, institutions favored cooperation not only by offering Russian conditional resources under clear rules, but by keeping the western member states united on the rules and conditionality.[38]

In addition to linkage problems and competing views about new policies and procedures, the obstacles to cooperation in these cases included uncertainty about the future. German officials faced the problem of uncertainty about Russia's future, and Russian officials faced the need to reassure others in order to attract the necessary cooperation. In this regard, the solution was to integrate Russia (and other states of the former Soviet Union) into the system of international institutions in order to create a stake in that system for Russia and to diminish uncertainty in the west that Russia was gaining internal control and pursuing reform. A German official (24) said that if Russia can cooperate with the IMF and World Bank and agree with the Paris Club, western uncertainty will be diminished and then private investment will come. "We are trying to rope them into a system," said another official (38); "it is better to have them in our arms." Joining export control systems is not only about the controls, he went on, but is part of a political process: "With these [memberships] comes the readiness to discuss issues when they are raised by other governments—this is very important because this is something entirely new for them." I asked one official (62) why Germany did not simply defer Russia's debt: "Because we have to educate them about how these things are done, and we have to tie it to steps, to the reform and progress they make." Ultimately uncertainties about Russia could be reduced only by integration and development. Said one German official (57) on the prospects for nonproliferation: "We just do not know what will happen in the future. Who knows who will be in control of these governments in the future, or even what the governments in place will do? All we can do is try to support them, include them, and with all this international aid we are trying to help stabilize the democratic situation."

Therefore, the substantial, if uneven, record of international cooperation for Russian reform and control is due in large measure to the set of international institutions suited to coping with the problems of linkage and assurance. These institutions offered substantial and often crucial technical and financial resources very attractive to the reformist Russian government and (not least important) powerful domestic Russian eco-

38. Lisa L. Martin, "Interests, Power, and Multilateralism," *International Organization* 46 (Autumn 1992): 765–792.

nomic interests. These resources were far from costless and entailed an extensive set of rules and standards for membership and access to the benefits. Because of this mix of benefits and standards, Russian and German strategies focused on involving and integrating Russia in the set of international institutions that would help to cope with uncertainty about Russia's economic prospects and reformist intentions. Although these institutions sometimes changed to adapt to new circumstances and the lack of a regime for nuclear reactor safety was a major failure, the cases in this chapter provide clear support for the hypothesis that variation in underlying cooperation problems matters and that institutions are most effective when their forms and functions provide the appropriate instruments to cope with the obstacles at hand.

INSTITUTIONAL EFFECTIVENESS

Finally, was it the case that institutions more successfully supported cooperation where they were layered? Without the set of linked and reinforcing western institutions, cooperation for assistance in Russian control and reform almost certainly would have failed. The IMF was important for Russian officials not merely because of its resources and rules, but because it was linked to the G–7 and its assessments were used by G–7 countries contemplating other areas of economic cooperation. Even public Russian government statements were clear that all major Russian hopes and goals centered on eventual inclusion in the G–7.[39] The Paris Club was important to cash-strapped Russian officials not because of a principled commitment to pay debts, but because negotiating in the Paris Club meant negotiating with the G–7, with close attention from the EU, the EBRD, and the IMF as well. Export controls were important for Russian security, but even more important was the knowledge that failure to participate in a western-based export control regime had implications for Russian hopes to gain assistance from the G–7 and eventually to join GATT.

From the German point of view, this set of interlocking institutions protected Germany from having to cope with a weak and unstable Russia alone. The set of institutions forced compromises in dealing with Russia: Germany did not get the open trade regime it sought from the EU, but it did achieve constant attention to the problem of debt repayment. Germany and its allies often had different preferences, but they

---

39. See the reporting on Yeltsin's statements at the Munich G–7 meeting in "Myunkenskaya vstrecha," *Diplomaticheskiy vestnik*, no. 15–16 (15–31 August 1992), pp. 3–13.

held to common policies across the range of issues, rooted in the set of international economic and financial institutions with the G–7 at its core. Ultimately, it was the scope of the problem of Russian stability, control, and reform that made the complex set of international institutions necessary for German cooperation with Russia.

The cases of control and reform in German-Russian relations show that layering is important for linkage and assurance problems. It was not merely the promise of any one benefit in the short term but the importance of a range of economic and political benefits at stake that influenced Russian strategies and made control and reform possible. The G–7 was the fulcrum of relations with the west, and all negotiations with the EU, the IMF, the Paris Club, the EBRD, and GATT were related as a result. This was partly because of the interlinked nature of the institutions created by the west during the cold war, but it was also because the problems of control and reform were substantively interlinked themselves. Progress on trade made little sense without a convertible ruble; therefore the Russian strategies for dealing with inflation and debt could not be chosen without regard for their effects on Russia's trade ambitions. This linkage extended to issues of nuclear and export control, because these were not merely security issues, but also issues of trade and integration given Russia's "G–8" aspirations.

The question of institutional effectiveness and layering brings us back to where we began in Chapter 2: institutions are valuable to states because they help decision makers cope with uncertainty about their security environment, the intentions and choices of other states, and the effects of their own choice of strategies. For Russian officials, the set of interlinked institutions established what could be expected by the Russian government and what was expected of it. Because of the institutional context, Russian officials were not faced with one-shot decisions and short-term injections of aid or advice, but instead with the process of regular meetings and negotiations, centered around yearly G–7 summits. For German officials, the interlinked institutions upon which Germany relied and in which it is embedded provided for ongoing discussions and negotiations with the Russian government as a way to assess its policies and development. They provided a structure for gradually embedding Russia in relations from which it could increasingly benefit. Most important of all, this interlinked set of effective and powerful institutions was Germany's ultimate guarantee that it would not be left alone to cope with the risky and costly process of Russia's transformation after the cold war. Predictions that Germany and Russia would seek to escape the constraints of cold war institutions turn out to be fundamentally wrong.

[8]

Balancing Acts: Power,
Interests, and Institutions

As I was finishing this book, I happened to go to Leipzig during a research trip in Germany, and on a tourist foray visited the Völkerschlachtdenkmal. This "monument to the Battle of the Nations" was
inaugurated on the hundredth anniversary of that 1813 battle, the decisive defeat of Napoleon by combined European forces, among them
Russia and Prussia. The battle resulted in 120,000 casualties and was
the single most deadly in the European wars of the nineteenth century.
The monument has an ambiguous and even disturbing meaning, however; it was not created as a straightforward memorial of death and
war. It is massive, with internal decorations and sculptures that glorify
warriors as much as mourn their loss, and was a project of the German
Patriots' League. Far from expressing regret for Germany's role in war,
the monument warns against Germany's disunity and the destruction
wrought upon German people as a consequence: Saxony (the region of
Germany in which Leipzig is found) had fought as an ally of Napoleon's
France against other German states, including Prussia. An exhibition
inside showed that in the twentieth century the monument has been
used for disturbing purposes. It was a symbol of German nationalism
during World War I and the Nazis used it from the 1930s to symbolize
German supremacy and power and the dangers of enemies on all sides.
During the cold war, it was used by the communist regime to show
that the GDR was the true embodiment of the German nation, and to
establish the historical roots of GDR-Soviet friendship in the unity of
Prussia and Russia against enemies from the west and turncoats from
within.

As I climbed the monument and thought about its ambiguous images, it seemed to reflect the fundamentally open question of the nature of German-Russian security relations explored in this book. A monument against a war could be exploited by a movement reflecting features of Germany society which had made that country the center of two shattering wars; the same monument could be a symbol to justify a war against the Soviet Union, killing some twenty million of its citizens, and then to justify occupation and "friendship" by that same Soviet Union as rooted in history. No wonder scholars can come up with mutually contradictory predictions about Europe's future and the nature of German-Russian security relations. As this book has shown, however, it is not enough to know the history of Germany and Russia in which power and interests play a role in security to understand contemporary relations and the future. After the cold war, "history" includes international military, political, and economic institutions which are part of German-Russian security relations.

Institutional Effects

What does the record of German-Russian security relations from 1991 to 1996 tell us about the role that international institutions can perform in fostering security cooperation among states?

- A significant number of common interests was the necessary condition for German-Russian security cooperation.
- The mere potential for the use of force did not prevent German-Russian security cooperation: what mattered was its costliness and the likelihood of its use.
- Uncertainty was as much a problem for cooperation as were conflicting interests and use of force: institutions enabled German and Russian decision makers to reduce uncertainty about capabilities, intentions, and policies.
- Institutions affected German and Russian security strategies in three specific ways: in monitoring activity and providing information, in specifying rules and limiting bargaining, and in altering the costs and benefits of alternative courses of action through resources and norms.

First, common interests were a necessary condition for German-Russian cooperation in security relations. The existence of common interests by no means ruled out competing interests; the evidence showed that even in areas of agreement such as the problem that instability in the former Soviet Union posed for security, German and Russian officials had competing views about what kinds of settlements or Russian involvement were desirable. That common interests are the starting point for cooperation may be obvious, but it is not trivial: it explains failure to restrain conventional arms sales. The analysis in Chapter 3, as well as concrete examples in subsequent chapters, showed that the condition of common interests was easily met given the security environment and the countries' national interests. In particular, the distinction both German and Russian officials made between security "threats" and "risks" is a concrete example of how the degree of common interests varies, and how it can often be quite substantial even in core security areas.

Second, the evidence presented in this book shows that the mere potential for the use of force did not prevent German-Russian security cooperation: what mattered was its costliness and the likelihood of its use. Force is not nearly as usable as a stark image of anarchy and self-help might imply. German and Russian officials assessed the use of force as too costly or ineffective for coping with many security problems; this made security cooperation a rational, viable alternative. Furthermore, this appraisal did not spring from naive or optimistic views held by these individuals. Russian officials clearly saw more scope for force in CIS conflicts and ultimately did not hesitate to employ it. The discussed in Chapter 6 show that the high salience of Russian military force in the former Soviet Union did undermine both communication and coordination, as realist theories would expect.[1] Nor were German officials simple pacifists: they sought to enhance Germany's capacity for out-of-area and Eurocorps military missions. The evidence shows, however, considerable variation in German and Russian assessments of the wisdom of employing force, and where it was deemed costly or ineffective, security cooperation was a viable strategy.

Third, uncertainty was as much a problem for cooperation as were conflicting interests and use of force. "Optimistic realists" also would expect that substantial common interests and the high cost and low effectiveness of using force would be conditions that facilitate security cooperation.[2] However, even when the "objective" conditions are present, uncertainty can still undercut cooperation if states cannot be confident about common interests, low threat, and the limited usefulness of force.

---

1. James Morrow, "Modeling the Forms of International Cooperation, Distribution versus Information," *International Organization* 48 (Summer 1994): 387–429, at pp. 413–414.
2. Charles L. Glaser, "Realists as Optimists: Cooperation as Self-Help," *International Security* 19 (Winter 1994/95): 50–90.

In principle, uncertainty could be reduced in many ways, but one of the best ways, as we have seen, in the German-Russian case was through institutions such as the CFE, which put clear limits on military forces, and NATO and the OSCE, which stabilized expectations and understandings about nonthreatening intentions. Institutions may not be a necessary condition for benign security dilemmas, but they happen to be a primary reason for the benign security dilemma in German-Russian relations after the cold war. A benign security dilemma was not itself a sufficient condition for German-Russian security cooperation, because it was a product of international institutions, as my evidence clearly shows.

Reducing uncertainty is crucial to the choice of rational security strategies. Anarchy cannot be changed by institutions short of world government, but its deleterious effects can be managed if uncertainty is reduced. The realist tradition is right that states worry about security lemons: they fear being exploited because with survival at stake, self-help is the ultimate recourse. Perhaps more than any other two countries in Europe, Germany and Russia have ample reason to fear that the other is a security lemon, bent upon expansion, conquest, and destruction. But German and Russian officials are not helpless in the face of post–cold war uncertainty and historical memory, in large measure because their foreign relations are conducted within a web of military, political, and economic institutions that give them a valuable source of information about capabilities, intentions, and policies. Although nearly all the important institutions were created under a different configuration of international power, they remained valuable, even though far from perfect, in the new international system. German-Russian security cooperation was not a matter of trust, it was a matter of information, facilitated by international and European institutions.

Therefore, on the point where institutionalist expectations diverge most clearly from those of both pessimistic and optimistic realism, the evidence from the German-Russian case clearly supports the institutionalist hypothesis. Institutions provide information that reduces uncertainty in security relations, making cooperation possible. Institutions do not force states to choose strategies contrary to their security interests, and this is not the standard for evaluating institutional effects in security relations. The standard is whether choices and outcomes were different from what they would have been in the absence of institutions. The evidence is that institutions affected the calculations and strategies chosen by German and Russian decision makers.

Fourth, institutions affected security strategies in three specific ways: in monitoring activity and providing information, in specifying rules and limiting bargaining, and in altering the costs and benefits of alternative courses of action by offering resources and establishing norms.

Institutions enabled decision makers to pursue desired outcomes when unilateral choice of cooperative security strategies would be risky, irresponsible, and even irrational because they allowed for monitoring mutual restraint and good behavior. This was the case with conventional and nuclear arms control: unilateral restraint will not be chosen if it will be exploited, but arms control regimes supported self-interested restraint and reductions by making them multilateral. Even where German and Russian officials were not highly suspicious of one another's intentions, institutions such as the CFE treaty and its extensive implementation rules and verification procedures made the choice of cooperative strategies possible by creating assurance about other states' intentions and actions.

In specifying rules and establishing focal points, institutions affected German and Russian strategies by narrowing the range of competition and bargaining. This effect was especially important given the systemic and structural changes with the end of the cold war, combined with the revolutionary changes at the state level with German unification and Soviet dissolution. It would not have been surprising if everything in German-Russian security relations had been up for grabs by 1992; that very little ultimately was is due in large measure to the governing and stabilizing effects of multiple institutions. There was a great deal of hard bargaining and pursuit of national advantages across a substantial range of issues, including troop withdrawals, the CFE treaty, nuclear proliferation, Soviet/Russian debt, and related economic issues. This bargaining, however, most often produced mutually acceptable outcomes rather than failure to agree. The primary reason for the success of the transition was that Germany and Russia were constrained by the rules of the game embodied in institutions that made renegotiation difficult and refusal to compromise risky. Institutions provided effective and resilient focal points, and their absence would have led to the kinds of unstable relations and failure to cooperate predicted by realism.

Institutions altered the cost-benefit situation to favor otherwise unappealing choices. This was most clear in linkage problems: the Russian choice, for example, to adopt a system of technology export controls that constrained revenues but opened the way to western high technology trade. Institutions could not force Russia to make choices harmful to the national interest. Instead, institutions such as the Paris Club raised the costs of defection and the benefits of cooperation. In addition to offering real resources such as access to trade and financing on the condition of adherence to institutional rules, institutions altered costs and benefits by enunciating norms that states would either visibly live by or visibly violate. By establishing norms and procedures on a multilateral basis, NACC assisted the CIS states in coming to a settlement on their CFE allocations, as we saw in Chapter 5. Even political institutions that are not terribly constraining, such as the OSCE, increased the reputational and linkage costs of being the "holdout" and of violating norms.

Thus, security institutions did matter: they were independent factors that affected the choice of strategies, themselves not solely determined by the power and the interests of the two states. States do not always seek to cooperate in security affairs. German and Russian officials were uninterested in multilateral strategies when they had no common interests (conventional arms sales) and when they believed that force was usable, low-cost, and effective (early in conflicts in the former Soviet Union). In other cases, however, where cooperation was desirable but not easy and where there were shared interests, institutions supported multilateral cooperation in managing military balances, preventing and managing conflicts, and negotiating the process of control and reform in Russia.

INSTITUTIONAL EFFECTIVENESS

How did institutions matter?

- Institutions were least important in collaboration problems and most important for assurance, coordination, and linkage problems.
- Institutions were more effective when their forms and functions matched the security tasks that confronted Germany and Russia, but the relationship is more complex than that proposed in Chapter 2.
- Institutions were more effective when they were layered, but only if states were clear on the problems they faced and did not allow "interlocking" institutions to become "interblocking."

First, perhaps surprisingly given the general acceptance of Prisoner's Dilemma, neither fear of exploitation nor temptations to defect played a large role in German and Russian strategies. This is not to say that German and Russian officials did not have in mind the need to protect themselves against a hostile Russia and Germany, respectively. These officials were realists enough to know that exploitation and defection must always be guarded against.

[198]

What is remarkably clear from the evidence, however, is how little these concerns plagued the German and Russian governments. I fully expected to find that military balances and military conflicts preoccupied German and Russian officials with classic Prisoner's Dilemma concerns, that attempts to cooperate would be thwarted by defection, and that only sanctioning and monitoring could hope to overcome such concerns. Instead, as Chapters 4–6 showed, the primary problems officials spoke of in thinking about military balances and conflicts were competitive bargaining (coordination problems) and the pervasive problems of uncertainty and information (assurance). The reason for the absence of collaboration problems and predominance of coordination and assurance problems goes back to one of the central findings in Chapter 3: Germany and Russia were not confronted with threats but rather with risks as their main security issues.

Indeed, where collaboration problems played the largest role was in Germany's relations with its western allies in cooperation on Russian economic reform. These aid programs could have a chance of being effective only if Russia faced a united front of western donors offering assistance on consistent conditions. "Defections," either making separate deals or failing to contribute, would leave Germany exposed and vulnerable, and would undermine the fundamental premise of its security policy toward Russia, market reform and international integration.

Similarly, where temptation to defect played a role in Russia's security strategies, it was not in relations with Germany, but with Russia's new neighbors. For the most part, this meant potential Russian exploitation of its weaker neighbors through unilateral action. But Russia's neighbors held some cards as well and could make Russia's life difficult through noncooperation in conventional arms, nuclear arms, proliferation, and economic issues tied to the effects of the Soviet breakup.

So for collaboration problems, institutions played a role not in direct German-Russian relations, but in affecting relations among the western countries in dealing with Russia and among the post-Soviet countries in managing their transition to independence and sovereignty. Germany's reliance on the network of western international economic and financial institutions was pervasive and effective in coordinating western policies, maintaining western involvement, and enhancing the credibility of conditionality that Russian officials had to face. The record in relations among the CIS countries was more mixed. In the case of the CFE and NPT treaties, institutions were quite effective in managing the process. In addition, international principles and norms played a supporting role in Russia's withdrawal from the Baltics. In the case of conflict management and resolution, however, Russia's neighbors proved far less able to count on institutions such as the UN and the OSCE to encourage Russian restraint, although Russia turned increasingly to those institutions for legitimacy and resources as its unilateral policies failed to resolve conflicts to its satisfaction in Abkhazia and Nagorno-Karabakh.

Far more important to the course of German-Russian relations were the three obstacles to cooperation less studied in institutional theory to date. The problems of assurance, coordination, and linkage were the focus of German and Russian concerns, and were the real difficulties with which the officials and politicians I interviewed struggled. Assurance was central because of the overwhelming importance of uncertainty about intentions and balance after the cold war. Coordination problems infused virtually all the issues in German-Russian relations because change in international conditions and in Germany and Russia themselves brought into question bargains that had been achieved with great difficulty under very different circumstances, raising the possibility of instability and disintegration of established expectations. And linkage was important because it was the underlying bargain of German-Russian relations: long-term security would be assured by reforming Russia and integrating it in the international system, and Germany would play a major political and financial role in this process.

The predominance of assurance, coordination, and linkage issues may be an artifact of the time in which this case study was conducted. Because my research looked at a period of fundamental structural change in the international system and revolutionary change in the German and Russian states, uncertainty and the attendant potential for instability were both pervasive problems. Therefore, it may not be surprising that the main problems officials faced were questions about the intentions, capabilities, and policies of other states, and that previously agreed-upon matters, such as Russian troop withdrawal and the CFE treaty, were thrown into question and might need to be renegotiated. However, we cannot dismiss the role of institutions in supporting security cooperation as just a unique feature of German-Russian relations at this unusual point in history, because institutions should (according to realist theories) be least relevant in such periods of change. That old institutions were valuable to both Germany and Russia in such a period is strong support for institutional hypotheses on how institutions matter.

Second, institutions were more effective when their forms and functions matched the security tasks that confronted Germany and Russia, but the relationship is more complex than the one I proposed in Chapter 2. In the cases of control and reform, institutions with the appropriate forms and functions were crucial to effectiveness. Where preexisting institutions combined the promise of resources, the threat of withholding them, and clear rules of conditionality and performance, linkage obstacles were substantially overcome. Institutions such as the EU, the IMF, the Paris Club, the NPT regime, and the evolving technology control regime offered Russia substantial benefits in exchange for adapting to well-established and clear rules. Furthermore, the clarity and stability of these institutions were important for the forging of substantially common policies by western countries. The negative case of nuclear reactor safety underlines that appropriate institutional form and function can be crucial to security cooperation.

For troop withdrawals and military balances, institutions were effective in supporting security cooperation because they helped to overcome problems of assurance and coordination by providing information and establishing focal points and rules that limited instability and renegotiation. However, the institutions had not been created to deal with assurance and coordination problems: the troop withdrawal agreements, the CFE treaty, the nonproliferation regime, and even institutional mechanisms to limit Germany's military activities had been designed to overcome the more difficult problems of monitoring and sanctioning. These institutional rules and procedures read as a textbook case of mechanisms to create incentives for cooperation in repeated Prisoner's Dilemma: monitoring, sanctioning, repeated interaction, and small steps in the process.[3]

The reason why institutions designed to overcome collaboration problems proved effective for assurance and coordination has to do with the difference between specific and general assets of institutions. Features such as information, ongoing interactions, and established rules and procedures are general assets, as long as they are symmetrical. They are features of all international institutions, so any arms control regime designed to overcome collaboration problems will be useful for transparency and bargaining as well. But sanctioning is a very specific asset: if an institution does not have it, that institution cannot be useful for collaboration problems which require threat of retaliation or sanction to work.

Similarly, linkage institutions, such as the IMF, the World Bank, and the Paris Club, embody specific assets: they include not only the general

---

3. See Robert M. Axelrod and Robert O. Keohane, "Achieving Cooperation under Anarchy: Strategies and Institutions," in *Cooperation under Anarchy*, ed. Kenneth A. Oye (Princeton: Princeton University Press, 1986), for this list of institutional features.

institutional assets of information and rules to constrain bargaining, but also positive and negative sanctions in the forms of access to or denial of financial and technical resources. In this regard, linkage mechanisms are more akin to those for collaboration. Transparency and coordination measures will not be useful when linkage issues are the problem because they do not provide the leverage needed to create incentives for altering strategies. This explains the failure of nuclear reactor safety: both the absence of a specific institution, and the weakness of G–24 in terms of offering rewards and sanctions.

More problematic for the hypothesis is the mixed evidence of cooperation and institutional effects in the cases of conflicts discussed in Chapter 6. Despite the availability of a wide variety of institutions with functions and forms for sanctioning (UN Security Council), aid in negotiation and conflict resolution (UN peacekeeping and "good offices"), and transparency (the OSCE), there were many failures to cooperate multilaterally to prevent or resolve conflicts in Yugoslavia and the former Soviet Union. Some successes occurred, including Macedonia, the avoidance of competitive intervention on the part of the great powers, and eventual Russian acceptance of international oversight of its peace operations in the former Soviet Union. These limited successes all have in common one element: they were successful efforts to promote transparency, assurance, and legitimacy through the looser institutions of the UN and the OSCE.

The failures to sanction aggression in Yugoslavia, to prevent Russian unilateralism in the CIS, and to use effective peacekeeping when the model and institution already existed are major failures of institutional support for multilateral security cooperation. However, as I noted in Chapter 6, the cases suggest that cooperation failed for institutional (as well as realist) reasons: the mismatch of institutions to tasks. In Yugoslavia, states could not agree on whether the conflict was a matter of aggression or instability, which meant that there was never a consistent policy of either sanctioning or conflict resolution. In the cases of Russian unilateralism, where power and self-interest loom large as explanations, part of the Russian argument for unilateral strategies was that multilateral peacekeeping was not effective since it required consent and impartiality, and these conditions could not be met in CIS conflicts.

The significance of appropriate form and function for different kinds of security problems is also supported by the substantial evidence that German and Russian officials took NATO's form and function quite seriously. NATO was not useful for security problems involving risks, both German and Russian officials told me, because it is an alliance for collective defense and has an exclusive membership. Changes in functions and increase in membership would make NATO "just like the OSCE," a de-velopment Russians did not mind but most Germans sought to avoid. The more important point is that officials and politicians in both coun-tries saw a very strong relationship between institutional form, function, purpose, and effectiveness.

Third, institutions were more effective when they were layered, but only if states were clear on the problems they faced and did not allow "interlocking" institutions to become "interblocking." Because of multi-ple institutions with different forms and functions, Europe now has a dense security regime that addresses multiple security tasks and makes cooperation in any one area less risky. The effectiveness of this regime lies precisely in its comprehensiveness. There is no one single security problem (aggression, bargaining, transparency, linkage), and hence no single solution (monitoring/sanctioning, coordination, transparency, conditionality). Although similar in a sense to the Concert of Europe, this regime is more stable and substantial because it does more than offer a mechanism for restraint and consultation among the great pow-ers. The debate about whether collective defense, or collective security, or a concert system is best for security misses the point: they are useful for different things, and have intrinsic weaknesses as well.[4]

Layering was effective in supporting German and Russian coopera-tion for slightly different reasons, however. For Germany, the multiplic-ity of institutions in which it was a member made cooperation in one arena, for example conventional arms control, less risky. Should Russia defect, Germany could rely upon its political and military alliances to cope with the effects of such failed cooperation. For Russia, layering did not provide this asset, and Russia would have to fall back upon its own resources. Instead, layering was effective because it linked issues in many different areas of military, political, and economic relations, creat-ing incentives for the west to deal with Russia on a comprehensive basis and the opportunity for Russia to use the west's interest in security and stability to obtain resources and cooperation. States are not altruistic, so the G–7 countries were involved in the question of Russian reform at this time because the G–7 increasingly managed a set of military and politi-cal issues including terrorism, nuclear proliferation, and other more tra-ditional security concerns. The G–7 itself was the connection not only to

---

4. For discussions of the relative strengths and weaknesses of different systems, see Charles A. Kupchan and Clifford A. Kupchan, "Concerts, Collective Security, and the Fu-ture of Europe," *International Security* 16 (Summer 1991): 114–161; Richard K. Betts, "Sys-tems for Peace or Causes of war?" *International Security* 17 (Summer 1992): 5–43; Robert Jervis, "From Balance to Concert: A Study of International Security Cooperation," in *Coop-eration under Anarchy*, ed. Oye.

financial and economic institutions, but to political and military institutions including NATO, the UN Security Council, and regimes for nuclear weapons control. Layering was an asset not for fallback positions, but for extending Russia's reach and significance in the process of international governance so common in relations among the western great powers.

Nonetheless, these cases show that there is an important problem with layering. The mix of multiple institutions with different and overlapping forms and functions can itself be an obstacle to effective security cooperation if states are not clear on the problems they are facing and what are the appropriate instruments to deal with them. This was demonstrated in Chapter 6; disagreements and confusion on whether conflicts in Yugoslavia and the former Soviet Union required forceful action (peace enforcement) or cooperative intervention (peacekeeping) were compounded by the involvement of multiple security institutions with incompatible missions. This is also the core dilemma of NATO enlargement: will the NATO of the twenty-first century have clear missions with appropriate institutional form and function, or will it become an ineffective mix of incompatible ambitions and purposes? Institutions are not substitutes for clear-headed and realistic assessment of power and interests, and can contribute to policies of appeasement, buck-passing, and defection which can come to characterize any diplomacy.

FURTHER INSTITUTIONAL RESEARCH

The most important finding of this book that warrants further work in institutional theory is the significance of institutional variation for understanding the prospects for cooperation. In particular, institutional theory has not looked carefully at the question of how institutions may themselves hinder effective cooperation when they have inappropriate forms and functions. These cases are ever more apparent in the real world, especially given the increasing frequency of internal and ethnic conflicts, and provide a new take on cooperation failure. If the international community is going to get involved in conflicts such as those in Yugoslavia and Somalia, the least it can do is do no harm. An understanding of institutional variation and its relation to form and function might also help scholars to explain why not all institutions and institutional actions are seen by all states as benign, a fact that seemed to escape too many for too long in the proposals for NATO enlargement.

Another important result of this study neglected in institutional theory is variation in the degree of penetration of institutions in national strategies. Even before unification, Germany was a strong supporter of international organizations and took a leading role in European integration. Since the end of the cold war, Germany has supported reform of European institutions and their inclusion of eastern European and formerly Soviet countries. Scholars of Germany have long noted that the role of institutions in German policies is more than strictly instrumental and tactical: German officials and politicians almost literally do not contemplate any foreign policy without reference to the meaning and opportunities presented by international institutions.[5] Although I did not emphasize it in this book, I found this mindset as well and it is apparent in the responses and discussions I have related. Whether the degree of influence of institutions is such that one can say they affect the definition of Germany's national interests is a question I did not answer.

But even if one cannot substantiate an institutional influence on German national interests, the effect of institutions on Germany's foreign policy is clearly qualitatively different from that on Russia's. The evidence shows that institutions have a sustained and systematic effect on Russian calculations and strategies, and probably more of an effect than most would have expected. But it is clearly more instrumental and tactical than the all-encompassing, assumption-forming effect on German policies. Russian officials value and rely upon institutions to support the pursuit of Russian interests and many areas of security cooperation, and that they do so is in the interests of Germany, the west, and other members of the international system. But Russia seeks to avoid institutional commitments where it can if they are costly or inconvenient, as in dealing with its post-Soviet neighbors, in a way that Germany does not. One might attribute this disparity to differences in power, and here comparisons to instances of U.S. disregard for the niceties of institutional rules would be instructive. But it is not that simple, because Germany is certainly very powerful in economic affairs in Europe, and it does not behave in this manner. The qualitative difference in the depth and degree of institutional effects on Germany and Russia remains unexplained by realist or rational choice institutionalist approaches and is more suggestive of alternative explanations such as culture or the role of ideas in security affairs.[6]

5. Jeffrey J. Anderson and John B. Goodman, "Mars or Minerva? A United Germany in Post–Cold War Europe," in *After the Cold War: International Institutions and State Strategies in Europe, 1989–91*, ed. Robert O. Keohane, Joseph S. Nye, and Stanley Hoffmann (Cambridge: Harvard University Press, 1993).

6. Peter J. Katzenstein, ed., *The Culture of National Security: Norms and Identity in World Politics* (New York: Columbia University Press, 1996); Martha Finnemore, *National Interests in International Society* (Ithaca: Cornell University Press, 1996).

The case of German-Russian relations also indicates that institutional theory should develop ideas about how institutions affect domestic politics and the definition of national interests. Although I chose to neglect this issue in this book in order to focus upon effects at the international level, my interviews suggested that institutions do affect the resources and ideas available to domestic political actors seeking to make their preferences and interests the basis for national policy. This is clearest in the case of Russian reform, where the promise of IMF loans improved the plausibility of reformist arguments within the government. But it was also true in Germany, where the prevalence of IMF and Paris Club negotiations enhanced the policymaking role of the finance ministry at the expense of the foreign office. A model of institutional effects on domestic politics and the definition of national interests would provide an alternative to constructivist work which has done more to question how the international system affects national security interests, rather than taking interests as given, as I have done.

The study of Russia and institutions also suggests the importance of issues of membership, form and function, and institutional design. Much of the thrust of these cases has been about including Russia in institutions, how such inclusion affects cooperation, and how inclusion affects the institutions themselves. To date, most work on institutional creation has focused on configurations of power and interests as explanations, with some input on institutional design. As we have seen, the problem of whether and how to include Russia in institutions as diverse as the IMF and NATO raises questions about how those institutions can maintain or adapt their original purposes while "swallowing" Russia. The carrot of membership has a one-shot effect, but it may be significant nonetheless in affecting both the target country and the functioning of the institution itself. If you cannot imagine a NATO that includes Russia, that inability implies strong assumptions about the relationship between institutional form and function which are incompatible with realist views on the irrelevance of institutions.

INSTITUTIONS IN INTERNATIONAL RELATIONS

The study of institutions in international relations has lagged behind that in other fields such as American and comparative politics. This is due largely to the predominance of the anarchy-power framework in international relations, which appears to eliminate interesting problems and paradoxes of social choice. One of the reasons for the development of institutional theory in American politics was the problem of Arrow's paradox: that under conditions of social choice, voting should produce unstable outcomes because for every winning coalition there is an outcome preferred by some other coalition. Because this is true for every possible coalition, no possible outcome will remain stable and choices will cycle in an unending pursuit of marginally superior agreements. Since we know that in fact there are many stable outcomes despite this incentive, something else must be affecting the process of social choice. Arrow's paradox is one of "preference induced equilibrium," and is in contrast to "structure induced equilibrium."[7] One source of stability that researchers have explored, therefore, is institutions.

In neorealist theory, all equilibria are "structure-induced," or preferences derive simply from structure (power). Therefore, the paradox of social "choice" does not exist: outcomes do not result from a vote, and preferences play no role. But if one allows that power does not determine preferences and structure will not determine outcomes, then institutions can play roles analogous in international relations to those in domestic politics. This is because it is not the enforcement features of institutions that solve Arrow's paradox, but the self-interest that parties have in reaching stable agreements. Therefore, any sensible theory of international relations which takes into account preferences as well as structure creates at the same time space for the role of institutions.

Furthermore, this book has shown that from any theoretical approach, theories of international security have to incorporate better the effects of information and uncertainty. This task has already been taken up in formal models that incorporate uncertainty and by realist scholars working in what Charles Glaser characterized as the "optimistic" tradition.[8] I have argued, and shown, that institutions affect uncertainty in security affairs, but they do not exhaust the possibilities, which include signaling, tying hands, sinking costs, and even traditional diplomacy. Institutions may be pervasive in Europe, but they are less so in other areas of the world and in other periods of time. What are the different sources of variation in information, and do they work in fundamentally similar ways? If so, then institutions are merely one part of a class of factors in security relations which need to be incorporated more directly in theories.

Another area where realist and institutionalist theories are now sufficiently developed to use the same concepts but offer different predictions is the relation between power, institutions, and distributional issues. Realists argue that institutions merely reflect underlying power

7. Kenneth A. Shepsle, "Institutional Equilibrium and Equilibrium Institutions," in *Political Science: The Science of Politics*, ed. Herbert Weisberg (New York: Agathon Press, 1986), p. 52.

8. Glaser, "Realists as Optimists."

and "settle" distributional conflict in coordination problems only to the extent that they reflect power, while institutionalists propose that institutions have an independent effect on outcomes, even after accounting for power. As Robert Powell notes, in a static situation it is not possible to assess which explanation holds, because power and institutions are coexistent. But as power distributions change, institutions will either adjust smoothly or will not reflect new power distributions, and the less they move the more they matter. So, he poses two questions: (1) do institutions adjust smoothly to changes in the distribution of power or does institutional history matter? and (2) what factors affect the stability or rigidity of institutions and the rates at which they adjust?[9]

The evidence in this book provides a clear answer to the first question and some suggestions on the second. For the most part, institutions did not shift smoothly with the change in the distribution of power, as we have seen. Institutional arrangements were in fact quite "sticky," including the agreements on troop withdrawals, the CFE treaty, the nuclear nonproliferation regime, and international economic and financial rules of the game. And in those cases where institutions have adapted—CoCom, NATO enlargement and change, and rules for peacekeeping and conflict resolution—power was far from the sole explanatory factor. In all those cases, officials argued that in one way or another, the existing institutions were functionally not suited to their tasks. CoCom was an export control regime designed to destroy the Soviet economy, not only an export control system. As for NATO, collective defense against Russia makes little sense, is far from urgent, and fails to address the problem of instability and "risk" in Europe. And for conflict resolution and peacekeeping, the rules of impartiality, consent, and self-defense which worked during the cold war were difficult to translate to internal ethnic conflicts.

In all three of these cases, power played a role in the shift. For peace-keeping, Russian determination to exert influence and stability on its terms was one reason why peace operations have evolved to allow Russian deployments with UN and OSCE observers, while in the case of a successor to CoCom and NATO enlargement, American power and preferences are important. But to attribute the changes only to power neglects cases where Russia and Germany as powerful countries were not able to shift the institutional status quo: Russia in the troop withdrawals and Germany in conceding to allies on trade and debt issues. Once

9. Robert Powell, "Anarchy in International Relations Theory: The Neorealist-Neoliberal Debate," *International Organization* 48 (Spring 1994): 313–344.

again, we have to understand that the question is not how institutions impose outcomes, but how they link issues and alter cost-benefit situations in a way that can favor cooperation. No institution can force Russia to move troops or reduce forces, but institutions did increase the value to Russian decision makers of doing so.

One reason why institutions are so sticky also explains why they are costly to create. James Fearon has pointed out that the long "shadow of the future" should make it more difficult for states to agree on a cooperative deal in the first place: it "can give states an incentive to bargain harder—to delay agreement in hopes of getting a better deal."[10] My evidence shows that German and Russian officials were aware of this, and it made them value existing agreements even more, even under changed circumstances. The temptation to bargain and to rely on power to get a better deal is countered by the recognition that the bargain may not ever be achieved, and that result would be worse than sticking with the status quo.

More generally, the role of institutions in the politics of bargaining, linkage, and information among states concerning security issues suggests that a return to traditional studies of the diplomacy and politics of international relations need not sacrifice analytical rigor for empirical insight. One of the reasons Kenneth Waltz offered for his parsimonious structural theory of international politics was to render it scientific and falsifiable, in contrast to classical realism, which imposed little in the way of predictive power on its explorations of security relations. But in doing so, Waltz developed a model of security affairs in which politics plays no discernible role: outcomes are determined by structure and rigid preferences. Understanding the effects of uncertainty and a variety of security problems in addition to power and anarchy offers the possibility of returning to the systematic study of international politics without merely resorting to the less structured study of foreign policy.[11]

The case of German-Russian security relations is only one test of institutionalist expectations about the responses of states to changes in their security environment which shift the distribution of power and increase uncertainty. We need to test institutionalist expectations in other regions and for other countries. One very hard test for institutionalism would be in relations among the newly independent states of the former Soviet

10. James Fearon, "Cooperation and Bargaining under Anarchy," *International Organization* 52 (Spring 1998): 269–306.
11. Kenneth N. Waltz, *Theory of International Politics* (Reading, Mass.: Addison-Wesley, 1979), chap. 2. Colin Elman, "Why *Not* Neorealist Theories of Foreign Policy?" *Security Studies* 6 (Autumn 1996): 7–53.

Union, either in terms of the CIS itself,[12] or in terms of the effectiveness of European institutions and norms among post-Soviet countries.[13] Another harder test of institutional hypotheses would be in Asia, where the security dilemma is greater and the level of institutionalization lower. Work by Yuen Foong Khong and Iain Johnston on the question of security cooperation in Asia has found that institutions have had an important and consistent role in reducing the destabilizing effects of uncertainty: Khong in the effects of the Association of Southeast Asian Nations (ASEAN) on the incidence of conflicts among member states, and Johnston in those of the ASEAN Regional Forum in creating incentives for wary Chinese participation.[14]

The contemporary historical context of German-Russian security points toward a more positive and constructive set of relations than those the two experienced in the past, which should reassure the neighbors of these two great but problematic countries. Power, national interests, and geopolitical realities are constants in their security relations, but history has carved out for them other factors that play a role in the assessments and choices of decision makers as well. Among those are a variety of international institutions which have survived structural change in the international system, and which often, although not always, support the choice of rational and self-interested cooperative security strategies. I began this chapter by explaining how the Völkerschlachtdenkmal had been manipulated by different German governments to support contradictory messages about the lessons of war and the meaning of Germany's historical relations with Russia. It should be a positive sign for those who believe that historical insight matters to know that the current German government has resisted the temptation

---

12. James M. Goldgeier, "Bilateralism Matters: Cooperation under Anarchy in the Former Soviet Union," paper presented at the International Studies Association meetings, Washington, D.C., March 1994.

13. Jeffrey T. Checkel, "Between Norms and Power: Identity Politics in the New Europe," unpublished manuscript, ARENA (Advanced Research on the Europeanization of the Nation-State), University of Oslo.

14. Yuen Foong Khong, "ASEAN's Security Discourses: An Alternative Model for Organizing Security in the Asia Pacific?" paper prepared for the Institute of Southeast Asian Studies and Stiftung Wissenschaft und Politik conference "Strategic Concepts and Strategic Cultures in East Asia and Europe," 10–11 November 1995, Singapore; Alastair Iain Johnston, "The Myth of the ASEAN Way? Explaining the Evolution of the ASEAN Regional Forum," in *Imperfect Unions: Security Institutions in Time and Space*, ed. Helga Haftendorn, Robert O. Keohane, and Celeste A. Wallander (Oxford: Oxford University Press, forthcoming).

to use it for any agenda, and has left it as the ambiguous and troubling monument to Europe's not-so-distant past that it truly is. Germany and Russia have a broader, if more complex, choice of security strategies than they faced the past because international institutions have altered their balancing act.

Appendix: Interviews

For this project, I conducted 124 interviews with German and Russian officials, politicians, and scholars in Bonn, Berlin, Brussels, and Moscow. In Germany, I interviewed officials in the federal ministries participating in foreign policy toward Russia (including the chancellor's office), military officials of the Bundeswehr command in Berlin, officials of Germany's permanent representations in NATO and the EC, and members of the Bundestag and their staffs. The method in Russia was not as systematic because of the chaotic nature of the government and politics and the lingering effects of the Soviet system on the willingness of some officials responsible for security affairs to meet with a foreigner—even an academic. I often relied in Russia on a method known as "cascading": I used my contacts to get interviews, and then those interviews to obtain more contacts for more interviews. I interviewed officials in the foreign, foreign economic relations, and defense ministries; politicians holding office, their staffs, and advisers; and several scholars at various international relations institutes, most of whom were also political figures.

Most of the interviews were conducted in 1992, with additional ones in Russia in 1993 and 1994, and in Germany in 1996. In August and September 1994, Oksana Antonenko-Gamota conducted 17 additional interviews for the project under my direction with a set of officials and politicians with whom I had not been able to meet the previous May. While these supplementary interviews are not strictly equivalent to those I conducted in 1992, I use them to confirm or qualify my earlier findings. In June and July 1992, I also conducted a limited set of interviews with Ukrainian officials in Kiev to test whether the study could be extended to cover Ukrainian relations with Russia and Germany as well. I did not extend it because I decided doing so would make for an unwieldy project, but I refer in Chapters 5 and 6 to information obtained from those meetings.

The 141 interviews were with 140 individuals: in only one instance did I interview the same person twice. All interviews were conducted on the condition of anonymity. Of all my interviews in Russia and Germany, only two were with women, one in each country. This reflects the extremely low participation of women in both countries' professional and official circles, especially in security affairs. Because it would therefore be relatively easy to identify those two individuals, I use the pronoun "he" in referring to them in the text so as not to compromise their anonymity.

The purpose of the interviews was to obtain reliable data on official policy beyond that which was publicly available, on the reasoning behind official policy, and on how alternative strategies were weighed and chosen. Conducted on the condition of anonymity at the time policy options were being formulated and strategies chosen, this method avoids the problems posed by imperfect memory, post hoc rationalization, and posturing inherent in after-the-fact interviewing and public statements.

The interviews that form the empirical core of this book, it must be emphasized, reflect the policies of the German and Russian governments at the time. Often enough, individuals with whom I spoke expressed their personal views, but when they did so they almost always flagged those views as such. If they did not flag them, I would ask to be certain whether what I was told was official policy (either of the government as a whole or of the individual's ministry or party). In addition, I distinguished between information and policy that were official as opposed to personal by checking at least two other sources (either other interviews or in some instances public information or internal documents given to me by people I interviewed). In instances where there was divergence of views or the individual's expressed views were distinctive for some reason, I included them to make clear that a range of views existed within official and political circles as policy was being worked out, or to convey a particularly striking way something was explained to me. However, I never included anything I was told I could not use even off-the-record, which did happen.

Where they were important or publicly available, I refer as well to public statements and documents on official policy in support of the interview evidence.

Russian Interviews

Starred interviews were conducted by Oksana Antonenko-Gamota under the direction of the author. All interviews took place in Moscow.

1. Official, department on foreign economic relations, Ministry of Foreign Affairs. October 1992.
2. Official, department on foreign economic relations, Ministry of Foreign Affairs. October 1992.

3. Official, department on foreign economic relations, Ministry of Foreign Affairs. October 1992.
4. Researcher, Institute of the USA and Canada. October 1992.
5. Staff assistant to the chairman of the Supreme Soviet. October 1992.
6. Official, department on political relations, Ministry of Foreign Affairs. October 1992.
7. Member of the Supreme Soviet. October 1992.
8. Official, department on international organizations, Ministry of Foreign Economic Relations. October 1992.
9. Researcher, Institute of the USA and Canada. October 1992.
10. Senior official, department on political relations, Ministry of Foreign Affairs. April 1992.
11. Senior official, department on political relations, Ministry of Foreign Affairs. April 1992.
12. Official, department on political relations, Ministry of Foreign Affairs. April 1992.
13. Official, department on political relations, Ministry of Foreign Affairs. February 1992.
14. Researcher, Institute of the USA and Canada. February 1992.
15. Researcher, Institute of the USA and Canada. February 1992.
16. Official, department on political relations. February 1992.
17. Researcher, Institute of the USA and Canada and adviser to Supreme Soviet committee. April 1992.
18. Researcher, Institute of the USA and Canada and adviser to Supreme Soviet committee. April 1992.
19. Researcher, Institute of the USA and Canada and adviser to Supreme Soviet committee. April 1992.
20. Researcher State University Institute of International Relations (MGIMO). February 1992.
21. Researcher, Institute of the World Economy and International Relations (IMEMO). February 1992.
22. Official, department on political relations, Ministry of Foreign Affairs. April 1992.
23. Official, department on political relations, Ministry of Foreign Affairs. April 1992.
24. Official, department on political relations, Ministry of Foreign Affairs. April 1992.
25. Researcher, Institute of Europe. April 1992.
26. Official, department on political relations, Ministry of Foreign Affairs. February 1992.
27. Official, department on political relations, Ministry of Foreign Affairs. February 1992.

28. Researcher, Institute of Europe. February 1992.
29. Researcher, Institute of the World Economy and International Relations (IMEMO). February 1992.
30. Officer, Ministry of Defense. May 1993.
31. Member of Supreme Soviet. May 1993.
32. Member of Supreme Soviet. May 1993.
33. Member of Supreme Soviet. May 1993.
34. Researcher, Institute of Europe. Moscow. February 1992.
35. Researcher, Diplomatic Academy of the Ministry of Foreign Affairs. February 1992.
36. Adviser to the Vice President. May 1993.
37. Official, department on political relations, Ministry of Foreign Affairs. June 1992.
38. Official, department on political relations, Ministry of Foreign Affairs. June 1992.
39. Official, department on economic relations, Ministry of Foreign Affairs. June 1992.
40. Official, department on political relations, Ministry of Foreign Affairs. June 1992.
41. Researcher, Institute of Europe. June 1992.
42. Researcher, Institute of Europe. April 1992.
43. Researcher, Center for Economic and Political Research. June 1992.
44. Official, department on international organizations, Ministry of Foreign Economic Relations. October 1992.
45. Officer, Ministry of Defense. October 1992.
46. Official, department on political relations, Ministry of Foreign Affairs. October 1993.
47. Researcher, Institute of Europe. September 1994.*
48. Researcher, Gorbachev Foundation. September 1994.*
49. Member, Presidential Advisory Council. September 1994.*
50. Official, department on political relations, Ministry of Foreign Affairs. September 1994.*
51. Researcher, Russian Foreign Policy Association. September 1994.*
52. Researcher, Institute of Europe. August 1994.*
53. Member of the State Duma. September 1994.*
54. Researcher, Association of Euro-Atlantic Cooperation. September 1994.*
55. Member of the State Duma. September 1994.*
56. Researcher, Institute of Europe. September 1994.*
57. Researcher, Institute of the USA and Canada. September 1994.*
58. Member of the State Duma. May 1994.
59. Official, department on political relations, Ministry of Foreign Affairs. May 1994.

60. Official, department on political relations, Ministry of Foreign Affairs. May 1994.
61. Official, department on political relations, Ministry of Foreign Affairs. May 1994.
62. Member, Presidential Advisory Council. May 1994.
63. Researcher, Institute of National Security and Strategic Studies. May 1994.
64. Official, Ministry of Defense. September 1994.*
65. Official, Ministry of Defense. August 1994.*
66. Member of the Federation Council. August 1994.*
67. Staff analyst, Foreign Affairs Committee of the Federation Council. August 1994.*
68. Researcher, Carnegie Endowment for International Peace. September 1994.*
69. Researcher, Diplomatic Academy of the Ministry of Foreign Affairs. August 1994.*

GERMAN INTERVIEWS

1. Official, department on foreign economic relations, Ministry of Finance, Bonn. October 1992.
2. Official, department on political relations, Foreign Office, Bonn. June 1992.
3. Official, standing mission to the European Community. Brussels. December 1992.
4. Official, standing mission to the European Community. Brussels. December 1992.
5. Official, German Embassy to Ukraine, Kiev. July 1992.
6. Official, department on foreign relations, Ministry for the Environment, Nature Protection, and Reactor Security, Bonn. November 1992.
7. Official, department on international cooperation, Ministry of Economic Cooperation, Bonn. November 1992.
8. Official, department on foreign relations, Ministry of Economics, Bonn. November 1992.
9. Official, department on political relations, Foreign Office, Bonn. November 1992.
10. Official, department on foreign relations, Ministry of Economics, Bonn. November 1992.
11. Official, department on foreign relations, Ministry for Research and Technology, Bonn. November 1992.

12. Official, department on political relations, Foreign Office, Bonn. July 1992.
13. Official, department on foreign relations, Ministry of Economics, Bonn. August 1992.
14. Staff analyst, FDP-Fraktion of the Bundestag, Bonn. December 1992.
15. Official, department on political relations, Foreign Office, Bonn. April 1992.
16. Member of the Bundestag, SPD, Bonn. December 1992.
17. Official, department on foreign relations, Ministry of Finance, Bonn. September 1992.
18. Officer, Bundeswehr Liaison Command, Berlin. November 1992.
19. Officer, Bundeswehr Liaison Command, Berlin. November 1992.
20. Official, department on political relations, Foreign Office, Bonn. April 1992.
21. Official, department on foreign relations, Ministry of Economics, Berlin. November 1992.
22. Official, department on foreign relations, Ministry of Finance, Berlin. November 1992.
23. Official, department on foreign relations, Ministry of Finance, Berlin. November 1992.
24. Official, department on political relations, Foreign Office, Bonn. December 1992.
25. Member of the Bundestag, SPD, Bonn. December 1992.
26. Member of the Bundestag, CSU, Bonn. December 1992.
27. Official, department on political relations, Foreign Office, Bonn. December 1992.
28. Official, department on political relations, Foreign Office, Bonn. March 1992.
29. Official, department on political relations, Foreign Office, Bonn. June 1992.
30. Official, department on political relations, Foreign Office, Bonn. June 1992.
31. Official, department on foreign relations, Office of the Chancellor, Bonn. November 1992.
32. Officer, Ministry of Defense, Bonn. June 1992.
33. Official, department on foreign relations, Ministry of Economics, Bonn. August 1992.
34. Staff analyst, CDU/CSU-Fraktion of the Bundestag, Bonn. November 1992.
35. Official, department on political relations, Foreign Office, Bonn. May 1992.

36. Official, department on economic relations, Foreign Office, Bonn. July 1992.
37. Official, department on foreign relations, Ministry of Economics, Bonn. July 1992.
38. Official, department on economic relations, Foreign Office, Bonn. July 1992.
39. Official, department on foreign relations, Ministry of Research and Technology, Bonn. November 1992.
40. Official, department on political relations, Foreign Office, Bonn. May 1992.
41. Official, department on foreign relations, Ministry of Finance, Bonn. November 1992.
42. Official, department on foreign relations, Ministry for Economic Co-operation, Bonn. November 1992.
43. Official, department on political relations, Foreign Office, Bonn. March 1992.
44. Official, department on economic relations, Foreign Office, Bonn. November 1992.
45. Official, department on political relations, Foreign Office, Bonn. May 1992.
46. Official, department on political relations, Foreign Office, Bonn. July 1992.
47. Official, department on foreign relations, Ministry for the Environment, Nature Protection, and Reactor Security, Bonn. November 1992.
48. Official, department on economic relations, Foreign Office, Bonn. July 1992.
49. Official, department on foreign relations, Ministry of Economics, Bonn. September 1992.
50. Official, department on foreign relations, Ministry of Economics, Bonn. September 1992.
51. Official, department on political relations, Foreign Office, Bonn. September 1992.
52. Staff analyst, SPD-Fraktion of the Bundestag, Bonn. March 1992.
53. Official, department on political relations, Foreign Office, Bonn. March 1992.
54. Official, department on foreign relations, Ministry of Economics, Bonn. July 1992.
55. Official, department on foreign relations, Foreign Office. September 1992.
56. Official, department on political relations, Foreign Office, Bonn. May 1992.

57. Official, department on economic relations, Foreign Office, Bonn. August 1992.
58. Official, department on economic relations, Foreign Office, Bonn. August 1992.
59. Official, department on political relations, Foreign Office, Bonn. October 1992.
60. Member of the Bundestag, CDU, Bonn. November 1992.
61. Official, department on foreign relations, Ministry of Finance, Bonn. September 1992.
62. Official, department on economic relations, Foreign Office, Bonn. May 1992.
63. Official, delegation to NATO, Brussels. November 1992.
64. Official, delegation to NATO, Brussels. November 1992.
65. Senior official, department on political relations, Foreign Office, Bonn. May 1996.
66. Official, department on political relations, Foreign Office, Bonn. May 1996.
67. Official, department on foreign relations, Office of the Chancellor, Bonn. May 1996.
68. Official, department on political relations, Foreign Office, Bonn. May 1996.
69. Senior official, department on political relations, Foreign Office, Bonn. May 1996.
70. Official, department on political relations, Foreign Office, Bonn. May 1996.
71. Official, department on political relations, Foreign Office, Bonn. May 1996.
72. Official, department on economic relations, Foreign Office, Bonn. May 1996.

Index

CORNELL STUDIES IN SECURITY AFFAIRS

edited by Robert Jervis, Robert J. Art, *and* Stephen M. Walt